Sustainable Community
Learning from the cohousing model

Community

As we tear down the fences
of our western ideals,
look through the holes
and wonder how it feels
to know your neighbours,
to know their family (they're family),
to be a part of a greater community.

I've lost my culture, lost my pride,
I've lost a fire deep inside,
It's good to be alone
but not to run and hide,
I want to be a thread
in the web of humanity,
I want to be a part of a greater community.

Loren Dent,
singer-songwriter,
Byron Bay, Australia

Sustainable Community
Learning from the cohousing model

Graham Meltzer PhD

Supported by the Graham Foundation
for Advanced Studies of the Fine Arts

TRAFFORD

USA • Canada • UK • Ireland

© Copyright 2005 Graham Meltzer.
All rights reserved. Unless otherwise acknowledged, all photographs and diagrams appearing in this book are by the author. No part of the book may be reproduced for the purposes of resale or republication without the written permission of the author except by a reviewer who may wish to quote short passages or reproduce illustrations in a review. Contact the author by email at: graham@grahammeltzer.com

However, it is the author's intention that the material within be freely available for the purpose of advancing sustainable development, cohousing, ecovillages, and intentional communities. Hence, any non-profit group (such as a cohousing group) may reproduce and distribute excerpts provided their combined length does not exceed 5,000 words or 20 pages and the source is duly acknowledged. Similarly, individuals may reproduce and distribute such excerpts amongst friends and associates provided the exchange is non-commercial (except to recover costs).

Cover images:
Front cover: Marsh Commons Cohousing, Arcata, CA.
Back cover: Top left: A common meal at Berkeley Cohousing, Berkeley, CA.
Top right: A work day at Puget Ridge Cohousing, Seattle, WA.
Bottom left: Thanksgiving games at Songaia Cohousing, Bothell, WA.
Bottom right: Christmas gift giving at N Street Cohousing, Davis, CA.

Note for Librarians: a cataloguing record for this book that includes Dewey Decimal Classification and US Library of Congress numbers is available from the Library and Archives of Canada. The complete cataloguing record can be obtained from their online database at:
www.collectionscanada.ca/amicus/index-e.html
ISBN 1-4120-4994-6
First published: May 2005
Trafford catalogue no: 04-2802

TRAFFORD

Offices in Canada, USA, Ireland and UK
This book was published *on-demand* in cooperation with Trafford Publishing. On-demand publishing is a unique process and service of making a book available for retail sale to the public taking advantage of on-demand manufacturing and Internet marketing. On-demand publishing includes promotions, retail sales, manufacturing, order fulfilment, accounting and collecting royalties on behalf of the author.

Book sales for North America and international:
Trafford Publishing, 6E–2333 Government St.,
Victoria, BC V8T 4P4 CANADA
phone 250 383 6864 (toll-free 1 888 232 4444)
fax 250 383 6804; email to orders@trafford.com
Book sales in Europe:
Trafford Publishing (UK) Ltd., Enterprise House, Wistaston Road Business Centre,
Wistaston Road, Crewe, Cheshire CW2 7RP UNITED KINGDOM
phone 01270 251 396 (local rate 0845 230 9601)
facsimile 01270 254 983; orders.uk@trafford.com
Order online at:
trafford.com/04-2802

10 9 8 7 6 5 4 3

Foreword

The great moral challenge of this century is to redirect the trajectory of human development onto a path that would be sustainable into the distant future. That will involve deep technical, social and political changes, since many current trends are headed in the wrong direction.

Housing is a very good example. Progressively, fewer people occupy the average dwelling with the most common Australian household now containing only one person; households with one or two people now account for more than half of the total. At the same time, houses are getting larger. Three-bedroom houses are now seen as small, with four and five-bedroom houses quite common. Larger houses tend to be equipped with more domestic appliances. Expectations are continually increasing. A letter in the Brisbane daily newspaper in 2004 even suggested that air conditioning is now essential domestic equipment!

As a direct result of these trends, more and more energy is required to build, maintain and operate our dwelling space. Since most of the energy used in houses is electricity, produced by inefficient burning of coal, it contributes disproportionately to global climate change. ["Energy use is the dominant source of greenhouse gas emissions in Australia, contributing 67.5 per cent in 2002 of the nation's total emissions" – Australian Government Greenhouse Office.] The science shows that global emissions of carbon dioxide need to be reduced to less than half the present level to stabilise the climate, so there will have to be improvements in all areas – including housing.

There are attractive alternatives. As this book shows, cohousing offers technical, social and environmental advantages. The approach uses resources and energy more efficiently, especially by sharing equipment that is only used a few times a month and making more economic use of living space. The social support it provides contrasts vividly with the isolation and alienation of modern suburbs in which people usually don't know even the names of others living in the same street. The case studies from a range of countries show that the broad approach has wide applicability. They also show that cohousing projects are as diverse as detached houses. The general principles can be applied in radically different ways to suit the people involved.

Graham Meltzer has done us all a distinct service by researching, writing and publishing this book. Its case studies show a range of practical responses to the task of sharing living space. The analysis reveals the underlying principles that determine how successful particular projects are likely to be. I hope the book inspires readers, not just to imitate proven designs but to improve on what has already been done. The road to the sustainable future consists of many small steps. We have to improve our housing, transport, urban planning, energy supply and use, food production and so on. If this book encourages more people to explore innovative ways of sharing living space, it will have made a real contribution to a better future.

Ian Lowe AO

Emeritus Professor of Science, Technology and Society, Griffith University
President, Australian Conservation Foundation

Contents

Foreword v
List of Tables vii
Acknowledgements viii
Preface ix
Chapter 1 Introduction 1

PART ONE
Chapter 2 Quayside Village Cohousing 21
Chapter 3 WindSong Cohousing 29
Chapter 4 Songaia Cohousing 37
Chapter 5 Puget Ridge Cohousing 45
Chapter 6 Marsh Commons Cohousing 53
Chapter 7 N Street Cohousing 61
Chapter 8 Berkeley Cohousing 69
Chapter 9 Swan's Market Cohousing 77
Chapter 10 Earthsong Eco-Neighbourhood 85
Chapter 11 Cohousing Cooperative 93
Chapter 12 Cascade Cohousing 99
Chapter 13 Kyōdō no mori Cohousing 107

PART TWO
Chapter 14 Circumstance: physical setting and managed systems 114
Chapter 15 Interaction: interpersonal influence and exchange 129
Chapter 16 Relationship: close sharing and social support 137
Chapter 17 Engagement: from belonging to efficacy 146
Chapter 18 Empowerment: lessons from the cohousing model 153
Chapter 19 Sustainable Community: applying the lessons 163

Bibliography 173
Index 175

List of Tables

Table 2.1: Community Data, Quayside Village Cohousing	21
Table 3.1: Community Data, WindSong Cohousing	29
Table 4.1: Community Data, Songaia Cohousing	37
Table 4.2: Songaia's ten-year development journey	38
Table 5.1: Community Data, Puget Ridge Cohousing	45
Table 6.1: Community Data, Marsh Commons	53
Table 7.1: Community Data, N Street Cohousing	61
Table 8.1: Community Data, Berkeley Cohousing	69
Table 9.1: Community Data, Swan's Market Cohousing	77
Table 10.1: Community Data, Earthsong Eco-Neighbourhood	85
Table 10.2: Projected average household cost savings, Earthsong Eco-Neighbourhood	91
Table 11.1: Community Data, Cohousing Cooperative	93
Table 11.2: Rostered car pooling and childcare arrangements, Cohousing Cooperative	96
Table 12.1: Community Data, Cascade Cohousing	99
Table 13.1: Community Data, Kyōdō no mori Cohousing	107
Table 14.1: Prior and current locations of cohousing households	116
Table 14.2: Reported changed ownership of vehicles and bicycles	117
Table 14.3: Density analysis	119
Table 14.4: Dwelling size (in m^2) by numbers of bedrooms	122
Table 14.5: Cohousing household's current and prior dwelling types	122
Table 14.6: Typical cohousing recycling protocol	125
Table 14.7: Food Preferences chart at Berkeley Cohousing	127
Table 15.1: Demographic characteristics of the American cohousing population	131
Table 15.2: Distribution of vocations in American cohousing	131
Table 15.3: Gross annual income of residents with full-time employment	132
Table 16.1: Changes in household ownership of goods	138
Table 16.2: Lending list of household items available to others	138
Table 16.3: Schedule of existing and proposed common facilities	140
Table 16.4: Area analysis of common versus private space	141
Table 16.5: Cohousing affordability analysis	144
Table 17.1: Development timeline for each project	149
Table 17.2: Reported participation in community activities	150

Acknowledgements

My deepest, most heartfelt thanks go to Jane, Anna and Liberty Meltzer for their love and support over ten years of continuous study and research. At times I was obsessively immersed in my work and I acknowledge certain sacrifices they bore as a result. To my PhD supervisors and good friends, Greg Bamford and Bill Metcalf – thanks guys, your feedback and critical insight were invaluable. For their collegial support, I owe a huge debt of thanks to staff and post-grads of the then *School of Architecture* at *The University of Queensland* where I was a student and to the staff of the then *School of Architecture, Interior and Industrial Design* at the *Queensland University of Technology* (QUT) where I was a lecturer. Particular appreciation goes to the then Head of School at QUT, Gordon Holden, for his support and encouragement. I'd like to thank Tomo Takada and Ayako Suzuki for their friendly assistance in interpreting some Japanese data and Mandy Fletcher for her dedicated proofreading. The travel this book required was generously funded by the US based *Graham Foundation for Advanced Studies of the Fine Arts*. Finally, my extreme gratitude goes to the cohousing fraternity for the time and effort that members so willingly contributed to the making of this book. You folk and your communities are truly inspirational.

Preface

This book marks the culmination of a personal journey – a lifelong involvement with communal or shared living. I grew up in Auckland, New Zealand where my family was one of six that shared a green space at some distance from the road. We kids roamed freely there as a 'pack' for hours after school and on weekends. The social cohesion and shared values of our post-war suburban community lent security and assurance to life. Added to this, a large extended family and close-knit Jewish community provided a wellspring of love and support from which I benefit to this day.

As a student during the late 1960s and early '70s I lived in politically radical urban communes where I first experienced shared ideology and purpose. This was followed by two years on kibbutz during which I became convinced of the immeasurable value of collaboration as a means of achieving both social and material satisfaction. There seemed to me at the time to be a profound connection between the psycho-social and the material dimensions of community life. It took thirty more years of experience and investigation before I could fully articulate what was then, just speculation.

I returned to Australia in 1976, seeking a communal lifestyle. I soon met and married my equally idealistic partner, Jane, and together we joined Australia's largest and best know intentional community, Tuntable Falls, near Nimbin in Northern NSW. The late 1970s in Australia was a halcyon period of greatest 'new-age' idealism. At the time, Nimbin was at the epicentre of the dream. We were going to change the world by our example…of an environmentally responsible community of communities, as self-sufficient as possible: materially, culturally, socially and economically. And for a time there, we were on track!

Living at Tuntable cemented my belief that a nurturing extended family or 'tribe' is the ideal social grouping for the human species and that a socially cohesive group of individuals (some related by blood but most, probably not) *has the potential* to be a profound milieu for the socialisation of both children and adults. Furthermore, an appropriately sized group, thus socialised, has the opportunity to create a truly civilised and civil society. I saw communalism as *the* best chance of fulfilling our individual and collective potential for creativity, intelligence, compassion and love – all those wonderful human attributes that, for the most part, remain sadly unfulfilled.

After eight years at Tuntable I returned to university to study architecture. I anticipated becoming one of those 'barefoot' architects dedicated to environmental and/or community architecture. As it happened, I moved quickly into post-graduate study and a full-time academic position. Academia offered the opportunity to apply rigour to previous musings about a link between the social and the material…or as I then saw it, the communal and the environmental. At that time, in the early '90s, there was considerable literature highlighting the incapacity of well-intentioned 'greens' to 'walk their environmentalist talk'. Yet, there was little investigation of the role of social relationships and social satisfaction in underpinning people's environmental behaviours and practices. I set about such an investigation.

Eight years of part-time research and analysis resulted in the completion of a PhD that, indeed, substantiated a connection between the social cohesion of a human group and the capacity of its members to enact their environmentalist aspirations. This book required four more years of occasional fieldwork and part-time writing. In total, the fieldwork comprised eighteen months of living in cohousing in Denmark, North America, New Zealand, Australia and Japan. I hope readers find the book revealing and inspiring, as I have certainly found the journey taken in its creation.

Graham Meltzer
graham@grahammeltzer.com   www.grahammeltzer.com

This book is dedicated to:
my children, Anna and Liberty;
their children, should they have any;
and future generations of children to come.

The shared meal, cohousing style!

1 Introduction

> Environmental sustainability goes hand in hand with social sustainability. Towns and cities are first and foremost places where people live and work, not just as individuals but as communities. If urban areas do not provide civilised places for people to live and for communities to prosper then it will not matter how 'green' they are, they will not be sustainable.[1]

The missing link

Since the 1970s, environmental values, attitudes and practices have been thoroughly investigated in numerous popular polls and university surveys. Consistently in the West, about 90% of people claim to be concerned about the state of the environment. Furthermore, most appear to recognise that high levels of personal consumption contribute decisively to environmental degradation. Yet strangely, very few of those same people can claim to have modified their lifestyles accordingly. Little connection is found between people's professed concern for the environment and their consumerist behaviour. Even easily achieved behavioural changes, such as increased recycling or reduced driving, do not seem to occur as a result of raised environmental awareness.

Why is this so? Why do intelligent, informed, well-meaning people have such difficulty 'walking their environmentalist talk'? The principle intent of this book is to provide answers to this question and to suggest how things might be different.

The disconnection between environmental awareness and consumerist behaviour is perhaps not surprising given that affluence is widely invoked as an essential component of the 'good life' and the 'great' Australian or American or Western European dream. However, this book reveals further causes. It shows how the quality of our social relationships and our 'sense of community' are major determinants of our capacity for pro-environmental behavioural change. Thereby, it establishes a link between 'community' and 'sustainability'. The argument is eventually broadened to encompass issues such as urban form, mass housing and ecologically sustainable development.

Concepts and definitions

Throughout the book, frequent use is made of a number of terms that have been notoriously misused through popular usage and in the literature; 'sustainability' and 'community' are obvious examples. Yet, irrespective of problems of meaning, such terms can be useful as widely understood descriptors of powerful ideas; their very popularity being evidence for the power and currency of their usage. In this section, these and other key terms are identified and their meanings, as they're defined for the purposes of the book, are clarified.

The concept, *sustainability* originated in the early 1970s, being first articulated in the influential paper, *Blueprint for Survival*, published in the journal, *The Ecologist*. The introduction to *Blueprint* commenced with the words: "The principal defect of the industrial way of life is that it is not *sustainable*".[2] The authors detailed the multitude of ways in which unrestrained population growth combined with excessive material consumption was untenable, and if left unchecked, would inevitably undermine the prospect of human survival. They used the descriptors *sustainable* and *stable* almost interchangeably.

Over the last 30 years, experts and non-experts alike have used the word, *sustainable*, and its derivative, *sustainability*, in a multitude of ways, sometimes manipulating its essential meaning for self-serving or opportunistic ends. Interpretation is often based on the needs and proclivities of particular disciplines. Biologists, for example, use sustainability in reference to the adverse impact of human systems on biodiversity and the viability of ecosystems, whilst economists might measure sustainability in terms of the state of natural resources, based on the action of market forces. A cultural anthropologist's conception may well be based on the impact of human groups on their natural or built environment.

Popular usage has laid down further layers of emotive, moralistic and polemical connotation that further conceal the true meaning of the word. Indeed, there is no precise, universally agreed definition of sustainability. Therefore, in this book the fundamental dictionary definition of *sustainable* will be applied. That is, "able to be maintained at a certain rate or level".[3] This associates sustainability with the notions, continuity, futurity and viability, and aligns it with the widely accepted definition proposed by the United Nation's World Commission on Environment and Development, that is, *meeting the needs of the present, without compromising the ability of future generations to meet their own needs*.[4]

There is a similar lack of consistency amongst definitions of *community*, made worse perhaps, because historical and contemporary manifestations of community are so diverse. The classical definition incorporates three essential characteristics: social interaction, shared ties and common geographical location, but implies other attributes such as, human-scale, belonging, obligation, *gemeinschaft* etc.[5] Contemporary usage has broadened to include abstract association (eg. the scientific 'community' or the gay 'community') and to accommodate contemporary communication phenomena such as 'virtual community'.

If the criterion, "common geographical location" is accordingly disregarded or relaxed then community becomes characterised by the first two criteria, namely, a certain quality or measure of social interaction within a group and the shared ties or common interests of its members. For the purposes of this book, these will be the defining attributes of community. This fits well with the word's etymology. Words such as 'common', 'community', 'commune', 'communitarianism', 'communalism' and 'communism' originate from the French, *communer*, meaning 'to share'. The French word in fact derives from the Latin, *communis*; *com* meaning 'with' and *munius* meaning 'duties'. Thus, sharing is fundamental to community, as are close relationships and the notion of commitment.

An *intentional community* (as opposed to other types of community) is a group of mostly unrelated people living together and dedicated *by intent* to specific common values or goals. Again, this characterisation is based on the straightforward dictionary meanings of the words *intentional* and *intent*.[6] Intentional communities generally place a high value on the sharing of land, housing, buildings and facilities. Shared facilities symbolise communal values and goals, and serve to represent the group as a collective. Intentional communities are supposedly less propinquitous than communes, with members and households having greater autonomy than would be the case in a commune. Cohousing (to be introduced in detail below) is a new kind of intentional community. Cohousing groups form with the explicit *intention* of creating a socially cohesive and mutually supportive community.

Empowerment is a recently developed theoretical concept with relevance to any discussion of social change processes. It is generally associated with 'grassroots' or 'bottom up' participation in community organisation and is associated with challenges to dominant relationships of power in society. Empowerment is said to be an "antidote to the alienating and disempowering growth of our mass society and its institutions".[7] Again, there is a confusing array of definitions of empowerment, causing it to be misidentified with other psychological constructs such as self-efficacy or the gaining of self-esteem. Yet, all the various definitions are in some way consistent with the one offered by the respected Cornell Empowerment Group, namely,

> [Empowerment is] an intentional ongoing process centred in the local community, involving mutual respect, critical reflection, caring, and group participation, through which people lacking an equal share of valued resources gain greater access to and control over those resources.[8]

In other words, empowerment is the means by which individuals, acting collectively, gain understanding of their circumstance and, in the process, greater control over their lives. Closely allied to the concept of empowerment is that of *community development*, which is a broader conceptualisation of the way groups gain social coherence and develop a sense of collective strength and effectiveness.

Introduction to cohousing

Empirical evidence for the central propositions of this book (outlined at the beginning of the chapter) is gathered through an investigation of cohousing, a new form of intentional community that provides clues to the link between the social dynamics of such a group and the pro-environmental behaviours of its members.

Cohousing first appeared in Denmark during the 1970s and spread throughout Northern Europe during the '80s. In the '90s, it took root in the United States, Canada and Australia. More recently projects have appeared in Britain, New Zealand and Japan. Cohousing has attributes that link it to the long history and traditions of communal living. Residents share property, resources and aspirations. They eat, meet and recreate together. Cohousing communities network, publish and hold national conferences. Collectively, they constitute a resurgent communalist movement.

Cohousing has distinctive architectural and site planning features. Typically, purpose-built, attached housing is set within a purpose designed neighbourhood. Autonomous private dwellings are integrated with shared utilities and recreational facilities such as kitchens, dining halls, workshops and children's play facilities. Danish projects range from as few as six dwellings to more than a hundred, but most are between twenty and forty households. Several hundred such *bofælleskaber* (which literally translated means 'living community') have been built in Denmark. In North America, where they typically comprise twenty to thirty households, over eighty cohousing communities are now built and many more are on the drawing board or under construction. In Australasia there are just four projects of between ten and twenty households and in Japan, a single cohousing community of eleven households.

Cohousing has arisen in precise response to perceived social problems of the late twentieth century – personal alienation and the breakdown of community, in particular. Members seek to establish close, supportive social relationships and utilise their shared facilities to establish a rich community life of social, recreational, cultural and work activities. Probably the most important communal activity is the shared meal held regularly on particular nights of the week. Common meals are valued for their practical advantages and for the social interaction they offer. They are emblematic of the group as an *intentional community*.

Since the 1960s, countless groups have lived communally, most famously in places like Nimbin in Australia and Christiania in Denmark, but in fact throughout the Western world. Common to many such 'alternative lifestyles' has been a commitment to living more simply than 'normal' in smaller, less elaborate dwellings with fewer material possessions. By choice, daily life is less hectic, travel-dependent and prescribed. Usually, amongst practitioners of alternative lifestyles there is considerable social support and a palpable sense of community.

Most people living alternatively have strong pro-environmental values and, unlike many 'greens' in mainstream society, are generally able to apply their values in day-to-day life. They consume less, recycle more of their waste and generally live with much less impact on the environment. By definition however, such alternative lifestyles are neither attractive to, nor viable for, most mainstream folk. They will only ever appeal to a very small minority and therefore will not, in and of themselves, bring about mass change toward social and environmental sustainability. Perhaps their most important function is to model important aspects of a future sustainable society, demonstrating that consumerist values *can* be resisted if the circumstance and the will exist.

Cohousing members generally acknowledge the debt they owe to historical communities but would claim to differ fundamentally from communal experimentation of the 1960s and '70s. Foremost among these differences is the recognition that exclusivity and isolation from wider society can be socially and politically detrimental. Most cohousing is deliberately located within cities and deeply enmeshed with mainstream culture.

Cohousing provides the opportunity to investigate what is now understood to be the ecological interconnectivity of social and environmental factors. Through a focus on cohousing, this book argues for greater recognition of the importance of community in the process of attitudinal and behavioural change toward social and environmental sustainability. Cohousing demonstrates compact architectural form and efficient, innovative land use. It facilitates the sharing of resources and reduced household consumption.

Cohousing encourages human interaction and lends support to disadvantaged members of society. It provides a physical and social milieu that nurtures an awareness of the consequences of one's actions for others and for the environment. Cohousing suggests a way of rethinking the structure and fabric of urban life, which prompts a vision of a civilised and environmentally sustainable future.

Characteristics of cohousing

Cohousing is commonly said to have (at least) six distinguishing if not defining characteristics, first articulated by Kathryn McCamant and Charles Durrett in their seminal book, *CoHousing: A Contemporary Approach to Housing Ourselves*.[9]

1. Participatory process

Cohousing groups attach great importance to the *participatory process* whereby residents organise and participate in the design and development of their project. This can take between one and five years or even more, but typically, project development takes between two and four years from inception to the date of initial occupation. Thousands of hours of meetings and the participation of many people are involved in the process.

2. Neighbourhood design

Cohousing projects generally adopt one of four generic approaches to *neighbourhood design* – site planning intended to encourage and facilitate social interaction between residents. Figure 1.1 illustrates these different configurations, classified as: (a) the pedestrian 'street', (b) the courtyard, (c) a hybrid of the 'street' and courtyard types, and (d) the single building with an internal atrium which functions as a 'street' but is covered by a glazed roof. Generally, dwellings have a private backyard separate and remote from the shared community space.

With all of these configurations, and others less common, vehicles are confined to the edge of the site, both to improve the qualities of the outdoor social space and render it safe for children at play. As cohousing has evolved and spread around the world to regions with diverse climates, cultures and topography, site planning strategies have naturally diversified.

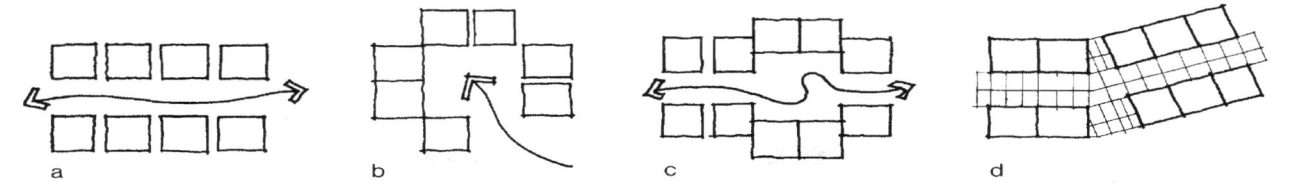

Figure 1.1: Generic cohousing site plans (after McCamant and Durrett (1994)).

3. Common facilities

The *common facilities* of almost all cohousing communities are concentrated in the 'common house' – a shared, centrally located building containing at least a kitchen and dining room large enough to allow common meals to be held regularly. Typically, these occur two or three times per week. In addition, most common houses contain a shared laundry, multi-purpose social space, children's room and workshop. Many communities share one or two guestrooms or a library or office. Some may have a room for teens or for games, crafts or exercise.

4. Self-management

In the spirit in which cohousing is designed and built, residents take full responsibility for the *self-management* of the project once it is completed and occupied. This involves them in almost all the decision-making as well as the activities and duties required for the day-to-day running of the community. Apropos their participation in community life, there is a further characteristic of cohousing not often found amongst other types of intentional community. Cohousing groups pay particular attention to what is called 'sustainable dynamics', which is primarily a function of their size. They aim to be large enough to allow members to occasionally withdraw from the group without jeopardising its social dynamics, but not too large that members cannot get to know one another through regular participation in community life.

McCamant and Durrett's original definition of cohousing, which appeared in the first (1988) edition of their book, comprised only the above four points. The following two were included in the second (1994) edition, presumably to distance cohousing from communes or intentional communities with charismatic or spiritual leadership and/or a common economy.

5. Absence of hierarchy

Cohousing is fiercely democratic in its decision-making processes. Consensus is universally utilised to ensure that all members have an opportunity for input. Although cohousing groups are started by a core of strong individuals, once the project is occupied these members take no more of a role in management decisions than others.

6. Separate incomes

Cohousing members and households do not pool their capital or financial resources. Indeed, a shared economy or 'common purse' is rare amongst intentional communities generally, being most likely to occur in sectarian communities. It is usual in cohousing to have a wide diversity of occupations and incomes. This creates significant challenges. Quite wealthy members and others on low or even subsistence incomes might have to reach consensus on such matters as increasing monthly levies, expensive infrastructure development and the cost of common meals.

There are at least two further characteristics that distinguish cohousing from many, if not most, other contemporary intentional communities. Cohousing communities place a stronger emphasis on the *balance* between community life and the privacy of individuals and households. Dwellings are self-sufficient, and household autonomy is symbolically expressed in architectural form, as is the importance of the common house with its "vital social and practical purpose".[10] Another fundamental characteristic not found in most intentional communities is the close relationship of cohousing groups to wider society. Members hold down conventional jobs, have mortgages and go surfing or skiing on weekends. Unlike its communal predecessors, cohousing is a *mainstream* option, and intentionally so. It is not an 'alternative' lifestyle, but one deemed appropriate for the broad majority of people. Communities believe they can maintain internal social cohesion despite the potential tension between members' commitment to community life and their association with the world beyond.

History of cohousing

Cohousing has developed in different world regions during different periods of time. It was spawned in Northern Europe in the 1970s and has continued to spread there ever since. In the late '80s it was imported into North America and has flourished there to this day. In the '90s, cohousing spread further west toward Australia and New Zealand and since then has appeared in Japan.

Denmark, Sweden and the Netherlands

Cohousing is popularly believed to have originated in Denmark, due mainly to the influence of McCamant and Durrett who coined the term 'CoHousing'. They argued that cohousing was a "Danish solution" to the social problems of late 20th Century post-industrial society.[11] It should be acknowledged, however, that throughout Northern Europe, organised collective urban living has a rich tradition stretching back at least two hundred years. Furthermore, during the 1970s when cohousing was first established in Denmark (where it is called *bofælleskaber*), very similar collective housing projects with comparable origins were being realised in the Netherlands (*centraal wonen*) and Sweden (*kollektivhuser*). Because all three countries enjoyed socially responsive and politically progressive cultures, the advantages of communal living demonstrated by communes of the '60s and '70s were widely recognised and quickly appropriated. In each country, cohousing developed as a *mainstream* housing option, despite being underpinned by many of the principles and practices of its predecessor communes. Importantly however, cohousing projects also varied significantly from their antecedents, the nature of these distinctions being different from country to country.

Photo 1.1: Typical Danish cohousing architecture: low-rise, neo-vernacular buildings with a separate common house (on the left).

Danish communes of the 1960s and '70s were unremarkable by comparison with their American counterparts. Few were sectarian or charismatic and the proportion advocating drug use and/or radical lifestyles such as complex marriage and bohemian or hippie alternatives, was relatively small. Most members or their households had their own private quarters. The accommodation was generally comfortable and material living standards were further improved through the sharing of resources. They were not ideologically or politically extreme but were generally proactive in supporting the disadvantaged, particularly the homeless, single parents and low-income students. They provided "a large measure of stability, warmth, genuine affection and a feeling that the individual member is indeed useful and wanted".[12] Most communards were well-educated middle-class citizens with conventional employment and recreational pursuits. They saw communal experimentation as a logical extension of a civil and tolerant Danish society and were generally well supported by neighbours and the authorities. Nonetheless, the first cohousing-like proposal, designed in 1964, met with considerable hostility from particular neighbours and was never built. Eventually, the political climate and radical social literature of the late sixties inspired two Danish cohousing groups to purchase properties in Hillerød (North of Copenhagen) and in Copenhagen, itself. Financial and practical difficulties delayed occupation of these projects until 1972 and 1973 respectively.

The differences between Danish and Swedish cohousing lie principally in their physical form and their socio-economic underpinning. Danish cohousing predominantly comprises low-rise (i.e. one or two storey) medium-density attached dwellings with a separate, detached common house (Photo 1.1). Commonly, the architecture takes a neo-vernacular character, its layout, form and materials being derived from rural building traditions. The common house is usually located centrally or at the entrance to the site, assuming a symbolic and functional importance. Swedish cohousing, on the other hand, is mostly found in medium to high-rise apartment blocks that appear little different from conventional mass housing types (Photo 1.2). Common facilities are often buried within the building, although their presence may be indicated by larger than expected windows or volumes.

Figure 1.2 (above): Extensive common facilities on the fifth floor of the Swedish communal housing project, Stacken. (Drawing by NOARK Architects).

Photo 1.2 (left): Typical Swedish collective housing: medium-rise buildings with common facilities within. (Photo by Dick Urban Vestbro).

Further significant differences are found in the social and economic imperatives which drive Danish and Swedish cohousing. Danish *bofællesskaber* originated (and continue to be built) in order to build better social relationships and a deeper sense of community. Swedish *kollektivhuser* originally had a more pragmatic *raison d'être*. Instigators sought to reduce the burden of housework, particularly for women entering the workforce, and improve the lot of children with working (often single) parents. This essentially feminist intent originally met with significant resistance from male-dominated Swedish housing institutions and political organisations. In a manner that never existed in Danish self-managed cohousing, professional services were commonly utilised to provide meals and undertake housework and childcare.

Dutch cohousing differs significantly from Swedish types in form, scale and social intent. Whereas Swedish *kollektivhuser* comprise substantial buildings with centralised common facilities and services, their Dutch counterparts occupy low-rise buildings similar in scale to Danish cohousing but with a more urban form and character (Photo 1.3). Because the Netherlands is significantly more densely populated, the degree to which cohousing projects blend with, and are integrated into, their neighbourhood is more carefully considered. Unlike both Danish and Swedish cohousing, *centraal wonen* usually have decentralised common facilities, with clusters of six or eight households sharing a kitchen and dinning room (Figure 1.3). In part, this is due to a humanistic Dutch architectural tradition with a "fascination for the manipulation of space and form in order to achieve intimacy".[13] In Dutch cohousing common dining tends to occur in small groups, not with the whole community, so is less noisy and more intimate. Theoretically, residents can join a cluster of households with similar aspirations (such as desired frequency of common meals per week) and move between clusters if necessary.

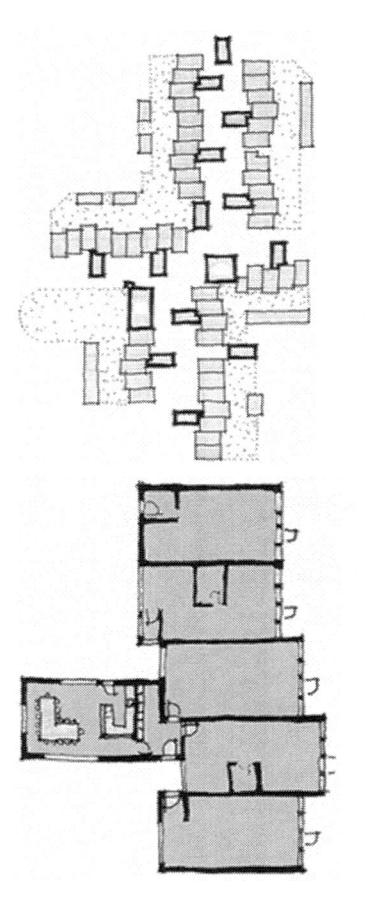

Photo 1.3: *Hilversum* is typical of Dutch *Centraal Wonen* projects in terms of its scale and urban character (Photo by Greg Bamford).

Figure 1.3: The site plan (top) and cluster plan (bottom) illustrate the decentralised nature of dining facilities at *Hilversum* (after McCamant and Durrett 1994).

Cohousing in the Netherlands originated in much the same way as Danish cohousing, through the radical social literature of the late sixties. Yet, its social intent and consequently the demographics of Dutch cohousing have always been different from the Danish and closer to the Swedish experience. It tends to be more focussed on the practical advantages of communal living, and so attracts a greater proportion of singles, single parents and the elderly. Dutch cohousing is readily accepted by neighbours as well as government and housing providers alike. Currently in the Netherlands, to a lesser extent in Denmark and lesser again in Sweden, little housing *of any kind* is built without reference to cohousing theory and practice. Housing projects in general, commonly incorporate some measure of neighbourhood design, centralised parking and shared spaces and facilities.

The USA and Canada

In the mid 1980s, Katie McCamant and Chuck Durrett returned to California from a study tour of Danish cohousing and in 1988 published their findings in *CoHousing: A Contemporary Approach to Housing Ourselves*. It sold 3,000 copies in the first month – such was the 'ripeness' of the idea. Over the next two or three years, McCamant and Durrett vigorously promoted cohousing in numerous public workshops and slide shows. One held in Davis, California in late 1988 spawned the first American project, Muir Commons, completed in 1991.[14] Within a few years, pockets of cohousing had been established in Northern California, Washington State, Massachusetts and Colorado. American projects incorporated most of the physical attributes of Danish cohousing (such as low-rise attached dwellings, centralised common facilities and peripheral parking), however they also adopted significant new variations of architectural character (Photo 1.4).

In Denmark, Sweden and the Netherlands, most cohousing is developed as social housing by non-profit organisations. This is rare in America. One project, Winslow Cohousing, was developed by an equity cooperative of residents and another by a non-profit organisation seeking to build cohousing for a low-income black community. Predominantly however, American projects are privately developed by the residents as a *condominium* whereby residents own their own home outright. Most groups use professionals and developers to expedite the design and procurement process. About 80% employ outside consultants while the remainder design and develop their own projects, usually with input from member professionals. About 30% work with property developers who typically undertake financing and project management roles. One development company in particular, Wonderland Hill, has largely been responsible for a wave of cohousing development in Colorado. American groups often employ a 'lot development model' whereby a site is carved up into house lots that are sold separately (together with a share of the commons) and developed individually. This results in cohousing projects with considerable diversity of architectural form, scale and character, the likes of which is not much found in European cohousing.

Photo 1.4: Diversity of architectural character amongst US cohousing projects as some adopt the neo-vernacular character or 'style' of their region: the Pacific North West (left), the South West (centre) and New England (right).

Chapter 1: Introduction

Another cohousing model, different from new-built projects, is known as *retrofit* cohousing (see Chapter 7 for an example). In suburban locations, longstanding neighbours create cohousing without relocating or building anew, opting instead to knock down the fences between existing dwellings, share backyards, and establish common facilities. In the process, such projects become a catalyst for broader social change. Blighted or tired inner-city suburbs are injected with fresh life by cohousing groups that have adapted, purposefully integrated with, and in some cases, politicised their neighbourhood.

The principal social intent of North American cohousing is similar to that of the Danish, namely, to develop supportive relationships with neighbours and a greater sense of community. In addition to that, widespread concern about profligate consumerism in the US has introduced there a strong anti-consumerist ethos. This has led, when coupled with American entrepreneurial flare and social innovation, to cohousing with extensive sharing and high levels of practical support. Residents live in compact building types (eg. townhouses and apartments) contrary to an overwhelming national preference for large detached dwellings. Cohousing dwellings are small by American standards – the average floor area being about half the national average for new housing (see Chapter 14). Perhaps more importantly, Americans living in cohousing have reconceptualized their domestic space needs, enjoying habitable spaces for their qualities and liveability, not their material content and associated status symbolism.

Another distinctive characteristic of North American cohousing is a propensity for communication and networking. Word of mouth, networking and ever increasing publicity has very effectively spread interest in cohousing. Many communities are now wired for internal (i.e. intranet) electronic communication and the World Wide Web is utilised intelligently to promote and provide support for development groups and communities. National and regional conferences are held regularly to exchange skills and knowledge. It is these attributes, above all else, that give the cohousing phenomenon in North America the feel and momentum of a genuine social movement.

Australia and New Zealand

In Australia, cohousing arrived without fanfare and has developed slowly, in stark contrast with the way it burst onto the scene in North America. The first project, Cascade Cohousing, was started in Hobart, Tasmania in 1991 (see Chapter 12). Since then, only two more projects have been constructed, one in Fremantle, Western Australia (1997) and another in Hobart (1999). Cohousing has been slow to establish in Australia for culturally specific reasons. Communal living, despite a long and rich history in Australia, has remained outside the mainstream range of lifestyle choices. Communal groups have mostly lived in remote locations (like Hobart and Fremantle) and been marginalised or discounted by a vast majority of the public. In good part, this is due to what political scientist, Denis Altman has called, "a uniquely Australian conservatism". Altman argues that an exaggerated emphasis on prosperity and home ownership has established 'two pillars' of Australian culture – the accumulation of property and an emphasis on privacy and family life.[15] The easy availability of land in Australia led to an early proliferation of low-density suburbs that reinforced this highly privatised social culture. Furthermore, post-war Australian attitudes and aspirations, in so far as there has been a consensus, have been predominantly based on middle class, bourgeois values (i.e. hard work, prosperity, respectability and family life) and the essential assumptions of liberal capitalism (namely, individuality, competition, consumerism and domesticity). The ubiquity of these cultural traits is one reason for cohousing being slow to establish in Australia. Altman argues too, that the "smallness of the Australian dream" has become a value in itself, creating suspicion of both intellectualism and visionary thinking.[16] Yet, distrust of one need not necessarily imply suspicion of the other. In the US, there is a similar anti-intellectualism, but a much stronger tradition of utopian thought and an historically derived vision of Americans as pioneers that has long fed entrepreneurial drive and innovation in that country. Their idealism and risk taking, which seem not be part of the Australian psyche, have no doubt contributed to the more rapid development of cohousing in the US.

Across the Tasman, New Zealand's first cohousing project is partially complete (see Chapter 10). *Earthsong Eco-Neighbourhood* has encapsulated in its name the intention to build a project with low environmental impact. In using the word eco-*neighbourhood* rather than eco-*village* the community is making the point that theirs is an integrated urban project, not an autonomous rural one. Their vision statement explicitly incorporates the intention to design and construct buildings and services that "demonstrate the highest practical standards of sustainable human settlement". Furthermore, they seek to "assist in the education and public awareness of sustainability by demonstrating and promoting innovative community design and environmentally responsible construction".[17]

Japan and Korea

A unique adaptation of cohousing principles to suit local circumstances has occurred in Japan. In Tokyo, there are two communal housing projects directly inspired by Danish and Swedish exemplars, one funded privately (see Chapter 13) and the other, publicly (Photos 1.5-1.8). The former is *bone fide* cohousing; the other is not, for lack of a participatory design process. Both have taken unconventional approaches to common meals to suit the stressful lifestyle and late working hours of Japanese employees. The former irregularly utilises a barbeque pit set within its shared rooftop garden, the other commissions serviced meals twice a day, six days a week.

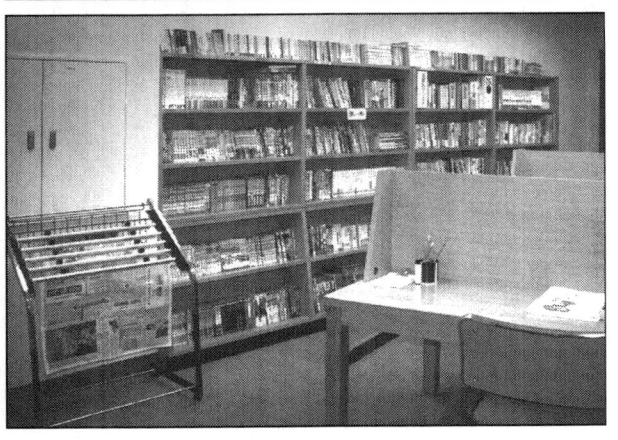

Photos 1.5-1.8: Common facilities in Tokyo's publicly funded 'cohousing-like' communal housing project: the dining room, crèche, library and traditional guest room (clockwise from top left).

Chapter 1: Introduction

In Kobe, when new dwellings were required quickly and in vast numbers following the 1995 earthquake, the authorities built what are known as *Fureai* houses (meaning 'places of friendship'). There are about 300 units in ten projects of between 6 and 71 units each (Photos 1.9-1.12). They are occupied predominantly by low-income singles and couples, mostly elderly. In recognizing the value of collaboration and social support as a means of overcoming hardship and material need, the *Fureai* houses were equipped with common spaces and facilities for residents to share. Admittedly, these are not cohousing projects, as such. Many would argue that without a participatory design process, no amount of common facilities, material sharing and social interaction can *create* cohousing. "Build it and they will come" perhaps, but it's likely that they, the residents, will never cohere as a community in the way that cohousing groups become bonded through the usual cohousing design and development process. Nor will they develop the decision-making and conflict resolution skills that operate so effectively in most cohousing communities. This is borne out in the case of the *Fureai* houses where the common spaces are not well utilised and, indeed, resented by some residents as an extra expense and maintenance burden. According to Dr Namiko Minai, a researcher at the National Institute of Public Health, "residents struggle amongst themselves, as they were not really organized or trained before they started their life in those flats".[18] Dr Minai and her team are now attempting to improve the social dynamics of the *Fureai* Houses by implementing participatory measures drawn directly from the cohousing literature.

Photos 1.9 -1.12: Kobe's *Fureai* Houses; four examples of diverse type and scale.

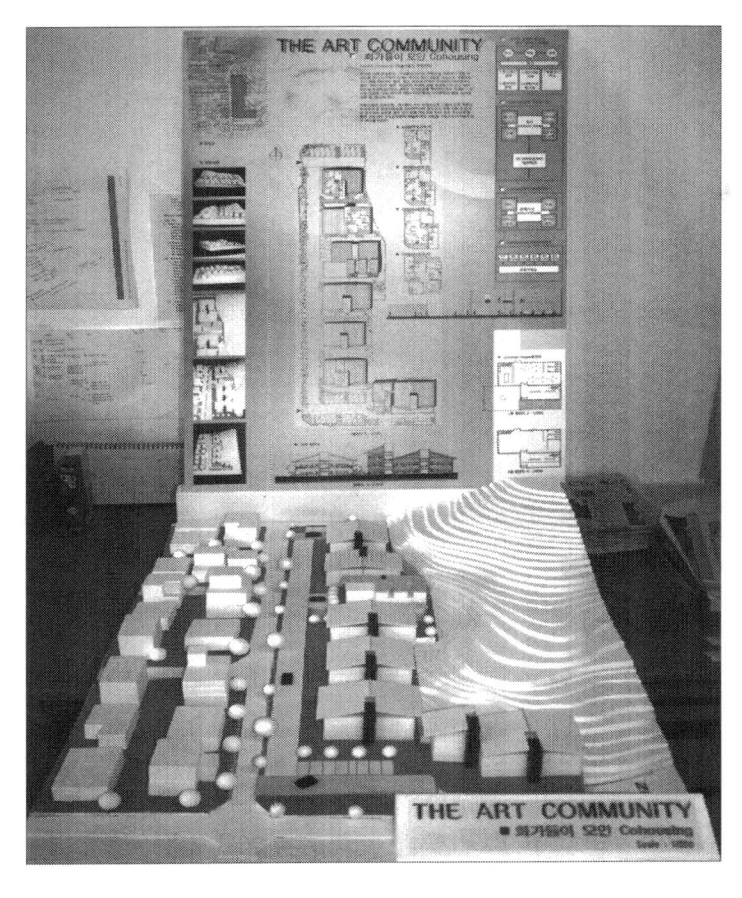

Photo 1.13: The work of Korean architecture students based on the cohousing model.

In Korea there is a similar growing awareness of the theory and practice of cohousing, at least amongst academics, if not the general public. A sociology professor has recently published a book about cohousing, incorporating examples from Europe, America and Australia.[19] A professor of architecture has published an article about cohousing in the journal of the Korean Housing Association.[20] His students, the next generation of Korean architects, have been designing cohousing projects in the teaching studio. Knowledge of cohousing in Asia remains mostly theoretical. Only the private Tokyo project has been designed and built by participatory process. Yet, there is sufficient interest and commitment to suggest that others may soon follow.

Asian interest in cohousing theory and practice flies in the face of previous cohousing rhetoric. Cohousing has often been touted as an exclusively Western phenomenon with little relevance to non-Western societies presumed to be based on extended families and high ambient levels of social support. In truth, Asia has suffered devastating social disruption over recent decades through rapid and ill-considered Westernisation that has brought a breakdown of family and community structures as well as loss of cultural values. There is an appreciation now of the role that cohousing has played in addressing these trends in the West and a readiness to apply cohousing principals to address similar needs. Dr Minai writes,

> Japan has a quite different way of thinking about housing and community development from the United States and other Western countries. On the other hand, we do have common problems of small scale families and other related problems of community destruction. Children find it difficult to play outside, and they do not encounter different attitudes of adults. Many children do not have the chance to discuss their thinking with their neighbours. Cohousing may solve some of these problems.[21]

Cohousing in Africa?

Africa has similarly undergone huge social disruption over a long period of colonial domination and post-colonial aftermath. South Africans, to take an extreme example, have suffered unthinkable rupture to community cohesion and development at the hands of the Apartheid regime. The efforts of the post-Apartheid regime have failed to improve the situation in many respects. The provision of critically needed social housing, for example, has suffered for being based on an idealised

Western suburban model of detached, privately owned dwellings on separate plots of land. Subdivisions typically have reticulated power, water and sewerage for which the below ground infrastructure consumes 70% of the budget. Dwellings, therefore, are of least size and quality and located on tiny, barren plots of land (Photo 1.14). No consideration is given to the social implications of such development given the deep-rooted traditions for extended family dwelling patterns in South Africa.

However, there is awareness of the cohousing model amongst South African academics, and the lessons it provides for social sustainability. The Built Environment Support Group (BESG), a non-profit housing provider associated with the School of Architecture in Durban, designed and had built a pilot project, *Shayamoya*, incorporating numerous cohousing strategies (Figure 1.4). Another research initiative involving scholars from South Africa, Denmark and Australia has proposed that the cohousing model be adapted for the overwhelming numbers of HIV/AIDS affected families and orphans who, lacking social welfare, fall back into modified forms of extended family support.[22] Building social support networks (or 'social capital' or 'community capacity') is one of the most effective interventions in addressing the HIV/AIDS pandemic. It's an essential element of sheltered housing provision for sufferers, particularly those orphaned by the disease. Cohousing offers a precedent for the development of housing that might mitigate the catastrophe.

Photo 1.14: Government provided 'social' housing.

Figure 1.4: Shayamoya.
(Drawing by BESG)

These Asian and African developments illustrate the robustness of the cohousing model, i.e. its capacity for adaptation to suit different cultural conditions, social dysfunction in its various guises and instances of dire need. These latest developments have not been foreseen by cohousing experts. Yet, the extended family tradition is common to almost all cultures in one form or another, and furthermore, societies everywhere are suffering the breakdown of traditional social support networks. Cohousing has been able to adapt so spectacularly because its principles are so simple. The primary intention of the cohousing model is to build more supportive, sharing and caring relationships between neighbours. Cohousing carries no other ideology, credo or baggage. For this reason it will increasingly become, through the twenty first century, an important means of addressing social dysfunction and inducing positive social change.

Cohousing and sustainability

Cohousing has been chosen as the case-study vehicle for this book about sustainability, not simply because of its environmentally responsive architectural and urban design features. As noted, cohousing has developed in direct response to perceived *social* problems of the late twentieth century – personal alienation and the breakdown of community, in particular. Therefore, cohousing offers an opportunity to investigate what we now understand to be the ecological interconnectivity of the social and environmental dimensions of sustainability.

Certain scholars in the field of *community psychology* have looked at this phenomenon within circumstantial communities (eg. an urban neighbourhood) claiming that such research can provide unique insights into the relationship between physical context, social conditions and lifestyle. Community psychology, it is said, "continues to hold out the possibility that settings can be designed which maximise positive development and optimise the quality of life for their inhabitants".[23] New Urbanists, an amalgam of architects, planners and urban designers make similar claims of 'model' communities such as Seaside, Florida.

> When people talked about feeling like they belonged, they frequently mentioned the presence and positioning of the porches in Seaside as well as the type of beach pavilions provided. These architectural enhancements provide opportunity for exchange with neighbours.[24]

The matter of whether design *per se* can help build a sense of belonging or a sense of community is extremely vexed. There is a long and much discredited history of *architectural determinism* which might once have held that strangers moving into an appropriately designed neighbourhood would likely cohere as a community. One need only browse the marketing material for the next gated housing development to be presented with this illusion, still. Gated 'communities', however, are generally designed without the involvement of future residents. The involvement of prospective residents in the design and development of cohousing, on the other hand, builds social cohesion and commitment within the group before inhabitation of the project. The process creates a sense of community up front that is absent from most other forms of, or proposals for, sustainable urban development.

The intentionality and social cohesion of cohousing communities facilitates ongoing manipulation of the built environment for social and environmental gain. Their social ties and level of commitment enable residents to act as a single entity when implementing particular technologies appropriate for consensual communities – centralised neighbourhood heating, for example. Such intermediate-scaled energy and waste systems are likely to function more efficiently and responsively than conventional ones.

> CoHousing's principle contribution to a sustainable society is that it offers another scale of social organisation – an intermediate scale between the single family and the town or municipality – thereby expanding the palette of technologies that can be applied.[25]

Social cohesion and trust facilitate sharing and collaboration that makes possible a range of practical savings, many with environmental consequences. There is potential, for example, for coordinated activity such as car pooling, bulk food storage and organic farming. The process is cyclical, since social relationships are built through residents working together to address practical needs. In cohousing, social cohesion engenders personal responsibility for one's actions through "its provision of a human scale, knowable society in which individuals have reflected to them, and recognise, the importance of their personal roles".[26] The community provides a touchstone. It "seeks to maintain itself as an ongoing entity, providing a fixed context against which to measure the changes in our personal microcosms, and of the ever quickening and often unsettling changes in the vast, global culture beyond the community".[27]

Chapter outline

The remainder of this book is in two parts. Part One (Chapters 2–13) offers descriptions of twelve cohousing projects located in five countries: Canada, the US, New Zealand, Australia and Japan. Each 'snapshot' represents the status of the community at a fixed point in time. These 'case studies' were selected for their distinctive and differing characteristics. They are not meant to typify cohousing, but rather, illustrate by their diversity and cultural specificity the adaptability of the cohousing model. In a sense, this book is intended to continue where McCamant and Durrett left off. The first (1988) edition of their book predominantly featured Danish cohousing. In the second (1994) edition, they incorporated the first North American examples. This book features North American examples built since, as well as some on the opposite side of the Pacific where cohousing has most recently arrived. This book is also intended to portray the robustness and adaptability of the cohousing model to suit different cultures so necessarily takes a more international perspective.

Part Two (Chapters 14–19) offers analysis and discussion ensuing from Part One. Chapters 14-17 present quantitative and qualitative case study data within four different domains or categories: 'circumstance', 'interaction', 'relationship' and 'engagement'.[28] Chapter 14 discusses *circumstance*, which comprises the physical *setting* of a community (ie. its location, site planning and architecture) and its coordinated *systems* such as recycling and composting. Chapter 15 investigates two kinds of interpersonal *interaction* in cohousing – *influence* and *exchange*. Chapter 16 examines *relationships* in terms of *sharing* and *support*. Chapter 17 considers *engagement* in terms of a sense of *belonging* and the personal *efficacy* that a sense of belonging can deliver. The remaining two chapters discuss a range of implications arising from the preceding analysis. Chapter 18 ties the threads of the analysis together with an holistic theoretical model, the Community Empowerment Model (CEM). Finally, Chapter 19 broadens the discussion, applying lessons learnt from the analysis of cohousing to issues of community development and sustainable human settlement, generally.

Notes:

[1] Rudin, D. and N. Falk (1999). Building the 21st Century Home: The Sustainable Urban Neighbourhood. Oxford, Architectural Press: 195.

[2] Goldsmith, E., R. Allen, et al. (1972). "A Blueprint for Survival". The Ecologist 2(1): 1-43: 2.

[3] The New Shorter Oxford English Dictionary (1993).

[4] Brundtland, G. H. (1987). Our Common Future. Brussels, World Commission on Environment and Development.

[5] Hillery, G. A. (1955). "Definitions of Community: Areas of Agreement". Rural Sociology 20: 111-123.

[6] It should be noted that in the last decade additional meaning has consistently been attached to the label, intentional community. Many have used it to distinguish particular contemporary communities from communes of the past or present.

[7] Perkins, D. D., B. B. Brown, et al. (1996). "The Ecology of Empowerment: Predicting Participation in Community Organisations". Journal of Social Issues 52(1): 85-110: 86.

[8] Perkins, D. D. and M. A. Zimmerman (1995). "Empowerment Theory, Research, and Application". American Journal of Community Psychology 23(5): 569-579: 570.

[9] McCamant, K. and C. Durrett (1994). CoHousing: A Contemporary Approach to Housing Ourselves. Berkeley, Habitat Press.

[10] McCamant and Durrett (1994: 10).

[11] McCamant and Durrett (1994: 12).

[12] Shey, T. H. (1977). "Why Communes Fail: A Comparative Analysis of the Viability of Danish and American Communes". Journal of Marriage and the Family 39/3(August): 612.

[13] Fromm, D. (1985). "Living-together Housing". Architectural Review(April): 63-75: 66.

[14] The matter of which was first is disputed; at least two cohousing projects started as intentional communities in the 1980s and later became known as cohousing.

[15] At about 70%, Australia has the highest rate of home ownership in the world.

[16] Altman, D. (1980). Rehearsals for Change: Politics and Culture in Australia. Melbourne, Fontana: 46.

[17] Earthsong Eco-neighbourhood (2000). Information Booklet. Auckland, Earthsong Eco-neighbourhood: 4.

[18] Personal communication.

[19] Dwelling Research Group (2000) Cohousing in the World: Dwelling with Neighbours. Seoul, Kyomunsa.

[20] Shin, Yong-Jae (2001) "A Study on the Harmony of Privacy and Community in Cohousing". Housing Research Journal, Korean Housing Association, V12/1: 45-56.

[21] Personal communication.

[22] Mullins, M., G. Meltzer, et al. (2001). Co-operative Models for HIV/AIDS Sheltered Housing in South Africa. XXIX IAHS (International Association of Housing Science) Congress, 21st to the 25th of May 2001, Ljubljana, Slovenia.

[23] Lorion, R. P. and J. R. Newbrough (1996). "Psychological Sense of Community: The Pursuit of the Field's Spirit". Journal of Community Psychology 24(4): 311-314: 311.

[24] Plas, J. M. and E. Lewis (1996). "Environmental Factors and Sense of Community in a Planned Town". American Journal of Community Psychology 24(1): 109-143: 137.

[25] Coldham, B. (1995). "The CoHousing Path to Sustainability". CoHousing: Journal of the CoHousing Network 8(3, Fall): 19-21: 19.

[26] Butcher, A. (1996). "The Marketing of Communitarian Values". CoHousing: Journal of the CoHousing Network 9(2, Summer): 6-7,13: 13.

[27] Butcher (1996: 13).

[28] Matters of methodology, such as the reasons for casting the analysis in terms of these particular domains, have generally been omitted from this book. Suffice to say, that the four categories represent the predominant influences (nominated by the survey respondents themselves) on the pro-environmental values attitudes and behaviours of cohousing residents. For a fuller explanation of the methodology see Meltzer, G. (2000). "Cohousing: Verifying the importance of community in the application of environmentalism". Journal of Architectural and Planning Research 17(2): 110-132.

Part One

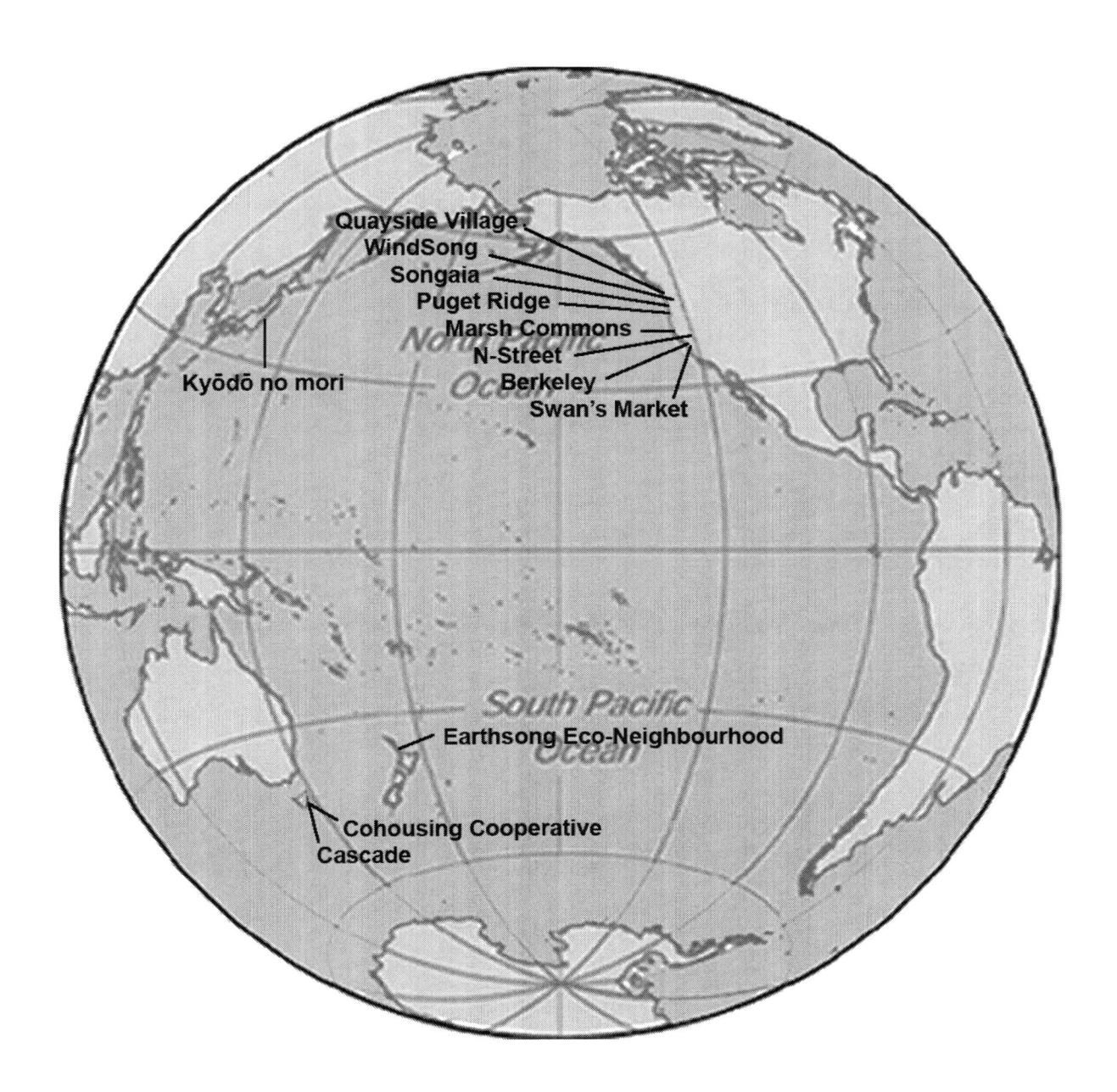

Quayside Village
WindSong
Songaia
Puget Ridge
Marsh Commons
N-Street
Berkeley
Swan's Market
Kyōdō no mori
Earthsong Eco-Neighbourhood
Cohousing Cooperative Cascade

Location of the cohousing projects featured in Part One

Photo 2.1 (above): The jaunty architecture of Quayside Village Cohousing.

Photo 2.2 (left): Internal courtyard with the common house at ground level.

Photo 2.3 (below): A father-and-daughter common meal cooking team.

2 Quayside Village Cohousing

The goal of Quayside Village is to have a community which is diverse in age, background and family type that offers a safe, friendly, living environment which is affordable, accessible and environmentally conscious. The emphasis is on quality of life including the nurture of children, youth and elders.[1]

Name	Quayside Village Cohousing
Address	510 Chesterfield Ave, North Vancouver, BC V7M 2L9
Context	Urban–residential neighbourhood. Walk to shops, schools, services and beach.
Households	19 (1xStudio, 8x1bd, 5x2bd, 5x3bd)
Adults	26
Renters	6
Developed	February 1995 – September 1998
Developer	The residents, incorporated as Quayside Village Cohousing Ltd.
Architect	Richard Valee of Courtyard Architects.
Funding	Member equity (25%) and a loan from North Shore Credit Union. The grey water system was funded by the Canada Mortgage and Housing Corp.
Site area	0.1 hectares / 0.25 acres
Common house	240 m² / 2,600 ft²
Ave. dwelling	80 m² / 860 ft²
Project cost	Can$3,600,000 / US$2,400,000[2]

Adults: 26; Children (under 18 yrs): 8
Renters: 6; Working from home: 3

Table 2.1: Community Data.

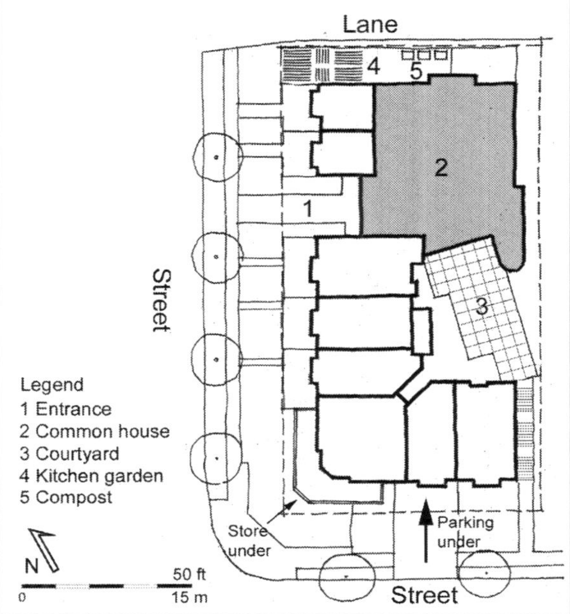

Figure 2.1: Site plan.

Legend
1 Entrance
2 Common house
3 Courtyard
4 Kitchen garden
5 Compost

Quayside Village Cohousing is characterised by its diversity. True to its mission statement (above) it enjoys a population of diverse age, income, ethnicity, spiritual orientation and life stage. Indeed, its founding members pro-actively sought single, elderly and disadvantaged residents – those often isolated members of society who most benefit from close community ties.

The children have been amongst the biggest beneficiaries. Of the six children under six, four are without siblings, but as a 'tribe', they enjoy close sibling-like relationships. In order to include lower-income households, the project incorporated five 'affordable' units (a quarter of the total number), four for sale at 80% of market value and one rental unit.[3] The group received no government subsidy for these units, but to improve their viability the City permitted an increased site density, reduced setbacks and fewer car parks.[4]

The project is located in the resurgent inner city neighbourhood of Lonsdale, North Vancouver. It is fifteen minutes from downtown Vancouver by ferry and an easy walk to the ocean, shops, schools, libraries, restaurants and community services.[5] The building is situated on a corner, flanked to the east by similarly scaled four-storey apartment buildings and to the west, by detached houses and duplexes. The somewhat jaunty architecture is richly detailed and brightly painted in 'brick dust', 'old linen' and 'tea leaf' colours. Individually expressed two and three-storey townhouses face the street, above which two levels of single-storey apartments appear to huddle under a massive gabled roof (Figure 2.2).

Figure 2.2: Western elevation (Drawing by architect, Richard Valee).

A pre-existing corner store, the Dome Mart, has been resurrected in the new building and its landmark copper dome reinstated above the corner (see Photo 2.1). The units are accessed from generous balconies facing into an intimately scaled, internal courtyard. These offer opportunities for gardening and informal social interaction. Balustrades support the 'vertical landscaping' of creepers and edible plants that provide food, shade and privacy (Photo 2.2). The common house at Quayside Village (Figure 2.3) is directly accessible from the street and the internal courtyard. Unconventionally, the entrance and principal social space are combined, creating an open and welcoming arrival experience. A fireplace centrally located within the space incorporates 'memory boxes' for display and a round timber bench for seating (Photo 2.10). Through recycled French doors is a generous multi-purpose space used for common meals, meetings, dancing, yoga etc. It is occasionally let for activities of the broader community, such as a health and parenting program for immigrants. A kitchen, office, guest room, bathroom, laundry and children's room adjoin. On an upper level, an octagonal domed reading room with stunning city and mountain views is available for reading, homework, craft and meditation (Photo 2.4).

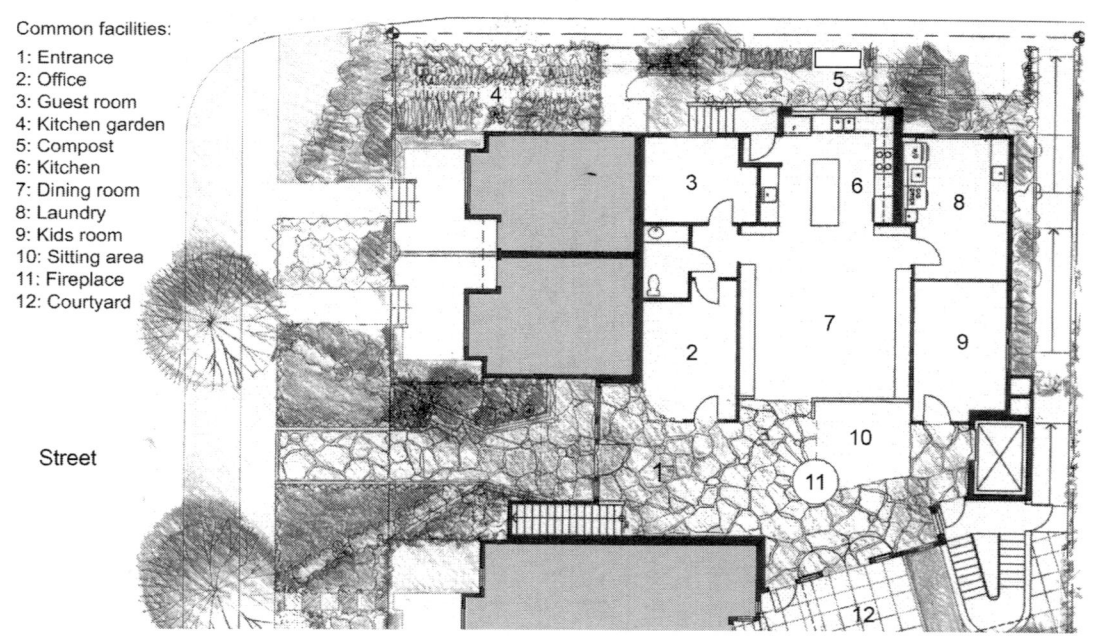

Common facilities:
1: Entrance
2: Office
3: Guest room
4: Kitchen garden
5: Compost
6: Kitchen
7: Dining room
8: Laundry
9: Kids room
10: Sitting area
11: Fireplace
12: Courtyard

Figure 2.3: Common house plan (Drawing by architect, Richard Valee).

In accordance with its mission statement, the group has incorporated many environmental strategies and technologies into the project. Most importantly, it is urban and dense. In this way, it uses valuable land efficiently and enables residents to 'work, live and play' in their locality. Six residents don't own vehicles, preferring to walk, bike and use public transport. The project has been designed to water and energy efficiency standards set by the BC Hydro 'Power Smart' and BC Gas 'Energy Efficiency' programs. A single water meter is deemed sufficient for the whole community. Their grey water recycling plant costing Can$230,000 was the first in Canada to be incorporated in a multiple housing project (Photo 2.5).[6] Flooring, leadlight windows and doors were recycled from pre-existing dwellings on the site (Photo 2.6). One hundred and sixty cubic yards of construction waste were voluntarily sorted by members and delivered to various local recycling facilities.[7] For all of these measures and more, the project won a 1999 Silver Georgie Award from the Canadian Home Builders Association, selected from 444 entries.

Photo 2.4: A domed recreation room with views to Vancouver.
Photo 2.5: Grey water system.   Photo 2.6: Recycled window.

If 'green' technology is the hardware, then the software of sustainability is also much in evidence at Quayside Village. Common meals held twice weekly are mostly vegetarian. In summer, they incorporate fresh organic vegetables from the garden. Organic milk and other produce are delivered to residents keen to take advantage of the economy of scale available in cohousing. The waste recycling program is amongst the most effective in cohousing, with potential to reclaim 90% of household waste (Photos 2.7 and 2.8). Tools and equipment are readily shared. Computers and printers move around the building. Kitchenware and garden tools have all been 'donated' to the community by individual households. Two households together own a car whilst others share their vehicles informally. Only one (disabled) member has a washing machine despite all the units being plumbed for the purpose. Clothes are passed down the line as children outgrow them…and passed on by expanding adults to those a size smaller. The community has its own on-site, licensed childcare centre. All furniture and toys in the centre have come from thrift shops, garage sales or donations.

Many of these outcomes have been instigated by individual, environmentally conscious residents who, in the process, have informed and mentored others. Carol, one of the retired residents, has scoured thrift shops for hand-towels for the childcare centre, and in the process acquired toys, furniture and clothing. Brian, said by one resident to be "a walking model of environmental practice," administers the recycling program. He collected unwanted bins from all over town for the recycling station (Photo 2.7) and circulated a plan of the ideal under-sink layout to each household. A resident mechanic and computer expert willingly donate their time and expertise, enabling others to maintain and optimise their equipment. One grateful member suggests that, "for people who are interested [in environmental practices] but without the knowledge or practical skills, the impetus and the motivation and the people to encourage you on, is definitely there".

Photo 2.7: Recycling station in the basement.

Photo 2.8: Notice above one of the bins.

Quayside Village offers, in accordance with its vision statement, considerable practical and social support for disadvantaged members. The building is fully accessible by wheelchair and the common areas and rental unit have additional universal design features.[8] The group deliberately sought to include members with special needs and, as a result, two intellectually challenged single men have purchased two of the affordable units. However, their integration into community life has not been easy. The group had difficulty communicating with their parents who, in advocating for offspring, were perceived by some to be interfering in community decision-making.

This is, perhaps, symptomatic of a more general malaise. Vexed communication and poor social cohesion have been worrisome from the outset. One resident explains: "the difficulties and divisions we have experienced are mostly due to people's knowledge and expectations upon moving in, that is, what they understood living in community to mean or be like. We are struggling with a philosophy of unanimity versus individual needs and expectations". In part this may be due to literature glowingly advocating for the project during its development phase, in suggesting that:

> By going through the planning, design and decision-making processes together, residents form the bonds which are the basis for ongoing community. Decision-making and responsibilities are shared by all members and decisions are made using consensus. This puts all members on an equal footing, avoids power struggles, encourages everyone to participate by communicating openly and ensures that all aspects of an issue are considered. Any fears about differences that arise as a result of diversity are alleviated through effective communication.[9]

This is an idealised view of the cohousing development process. A more realistic expectation is put by one of the now much wiser residents:

> North Americans that are moulded by an individualistic and private property model have a very romantic conception of community based on an idealisation of harmony. The idea that a functional community is one that doesn't have conflict is pure illusion. Conflict is not a sign that a community is not working. Conflicts and differences and disputes are always going to exist.[10]

With the benefit of this hindsight, the group may well have applied more effort to improving their decision-making and conflict resolution procedures. As it was, the enormous challenge of being the developers and project managers left little time and energy for the purpose, as one founder member recounts:

> We had a difficult development process, dealing with the complexities of construction in an efficient and fair way. We had tax arrears to deal with and problems of a legal and financial nature. A preoccupation with business led to a neglect of social communication that lasted for eighteen months afterward and has had ongoing social repercussions.[11]

Indeed, continued financial pressure has placed an unremitting strain on group cohesion. Costly levies have been introduced to cover ongoing maintenance and unanticipated, retroactive repairs. Collective decisions about the distribution of these costs to individuals and families has necessitated outside facilitation. Some of the difficulty has been structural. Initially, for the purposes of the development process, the group was a legally constituted corporation. At move-in, they adopted a conventional Strata Title but did not formalise an alternative 'cohousing-based' set of bylaws to deal with day-to-day issues. "We always believed, based on an unspoken understanding, that consensus and face-to-face negotiation would be enough. We had that level of naiveté," admits one resident. "In the progression from Corporation to Strata Title it's been difficult to develop a discourse about Strata versus cohousing versus socially cohesive community".

A particularly divisive clash developed over usage of the internal courtyard, said by some to be 'kid dominated'. Reverberant noise quickly became problematic for residents and adjoining neighbours, alike. A protracted conflict resolution process resulted in guidelines limiting noise at certain times. However, this is a complex issue that goes beyond the simple matters of decibels and times of day. It is underpinned by differences of opinion about child socialisation and the dissimilar lifestyles of families and elderly or single members.

The design of a cooking roster generated another vexed discussion over demands on members' time. Like the noise issue, this dispute results, in part, from the community's diversity. Some residents deal daily with a stressful cocktail of work life, child rearing, domestic responsibility and recreation. One such member comments: "I don't see friends in Vancouver because it takes all of my social time to be even minimally involved in this place. I underestimated the amount of time involved and over estimated my willingness to give it". Other members, on the other hand, are retired, have grown children and enjoy a relaxed lifestyle. Their approach is, naturally, quite different. "The more involved I am, the more I get out of community" suggests one such retiree.

The difficulty experienced with the cooking roster exemplifies the organisational pressures on smaller cohousing groups. Quayside Village has established thirteen committees to deal with the day-to-day management of the project: Administration and Finance, Community Building, Building Systems, Maintenance, Landscaping, Parents, Indoor maintenance, Room Rental, Unit Rental, Parking, Safety and Emergency, Recycling, Building Restoration. On average, each committee comprises three members. Therefore, 26 residents (some of whom are inactive) are required to fill 39

Photo 2.9 (top): The common house entrance adorned with candles for the Nepalese festival of Tihar.
Photo 2.10 (bottom): The community's main social space contiguous with the main entry beyond.

positions so most have to sit on at least two committees. Because most members have very busy lives, committees sometimes eschew scheduled meetings. This can be frustrating for others, given that anyone interested in a particular issue may participate in committee decision-making if they so wish. "They make decisions on the fly, in the elevator" suggests one resident. "Nobody knows where the lines of authority really are". If the experience of other cohousing groups is any indication, Quayside Village Cohousing will rationalise and fine-tune – if not completely overhaul – its management structure in the years ahead.

The diversity that Quayside Village deliberately sought is probably its biggest challenge, but it is also its greatest blessing. Age diversity, for example, is much valued. Children roam freely throughout the building, visiting a selection of surrogate grandparents. The elderly, who mostly live alone, treasure the contact in return. "I never imagined how much I would enjoy the children," comments one, "it's been way beyond my highest expectation". Ethnic diversity is valued for the opportunity it offers to participate in, and learn about, non-Western traditions. Abi, a Nepalese member, annually adorns the common areas with candles for the festival of *Tihar* (Photo 2.9). Jews help celebrate Christmas, and Christians enjoy *Hanukah*.

Collectively, the group celebrates birthdays, plays music and organises creative opportunities (such as a mask making workshop said by one resident to be profoundly moving and growthful). Some members encourage each other in fitness work; going to the gym together and having a yoga instructor visit once a week. The group collectively walk their dogs and organise occasional outings. The prospects are bright for this ambitious group. Their high level of commitment to each other and the project is almost certainly going to prevail over their early teething problems. This is generally the experience of other longer-lived groups whose history has been similar.

Notes:

[1] Community mission statement, which appears in much of the group's literature.

[2] The currency conversion is based on relative values at the time of construction (in 1998).

[3] Because real estate values in inner Vancouver are so inflated, these units are still not affordable to low-income families. They are available to households on 80% of medium income for the region, which is still reasonable by North American standards. Units can only be on-sold at 80% of market value.

[4] Site density: increased from 1.2 to 1.95 FSR. Setbacks: Front yard, 10 ft reduced from 20 ft; rear yard, 4 ft reduced from 20 ft; side yard, 7 ft reduced from 15 ft. Parking: 22 stalls reduced from 24 (1.2 per unit).

[5] Services include three high schools, five elementary schools and the Lion's Gate Hospital.

[6] The system was funded by the Environmental Research Division of the Canadian Mortgage and Housing Corporation as an experimental pilot project. It has, in fact been a considerable management and financial burden for the community.

[7] The waste included 105 yd^3 of wood, 23 yd^3 of cardboard, 13 yd^3 of metal, 9 yd^3 of paper, 8 yd^3 of Styrofoam and 0.5 yd^3 of carpet underlay. In total 51% of demolition material was recycled, the highest level ever achieved in the Vancouver area.

[8] Including an elevator, wider than standard doors, door levers and rocker light switches.

[9] Mathew, R. (1997). "Quayside Village Cohousing: Construction set to begin in mid July". <u>CoHousing: The Newsletter for Cohousing in Western Canada</u> **5**(3): 2,3: 2.

[10] Personal communication.

[11] Personal communication.

Photo 3.1: One of WindSong's two pedestrian 'streets' or atriums, as they're called.
Photo 3.2: Hanging out in the atrium.   Photo 3.3: A 'private' front entrance.

3 WindSong Cohousing

Our purpose is to create, build and sustain a supportive community. The community promotes a sense of belonging in its members by providing common facilities and by encouraging open communication and interaction amongst residents.[1]

Name	WindSong Cohousing
Address	20543 96th Ave, Langley, BC V1M3W3
Context	Semi-rural, increasingly suburban.
Households	34 (6x1bd, 1x2bd, 19x3bd, 8x4bd)
Adults	61
Children (under 18 yrs)	36
Renters	6
Working from home	12
Developed	February 1991 – August 1996
Developers	The residents, as The Windsong CoHousing Construction Co-op, and the contractor, Bill Hancock of Northmark Construction Co.
Architects	John Davidson & John Simpson of Davidson, Yuen & Simpson.
Funding	Member equity (20%) and a loan from Emerest Trust, guaranteed by the Canada Mortgage and Housing Corporation.
Site area	2.39 hectares / 5.89 acres
Common house.	557 m^2 / 6,000 ft^2
Ave. dwelling	115 m^2 / 1,240 ft^2
Project cost	Can$5,200,000 / US$3,800,000

Table 3.1: Community Data.

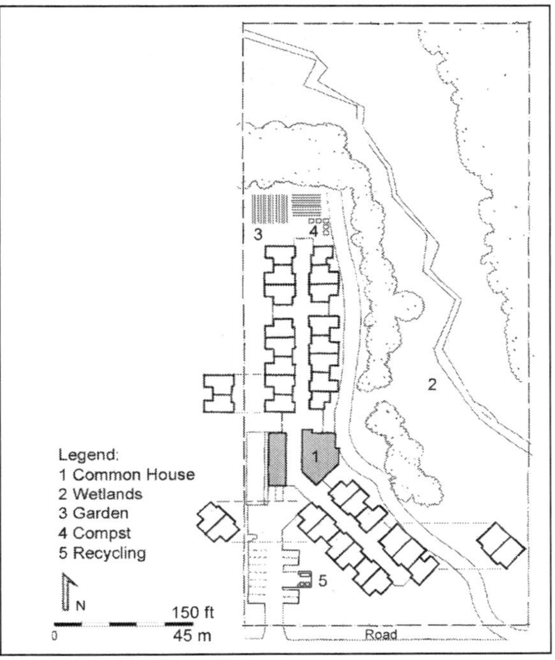

Figure 3.1: Site plan.

Legend:
1 Common House
2 Wetlands
3 Garden
4 Compst
5 Recycling

WindSong Cohousing community has no formal mission statement. However, the above declaration of purpose succinctly encapsulates the two most notable characteristics of this remarkable community – comprehensive interaction and open communication.

WindSong is located in Langley, BC, a one-hour drive southeast of Vancouver. Through the 1980s and '90s, the region was transformed from rural idyll into 'edge city'.[2] Productive farms and fecund ecosystems were subsumed by a creeping suburban landscape of tract housing and tarmac. In 1993, the group's founding members purchased a portion of riparian habitat that may well have suffered the same fate. The six-acre property was diagonally bisected by Yorkson Creek, home for millennia to breeding salmon, beaver, racoons, skunks, and countless varieties of birds and insects.

In consultation with professionals and their chosen contractor, the group considered a range of development options that would enable preservation of the wetlands. It quickly became apparent that economic viability and the footprint of land available for development imposed severe design constraints. The steering group adopted two fundamental strategies – very close clustering of the dwellings and basement parking. This suggested a previously unforeseen scenario, the construction of a single, extruded low-rise building.

Given the similarity of climate, the group adopted a Danish cohousing building type – a glass-covered pedestrian street separating two rows of attached townhouses (Figure 1.1(d)). In seeking

Chapter 3: Windsong Cohousing

development approval for the proposal, the group utilised the graphic shown in Figure 3.2. The image on the left shows the pre-existing house in the southwest corner of the property. The ecologically disastrous consequence of conventional lot development is shown in the centre, while the image on the right depicts the quite radical site planning option adopted by the community.

The project met significant cost overruns during construction. Some group members sold their homes or loaned monies at considerable financial risk. Northmark, the construction company, relinquished its profit to help save the project. Unit customisation, said by Bill Hancock, CEO of Northmark, to be "the crabgrass in the lawn of [a developer's] life", was minimised. With shared vision and commitment, group members, consultants and contractor together navigated a treacherous development course. The result was a unique building with a singular form and unified architectural language that metaphorically represents this truly cohesive community. It is perhaps no coincidence that WindSong is one of North America's most harmonious cohousing communities.

The project received a 1997 Gold Georgie Award for the most environmentally responsive (new) housing project in Canada. It was chosen from 550 entries on the basis of (a) the preservation of two thirds of the site as natural habitat, and (b) the inclusion of extensive shared facilities that enabled the building of comparatively small homes.[3] The common facilities include a kitchen, dining room, lounge, children's room, teen room, craft room, workshop, laundry, shared office, multi-purpose room, and guest room. All are accessible from Hancock Square – the entrance and central circulation hub through which residents and guests pass many times a day.[4]

The common house is located midway between two separate residential wings, each with a 110 m² (1,200 ft²) glazed pedestrian street that is ventilated in summer but unheated in winter. Passive solar gain tempers winter temperatures to some extent, but protection from the elements is its principal advantage. All along the *atrium*, as it is known, entries to dwellings are festooned with rugs, furniture and plants; like a strip of street cafés spilling onto the footpath. The colour and diversity of these contributions to the 'public realm' well represents the individuality of the residents and provide a necessary counterpoint to the unified and commanding quality of the architecture (Photos 3.1, 3.2 and 3.3).

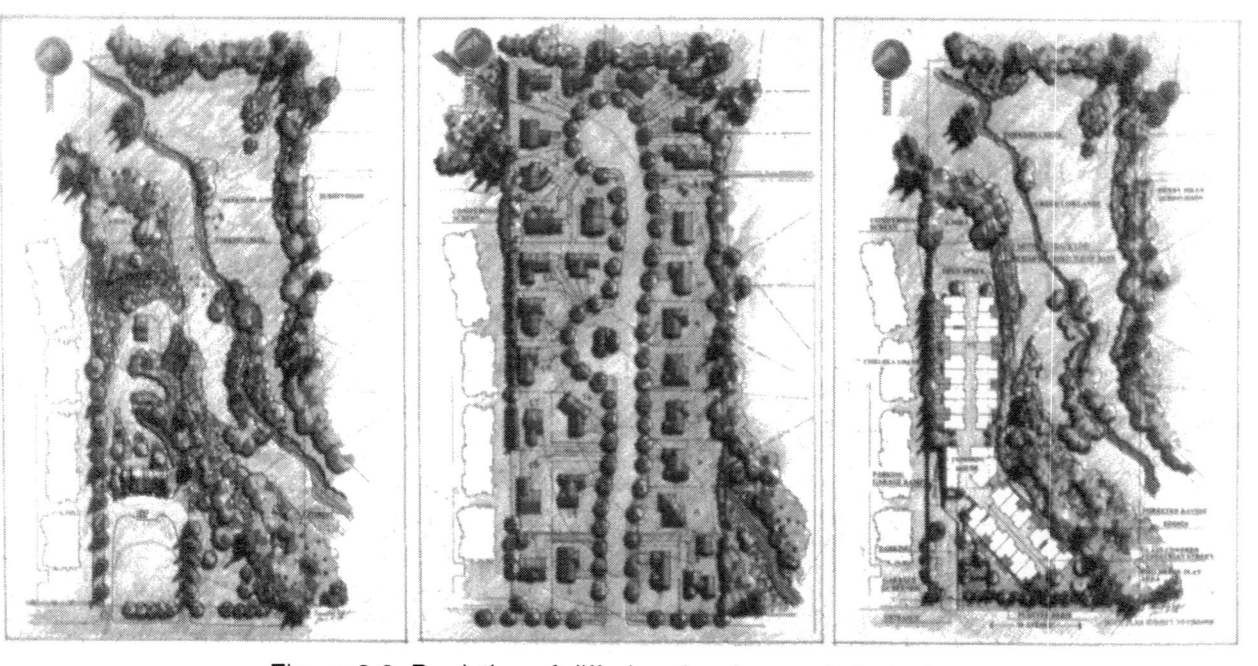

Figure 3.2: Depiction of differing development strategies.

Demographically, WindSong is not particularly diverse.[5] Yet, its most valuable and valued social characteristic is its rich diversity of talents and abilities. The range of skills and depth of experience at WindSong is such that members seldom have to seek outside advice or practical assistance. They have a resident accountant, architect, business coach, chaplain (retired), consultant, civic worker, college instructor, doctor, electrician, farmer, film maker, geologist, homemaker, journalist, librarian midwife, naturopath, nurse, nutritionist, office worker, physiotherapist, programmer, rolfer, salesperson, social worker, student, swim instructor, systems analyst, teacher, therapist, urban planner, waiter and x-ray technician.[6]

WindSong's diversity extends to members with esoteric, artistic and creative talent, who enthusiastically share their skills and passions with the community at large. Those with experience in Tai Chi, yoga, dance and areas of personal growth regularly run workshops. Jean, an acclaimed artist, holds regular watercolour courses. Musicians offer tutorial classes and wordsmiths promote creative writing. Artistic expression, whether by professionals, keen amateurs or novices, is readily shared with the whole community. A stage in a corner of the common house dinning room is a venue for dramatic and musical performances by young and old. "We enjoy being on stage for each other," writes one member, "it produces treasured 'WindSong moments'".[7]

WindSong 50's Dance
Saturday, April 8th, 2000

This will be the first in a series of decade themed dances. I will be putting together a tape of 50's music, so if you have any music you would like to give me, (Leah in #10). I will be creating a tape of great dance music from this decade. So dig up, look for, or find that old poodle skirt or white t-shirt and leather jacket, and come dressed in the 50's fashions. Plan to dance the night away. We will also be preparing a 50's Diner meal that night. We'll be serving hamburgers (or Garden burgers) fries and floats and/or milkshakes.
Look for the sign up sheet in the meals book. So lets Rock around the clock that night!

WindSong Cowboy Dinner

featurin' all yer fav'rite cowBoy foods
Beans, Beef, Biscuits, Beer.
Haul them cowboy duds out'n the closet,
git them ol' boots on, an'
make fer the dinin' room at

Dinner 6:15 pm
Saturday, April 29th

Live Music · Dancin' · Hootin' · Hollerin'
Bitchin' · Moanin' · Cryin'

All shootin' irons will be left at the door.

Bring a poem, song, story, etc.
See "Slim" (Larry S.)
for stage time.

CALLING ALL WINDSONG INSTRUMENTALISTS

Norma White would like to hear from all those who would be interested in performing from time to time within a small, sympathetic group of fellow players, the object being (1) to have regular relatively non-stressful occasions to work towards, and (2) to get used to playing for an audience. A move to eventually bring more WindSong talent out into the open and encourage our young people. Those interested, call Norma.[8]

GET INTO THAT TRIBAL FEELING!

The Conlins had such a wonderful time learning African Drumming while on holidays; we thought it would be a great experience to share it with our WindSong family. It's also a way to bring friends and neighbours in to play with us – it's relaxing and energizing at the same time. No previous drumming experience required. All ages, 9 and up. We are considering a performance in the evening. Cost $20. Common House, 1 pm, Oct 4th.[9]

Figure 3.3: Several notices from the community's newsletter, WindSong World, illustrating the breadth of talent amongst residents and their readiness to share.

There is also a critical mass of WindSong members with an interest in social and recreational pursuits. "We have a good representation of all ages in the community and therefore provide well for everyone's social needs. We have a book club, a Life Purpose Circle, a seasonal choir, keen groups of barbecuers and bridge enthusiasts, lots of vegetarians, recreational walkers, runners, gardeners, cyclists and tennis players".[10] In all these endeavours there is a strong ethos of unselfconscious sharing and having fun in a non-threatening atmosphere. The notices shown in Figure 3.3 were posted in *WindSong World*, the community's newsletter since 1997. *WindSong World* is an essential outlet for creative writing, especially for the children. It features articles, stories, poems and jokes by adults and kids, plus community news, advertisements and a monthly calendar of upcoming events. *WindSong World* is also an important vehicle for the dissemination of information and the discussion of community matters (Figure 3.4). Reports from management teams, a schedule of common meals and proposals for the next general meeting are also included.

Figure 3.4: Copies of WindSong World.

Figure 3.5: A notice on the community bulletin board.

Common meals at WindSong are different from the cohousing norm. For the initial few years of its existence WindSong was without a common house kitchen, so by necessity, shared meals were potlucks. Held six times per week, these were universally popular, not least because Norma, an accomplished pianist in her seventies, would play in the background and lead singing around the piano after the meal (Photo 3.7). "Norma can play almost every song written in the twentieth century," suggests one appreciative resident. Over time, potlucks became an established format and have since been retained for the majority of common meals. Some residents prefer them because they attract fewer members (about 12 – 16) and therefore provide an opportunity for more intimate conversation. Common meals prepared by cooking teams are more popular, attracting 20 – 40 members. These are commonly themed, providing further opportunity for collective fun through song, dance or performance (Figure 3.3).[11]

Photo 3.4: Vegetable garden.

Photo 3.5: Compost bins.

Photo 3.6: Bicycle storage.

Chapter 3: Windsong Cohousing 33

A further distinguishing characteristic of WindSong Cohousing Community is the concerted effort applied to effective communication. Open communication is deemed essential for improving and deepening social relationships. "Communication is the social juice of life," suggests one member. "It pays to communicate more openly, more deeply and more often even though the potential for conflict is greater. It generally leads to increased tolerance of difference and greater understanding of individual needs and wants". This in turn enables the community to function more effectively.

> We are striving to value and respect every person for his or her own unique qualities, to make decisions together for the good of the whole community, not just one or a few people, and to collaborate to solve problems and keep the community functioning in a wholesome way. It's a long slow process.[12]

Photo 3.7: Norma at the piano in the common house dinning room whilst others finish their meal. Note the intergenerational exchange occurring.

Whilst much communication happens informally, the group has established a range of options for structured exchange. Apart from *WindSong World*, there are bulletin boards in Hancock Square, a telephone messaging service to every household and *Communi-Link*, an intranet service that broadcasts messages, delivers the minutes from recent meetings and holds an archive of useful documents. By these means, writes one member, "we may hear a plea for the return of a child's favourite toy, a request for a work party in the large organic garden, announcements about an emergency meeting, [or hear about] prospective buyers joining us for a potluck or gift tickets for an outside event".[13]

Open communication unquestionably oils the wheels of governance at WindSong. Community meetings are held monthly. Proposals intended for discussion are circulated in advance, enabling smoother consensus decision-making. "We operate on the assumption that everyone has been informed of the upcoming proposals and therefore if they do not express an objection, they must support the decision being made by those attending the meetings".[14] That's not to say that decisions are necessarily made easily or quickly. "Juicy issues tend to attract more participants," one member observes. Contentious issues may linger for several meetings, simply because, "we...have a mature willingness to explore the ideas and views of others".[15] The fine tuning of their decision-making system has taken much time and effort, but eight years after moving in, WindSong members are truly reaping the benefit. "At meetings in the beginning, people would get angry, storm out and not speak to each other," recalls one member, "but now, everyone cracks up laughing over similar disputes. We have come such a long way!"

Notes:

[1] From "WindSong CoHousing Community Answers to Commonly Asked Questions". <u>WindSong Cohousing Information Package</u>, 1996.

[2] Garreau, J. (1991). <u>Edge City : life on the new frontier</u>. New York, Doubleday.

[3] At 115 sq. m. (1240 sq. ft) the dwellings are about half the size of new homes built in North America.

[4] Hancock Square is named in honour of Bill Hancock, for his critical contribution to the birth of the project.

[5] Windsong has only a few members of ethnic, disabled, disadvantaged or gay and lesbian minorities; fewer than most other cohousing groups.

[6] See the community's website, http://www.cohousing.ca/cohsng4/windsong/.

[7] McIntyre, V. (2000). "WindSong Cohousing". <u>CoHousing: Building Community...One Neighbourhood at a Time.</u> **13**(1): 57.

[8] WindSong World: Newsletter of the WindSong CoHousing Community, Sept.1997. **1**(6): 2.

[9] WindSong World: Newsletter of the WindSong CoHousing Community, Sept.1997. **1**(6): 15.

[10] http://www.cohousing.ca/cohsng4/windsong/.

[11] Themes have included an Experimental Food Night, a Midsummer Night Swedish Feast and a Wrap-it-up Rap Night.

[12] Kilgannon, G. (2003). *Living the cohousing lifestyle* in <u>Another kind of space: creating ecological dwellings and environments</u>. A. Dearling and G. Meltzer. Lyme Regis, Enabler Press: 155-157: 157.

[13] McIntyre, V. (2000).

[14] Kilgannon, G. (2003: 157).

[15] McIntyre, V. (1997). "Being here at Windsong". <u>CoHousing: The Newsletter for Cohousing in Western Canada</u> **5**(4): 1.

Photo 4.1: Making popcorn chains in the common house kitchen.
Photo 4.2: Songaians in full voice prior to the Thanksgiving feast.

4 Songaia Cohousing

We believe that intentional communities have a critical role in the future evolution of the planet and human relations. These communities can encourage sharing the responsibility of our planet with all other life forms, reclaiming ancient, symbolic relationships toward sacred space, conserve the earth's resources through sharing, and re-establish multi-generation/extended family groupings. To these ideals we are committed.[1]

Name	Songaia Cohousing Community
Address	22401 39th Ave, Bothell, WA
Context	Semi-rural, but becoming increasingly suburban.
Households	13 (3x1bd, 2x2bd, 8x3bd)
Adults 24	Children (under 18 yrs) 12
Renters 1	Working from home 1
Developed	April 1991 – December 2000
Developers	The residents as Songaia Association LLC
Architects	Rick Brown of Brown & Assoc.
Funding	Member equity plus a loan from Viking Community Bank
Site area	4.25 hectares / 10.5 acres
Common house.	325 m² / 3,500 ft²
Ave. dwelling	127 m² / 1,368 ft²
Project cost	US$2,700,000

Table 4.1: Community Data.

Legend:
1 Common House
2 Barn
3 Greenhouse
4 Vegetable garden
5 Compost
6 The commons
7 Forest

Figure 4.1: Site plan.

It is commonly said that cohousing communities, "espouse no ideology other than the desire for a more practical and social home environment".[2] If this truly is the case, then Songaia Cohousing Community is the exception to the rule. Songaia (meaning 'Song of the Living Earth') can be characterised, above all else, by its strongly held ideology. Indeed, it's likely that it would not exist as a cohousing community but for the ideals that sustained it through one of the most protracted development periods in the short history of North American cohousing.

Photo 4.3: Duplexes are the predominant housing form at Songaia.

In 1988, a fledgling community of four households moved to ten acres of rural land in Snohomish County, north of Seattle. Three years later, they initiated a program of growth and development based on the cohousing model that would bring ten more years of unrelenting struggle (Table 4.2). They started with a vision – an environmentally sustainable setting for a rich, integrated community life. They adopted the humanist design strategies of Christopher Alexander's *A Pattern Language*[3] and took a Cooperative legal structure as the one that best represented their social intent. The community swelled as new members were attracted to the dream. Early in the design process, architecture students from the University of Washington involved the group in a *charrette*, a community design process that enabled further design development. Having met the demands of the County and secured the support of neighbours, they completed a design proposal and sought estimates from contractors. The year was 1996; the process had taken five years, so far.

The outcome of the tender process was devastating. The cost per household was way too high for most participants to bear.[4] Within a short time, all but five families had departed. Morale hit rock bottom for a period that became known as the 'dark night of the soul.' "The hardest part," recalls one member, "was that so many good and committed people left for financial reasons. We attracted people who were living their dreams – a massage therapist, a woodworker, a yoga instructor – people not earning enough money to buy in". However, with renewed determination those remaining went 'back to the drawing board'. They initiated a rolling program of recruitment and intensified their relationships with consultants. At some sacrifice to the dream, they adopted cost saving design strategies and creative, if not risky, financing arrangements. They sought a new contractor willing to work for a fixed price and identified 'off-mortgage' (or sweat equity) projects to the value of $34,000. Finally, in the year 2000, the process culminated in the construction of five new duplexes and refurbishment of two pre-existing houses. Essential landscaping and aspects of construction were completed by the residents themselves. At different times during the ten-year process they had commissioned three development consultants, a financial advisor, two architects and two contractors. Twenty-seven households had been involved. Thirteen remained.

Songaia is one of a few cohousing communities to have evolved from a pre-existing intentional community.[5] The founders were members of the Institute of Cultural Affairs (ICA), a non-profit organisation involved in grass-roots community development around the world. The principles espoused by the ICA underpin the utopian vision that opens this chapter. Together with contemporary eco-spirituality they have shaped the community's values: i.e. to honour individual, family and community; to live a sustainable lifestyle; to share a rich spiritual life; to pursue life-long learning; to be open to diversity; to share responsibility; and to pursue community outreach.[6]

Dreaming and scheming	Dark night of the soul	Redesign and regroup	Final feasibility	Labour and delivery
1991 / 1992 / 1993 / 1994 / 1995	1996	1997 / 1998	1999	2000
Initial planning meetings / Formulate value statement / Initiate community culture / Initial feasibility study / Research eco-sensitive / Develop design concept / Research legal structure / Study A Pattern Language / Refine design with UW / Research financial options / Establish design programme / Second feasibility study / Apply for rezoning / Meet County requirements / Visit neighbours for support	Complete design proposal / Submit design for estimates / Establish financial structure	Recruit new members / Back to the drawing board / Research housing alternatives / Explore creative financing / Recruit new members / Work closely with consultants / Complete redesign / Rethink legal structure	Recruit new members / Change from Coop to Condo / Secure Bank financing / Retain fixed price contractor	Recruit new members / Work on off-mortgage projects / Monitor construction / Move in

Table 4.2: Songaia's ten-year long development journey (courtesy of Fred Lamphear).

Photo 4.4: American Indian symbolism at the entry to the community.

Figure 4.2: Songaian philosophy.

Figure 4.3: Songaia's songbook cover.

Chapter 4: Songaia Cohousing 39

Sustainability, Songaia style, is an amalgam of principles and practices derived from a biocentric (as opposed to an anthropocentric) worldview, a bioregional orientation and the tenets of 'voluntary simplicity'. (See Page 163 for an explanation of voluntary simplicity.) Theirs is a consciousness and a lifestyle based on: sharing resources; coordinating services; minimising consumption; buying locally and in bulk; and growing as much food as possible. An extensive organic vegetable garden supplemented by a large greenhouse provides home grown food all year round.

The food program is the most progressive in North American cohousing, being the type of system more commonly found in communes and shared houses. Adults contribute $80 per month to a kitty and for children the charge is $5 for every year of a child's age.[7] This covers the cost of common meals *plus* foodstuff for the home. At any time, members may access a community pantry stocked with grains, fruit, vegetables, soy products, canned food and other staples (Photo 4.5). In addition, the store meets household needs for toilet paper, toiletries, cleaners etc. "It's like having our own corner shop," says one resident. "Before we came here, we used to have four of five cupboards just for food. We don't need that any more". A committee of residents do the shopping. They purchase locally and in bulk - buying organic milk, eggs, fruit and vegetables as necessary.

Common meals, for which there is no separate charge, occur five times per week. Menus are posted well in advance so that the buying team can purchase non-staple ingredients for each scheduled meal. Members volunteer to cook or clean once a week, or alternatively, undertake the necessary childcare to enable others to do so. This third option is rarely formalised in cohousing although it happens informally in many communities. There is no requirement for residents to sign up for meals as everyone's attendance is assumed.[8] In terms of their common meals and food systems generally, Songaia functions very much like a family.

Songaians believe that nourishing the *spirit* is as important as feeding the *body*. Their spirituality is a loosely defined, eclectic mix of beliefs and practices, closely allied to the vision of a sustainable future outlined in the opening quotation. It draws on deep ecology, New Age spirituality and Native American mysticism. Established festivals are adapted to give expression to these beliefs. May Day, for example, is celebrated as Earth Day or the Festival of the Earth, when "we recognize

Photo 4.5: A corner of Songaia's community pantry.

our responsibility to care for the Earth" through tree planting, dedication, singing, dancing and feasting.[9] Earth Day is the biggest annual gathering at Songaia, involving as many as two hundred people. The celebratory centrepiece is a May Pole dance on 'the Commons' – the central lawn between the houses.

The Commons is home to another eagerly anticipated ritual held every New Years Eve. A 'sphere of dreams' containing individual and collective aspirations for the coming year is lowered from the top of the May Pole during the count down to midnight. "We bring in the New Year in a BIG way at Songaia. We…have lots of fun and make time to reflect on the past year and record our dreams for the coming year".[10] Thanksgiving, or the Harvest Festival, is the third core celebration. Members, family and friends gather before the feast to sing, read poetry and play games (Photo 4.2). "We express our gratitude for the harvest, for our family, friends and community, for our work, and for all facets of Life".[11] Over time these institutions have become Songaia's traditions – held to be "foundational to our group identity…to our group's culture".[12]

Honouring the different needs of individual, family and community is another tenet of Songaian philosophy. The same principle is recognised by all cohousing communities, though it is seldom expressed in the same terms. Provision for individual and household privacy ensures the essential balance of individuality and community that is cohousing lore. At Songaia, however, it takes a more esoteric tone. "We respect individual and family needs for privacy and alone time. We allow for the creation of private and sacred space that encourages contemplative and ritual activity, and we educate our children and youth to honor these".[13]

'Sacred space', by this usage, has metaphorical meaning; it's the psychic 'space' required for clear and open personal communication without fear of the consequences. At Songaia, there are regular opportunities for such interaction within different groupings. There are separate monthly 'sharing circles' for men, women and parents in addition to the monthly community 'Talking Circle', which is the principal vehicle for expression, exchange and bonding. There are occasional role-playing opportunities and separate annual retreats for men, women and the whole community. Community (or moral) support for individual members is epitomised in a modest but quite profound marking of birthdays. These are celebrated with a special meal, whereby the individual being honoured is invited to reflect on three things: events of the previous year; goals for coming year; and ways that the community might support those aspirations. "It's another way of connecting and bringing intention to what we do," suggests one member.

Friday nights are a time for games and having fun. "Songaians will do anything in the name of fun," suggests a resident known as the 'Queen of Fun'. "They are open-minded and willing to go with whatever it is we're doing. [They will] immerse themselves in whatever is going on". In that same spirit, almost all gatherings, celebrations and festivals at Songaia are punctuated with song (Photo 4.2). Community singing is one of the longest standing and most valued Songaian institutions, inherited as it was from practices of the ICA. The community songbook contains hundreds of items indexed by themes such as:

- Community eg. No Housing like Cohousing, New Community Bound;
- Family eg. On Children, Our House;
- Freedom eg. This Land is Our Land, We Shall Overcome;
- Love eg. When I'm 64, Black is the Colour;
- Nature eg. Rocky Mountain High, My Roots Go Down; and
- Spirituals eg. Amazing Grace, Rock My Soul.

The Songbook carries on its cover a symbol representing three pillars of Songaian culture: nature, fellowship and traditional (Native American) wisdom (Figure 4.3).

Photo 3.6: The well appointed and well used kitchen in the common house.

Life-long learning and openness to diversity are two more closely linked, Songaian values. Once again, these values are common in cohousing generally, though seldom are they meant as earnestly.

> We take the posture that everyone in the community, from infant to elder, is a learner as well as a teacher. Regardless of age or educational background, we all have experiences, ideas and insights that are worthy of sharing with each other. We see ourselves as a learning community.[14]

The enthusiasm with which Songaia's members embrace learning and personal growth, is again, linked to their vision. They see themselves as researchers into a lifestyle that is imperative for planetary survival. To that end, they eagerly seek knowledge and expertise from outside the community. This overlaps with another more general principle – community outreach. Songaians pro-actively seek interaction with neighbours and involvement in local affairs. Primary activities such as common dining, the sharing of resources and car pooling are openly extended to neighbours and associates. "We hold an inclusive posture, and choose not to isolate ourselves from society".[15]

Given the limited number of households at Songaia and the richness of its programs, responsibility for the workload assumes a greater importance than it might in a larger or less ambitious community. In principle, however, Songaia's management processes are little different from elsewhere in cohousing. Residents utilise consensus in formal decision-making and nominate committees to take care of business. There is no doubt, however, that the effort invested in social interaction, communication and celebration reaps added benefits. It so deepens the connection that residents have with the place and the people that taking personal and collective responsibility for community welfare becomes a natural and willing response. The management committees are:

- the *Navigators*, a steering committee that monitors the direction in which the community is moving, especially in relation to its vision;
- the *Fabulous Food Folks*, responsible for maintenance and expansion of the food program;
- the *Spirit Nurturers* who monitor social cohesion within the community and facilitate conflict resolution where necessary;
- the *Community Relations* committee, concerned with guests and relations with neighbours and

wider society;
- *Facilities*, a committee responsible for maintenance and further development of the property and buildings;
- *Community Works*, responsible for common house and community space logistics and usage;
- the *Biogaians*, responsible for landscaping and vegetable gardening; and
- *Kids Connections*, a committee responsible for parent and child support.

The management structure is a close reflection of the community's priorities (ie, its vision, food system, social cohesion, resources, gardens and family welfare) rather than an *ad hoc* or pragmatic allocation of chores and duties.

Songaia Cohousing Community is clearly different from the rest and not likely to suit everyone attracted to cohousing. Quips one member, "it's a little bit of summer camp, a little bit of college dorm life and a little bit of the TV show, *Northern Exposure*". Songaia is proudly and deliberately aligned with the intentional community movement, unlike other cohousing communities which, to varying extent, prefer to distance themselves from it. In some respects it is closer to being a commune than a cohousing community. Despite that, or perhaps because of it, Songaia Cohousing Community offers important lessons for the cohousing movement as a whole. It demonstrates that:
- small cohousing communities can be viable, given the requisite social cohesion;
- social cohesion can be crafted, given the requisite commitment; and that
- commitment can be garnered, given the requisite purpose.

Notes:

[1] From the community's Website: www.songaia.com, June 2002.

[2] McCamant, K. and C. Durrett (1994). CoHousing: A Contemporary Approach to Housing Ourselves. Berkeley, Habitat Press: 16.

[3] Alexander, C., S. Ishikawa, et al. (1977). A Pattern Language. NY, Oxford University Press.

[4] The fundamental pricing problem was one of scale and viability. The County had limited the project to a maximum of thirteen households, so the development and infrastructure cost per unit was excessively high.

[5] Sharingwood Cohousing Community in nearby Snohomish is another, as is N-Street Cohousing in Davis California.

[6] See Songaia's Web site, for a more comprehensive description.

[7] For example, the charge for an eight year old would be $5 x 8, or $40 per month.

[8] With few exceptions, all members attend or else, organise a take-out.

[9] www.songaia.com, June 2002.

[10] www.songaia.com, June 2002.

[11] www.songaia.com, June 2002.

[12] Lamphear, F. (2001). The Stuff of Community – Economics, Culture and Governance. Communities Magazine. Winter, 2001, 113.

[13] Lamphear, F. (2001).

[14] www.songaia.com, June 2002.

[15] www.songaia.com, June 2002.

Photo 5.1: A cooking team prepares a common meal.
Photo 5.2: The spacious common house dining room.

5 Puget Ridge Cohousing

Each of us comes to this group with a deep respect for both our shared values and our individual differences. Throughout this process, we hope to take joy in our similarities and differences, support each other's dreams and ideas, and thus strengthen the friendship that brings us together.[1]

Name	Puget Ridge Cohousing
Address	7020 18th Avenue Southwest, Seattle, WA 98206
Context	Suburban, .15 min ride from downtown.
Households	23 (3x1bd, 11x2bd, 7x3bd, 2x4bd)
Adults	41	Children (< 18 yrs)	12
Renters	3	Working from home	1
Developed	Jan. 1989 – Sept. 1994
Developers	The residents as the Puget Ridge Cohousing Assoc.
Architects	Lagergquist Morris Architects
Funding	Member equity and a loan from Key Bank, Washington.
Site area	0.98 hectares / 2.42 acres
Common house.	372 m² / 4,000 ft²
Ave. dwelling	95 m² / 1,022 ft²
Project cost	US$3,350,000

Table 5.1: Community Data.

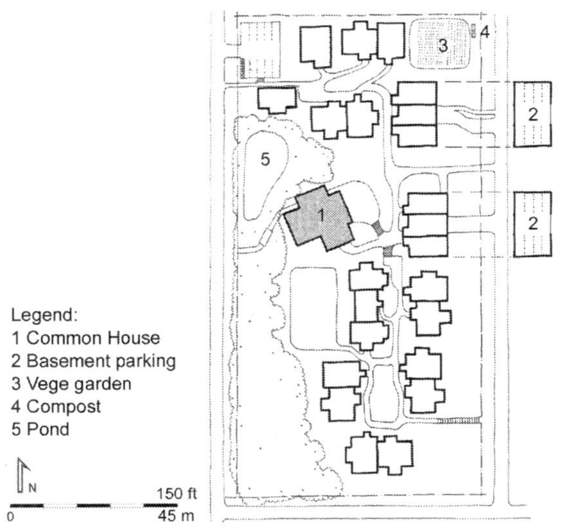

Legend:
1 Common House
2 Basement parking
3 Vege garden
4 Compost
5 Pond

Figure 5.1: Site plan.

Puget Ridge Cohousing lies in Delridge, just twenty minutes drive from downtown Seattle. It's an ethnically diverse suburb of low-cost, post-war dwellings, but like many inner city suburbs of large American cities, Delridge is subject to fast changing demographics and rising property values – a phenomenon otherwise know as 'gentrification'. The cohousing project is an architectural delight, invoking an image of a remote North Western lumber town of identical houses with stained Western Red Cedar siding, steep shingle roofs, porches and decks. The dwellings face inward onto a meandering pedestrian 'street' that broadens at each end to form two intimately scaled courtyards. A natural landscaping of groundcovers, shrubs and trees sensitively meanders between the buildings so as to interrupt the linear nature of the scheme (Photo 5.7). A towering common house dominates the middle of the site. All along the western edge, a corridor of native bushland containing a stormwater detention pond is home to native wildlife and migrating ducks. Cars are seemingly absent from the site. The project looks and feels like the setting for a radical social experiment – a collaborative approach to dense city living.

The unique qualities of this project can be attributed, in part, to an exemplary development process.[2] In 1989, following a slide presentation by McCamant and Durrett, a group formed to explore the possibilities of cohousing in Seattle. Apropos their meeting routine, they were known as the Sunday Evening Cohousing Group. Members spent the initial six months honing their goals and aspirations in preference to rushing headlong into the pragmatics of site selection and planning. Then, having established a collective vision and crafted a written agreement that defined their structure and purpose, the group was well placed to launch the next phase; they pro-actively lobbied City politicians and disseminated information about cohousing to bureaucrats and the general public.

This educative role is rarely taken as seriously by cohousing development groups, often to their detriment when seeking approvals from city staff who have never heard of cohousing. Within six more months, the group's scouts had located a vacant two-acre site owned by the City and earmarked for future housing. However, it was not quite large enough to come under the City's Planned Residential Development (PRD) regulations which would accommodate cohousing-like site planning strategies.

Fortunately, an adjacent half-acre site became available for private sale and several members formed a syndicate to make the purchase. This was an act of considerable faith since negotiations with the City over the larger site were far from finalised. Early in 1991, the group formed a non-profit corporation, the Puget Ridge Cohousing Association, which offered greater negotiating leverage and valuable tax benefits. The remainder of that year was spent in negotiation with the City and in dialogue with neighbourhood groups to gain their support for the project. Architects, Lagergquist and Morris, were engaged and preliminary design work commenced.

In mid 1992 transfer of the land was approved and the group moved forward with enthusiasm into the construction phase. In an inspired move somewhat counter to cohousing lore, they hired one of their own as project manager. Paul Fischburg was engaged (for "not nearly for as much as his time and effort was worth," according to one member) to guide the group through complex legal, financial and technical matters.[3] Planing approval, final design and documentation of the project, negotiation of a construction loan and the selection of a contractor delayed construction for another year. This enabled the saving of hundreds of plants that otherwise might have been bulldozed. In the meantime, the group grew from nine to 21 households.

At a cost of between US$87,000 and US$180,000, the dwellings of Puget Ridge were inexpensive by Seattle standards. Savings were achieved through standardised and modularised construction, tightly controlled customisation, the clustering of dwellings and 'sweat equity' – off-mortgage projects including the construction of porch roofs, paving and landscaping. For a period, these projects filled members' every weekend with truly collaborative 'hard labour.'

> Melinda led the paving team. Les took the lead measuring for and creating the forms. We took shifts filling pushing and dumping wheelbarrows full of sand, keeping just ahead of the raker and the pair who worked a special two-by-four to level the sand. Others carried bricks for still others to lay. Different members kept and eye on the pattern, swept sand into the cracks, made lemonade [and] did childcare.[4]

The personal and collective sense of achievement gained through working together as members of an 'orchestra' cannot be overestimated. It cements relationships amongst future residents and helps establish allegiance to place. It lays the groundwork and establishes a pattern for the building of a deep sense of community.

> At many…work parties, porch roofs went up one by one as well. When each of the completed eight units had a paver path to the front door and roof on the porch, there was a sense of satisfaction. If we didn't look down at the rest of the site, just up at the finished courtyard, cohousing was complete. Appreciation of the beauty and the friends abounded.[5]

Photo 5.4: The extensive range of co-owned garden tools at Puget Ridge Cohousing.
Photo 5.5: A community work day.　　　　　　Photo 5.6: Practicing in the common house.

Throughout the move-in period, which happened progressively as each precinct of houses was completed, a modest but profound ritual was repeatedly invoked. The community would gather, a candle lit for each new household to place in their kitchen window, and the contribution of the principal protagonists acknowledged open-heartedly.

> The mood was serious and passionate. ...As both men spoke of their admiration and gratitude for the other, they had tears in their eyes and they hugged. I felt gratitude for the fact that my seven-year old daughter, Allegra, was witnessing this

> tender moment between these two men who would now be a consistent part of her life. Without cohousing, that would never have happened.[6]

Ten years on, the project is as picturesque as ever. A decision to house vehicles within basement carparks has ensured that delicate qualities of site, architecture and landscape have been preserved. The buildings are well maintained, the landscaping has matured and the detention pond is teaming with wildlife. The topography, architectural cohesion and human scale prompt the metaphor of a mediaeval Italian hill town.

A magnificent common house – containing a dining room, lounge, teenagers' and kids' spaces, guest room and laundry – is the hub of community life at Puget Ridge. "The common house is the core of our existence," explains one member. "It draws people out of their homes". The dining room has cathedral-like qualities of space and light. Less desirable by far, are its cathedral-like acoustic properties, which to some extent, are tempered by baffles suspended from the ceiling (Photo 5.2). Common meals are held three or four times per week. In order to ensure that everyone can attend at least some shared meals, they are scheduled irregularly on different nights each week. For this to work, considerable coordination is required by a committee that schedules meals two months in advance and circulates a calendar of events to each household. The same concern for individual need ensures that allergies and dietary preferences are carefully considered. The committee designs each meal, posts menus on the community noticeboard and, once the number attending is known, calculates quantities of ingredients for those doing the shopping. The system may seem inflexible but it ensures a quality and balance to the common meals that, otherwise, might not occur. "We try and leave some room for creativity," explains a committee member. "In addition to the fixed menu, there are three *cooks' choices* per month".

Residents of Puget Ridge enjoy a rich and varied cultural life. "We have so many events now that it's hard not to double book," claims one member. On Friday nights, a video projected large on a wall of the common house lounge room transforms it into a mini-cine. Talent nights are particularly popular. Held every few months, they offer an opportunity for aspiring performers to overcome their fears and inhibitions in an atmosphere of trust.

> They started slowly but now we have so many people we have to cut the acts. It's getting better and better all the time. People trust that they won't be judged. They just want to express themselves, any way they can. There's a real comfort with the whole event and it's natural for your creative juices to start flowing when the talent show is coming up.

The social cohesion developed at Puget Ridge offers profound, if not life-changing benefits for some residents. A retiree in his mid-seventies explains:

> At the beginning I didn't feel I could socialise with the younger members. I was of a different generation. In fact it's the intergenerational nature of this place that has changed me. It's enabled me to do things that I never would have done where I used to live, in Chicago. I'm more active and healthier. All of my cohort back there are now either dead or infirmed. If I were still there, I would be sitting in the house all day. Now I get involved in everything. Here, there's always something exciting going on. We just had an incredible wilderness trip in Utah. The younger people asked me to come along. Cohousing has meant a whole new life for me.

There is a discernable maturity to the social intercourse at Puget Ridge that can only be found in some of the longer-lived cohousing communities. It's a subtle quality that develops imperceptibly over time. Such a maturity renders the community a family of sorts, where lives increasingly intersect, even at a subconscious level. A female resident in her fifties explains:

Photo 5.7: Meandering pathway running between close spaced houses.

> Our lives were once compartmentalised...colleagues at work, friends and family, all separate. Here too, at the beginning, our rhythms were disparate. There was little resonance within the community. But as time has gone on, that has grown. Our lives have merged together and are now more in sync. It's an unconscious process.

The maturation process at Puget Ridge has been accompanied by a growing self-realisation; collectively learning "who we are" as a community. Ironically, suggests one member, a healthy turnover (higher, probably, than the cohousing average) has contributed to the process.

> Some of the founding members left after two or three years when they found they were not really enamoured of the lifestyle. Those of us who stayed have learned how to talk with the new people in ways that enables them to assess what we're on about before they get involved. In the process we've become articulate about our needs and wants, because we've become cognisant of who we are.

As relationships have matured, trust within the group has accordingly grown. As a result, decision-making has become smoother and more efficient through increased delegation to committees. Expenditure under $500 is now simply a committee matter. The upkeep of buildings and grounds is coordinated by a new committee, Maintenance Management, which now fields much of the decision-making that once fell to the general meeting.[7] Indeed, over time, the decision-making focus of the group as a whole has shifted away from the physical, toward social and cultural matters. In the process, the nature of the consensus process itself has become subtler. "We are now more attentive to the finer points of a person's value system," suggests one resident. Improved understanding has been achieved, in large part, through an emphasis on open and transparent communication. A resident explains:

> It's really important to facilitate a meeting properly so that no one gets cut off, feelings are out on the table and nothing is concealed. In a consensus situation we want to know, "Why are you standing aside?[8] Let's get to the bottom of what this is all about". We don't let emotional things slide without closure. We want everything out in the open. But this is not easy to do without upsetting people. You almost have to be a psychiatrist to be a facilitator.

The group realise that the subtleties of effective facilitation require extra consideration. To that end, facilitators are aided by an 'emotional reader' who sits next to them at meetings and monitors emotions within the group in order to redirect the discussion if necessary.

Paul Fischburg describes the evolution of Puget Ridge in the following terms. At the beginning, the focus of the group was *vision*, then during the development process, the focus shifted to, "How do we *design* and *build* something that embodies that vision?" These were approximately two-year phases. Then, following move-in, the focus became, "How do we live together in this place?" During this phase, the discussion was necessarily about management, maintenance and pragmatics such as, "How should we divide the work fairly?" Fischburg believes that this phase has outlived its usefulness and that a new focus is now required.

> We've got the reality. We've got the place and the methods of operating. It's time to step back and have a retreat and ask our members, "What does community mean to you, *in your wildest dreams*? In your heart of hearts, how do you *really* want to live here?"

It will be fascinating to see whether the re-visioning process that Fischburg advocates will launch an exciting new phase for this inspiring community.

Notes:

[1] From a 'Statement of Community Values,' www.scn.org/pugetridgecohousing/, August 2002.

[2] Lindemann, D. (1996). "How They Got it Built". Cohousing: The Journal of the Cohousing Network **9**(3): 19, 22.

[3] Bird, S. (1996). "Rites of Passage". CoHousing: Building Community...One Neighbourhood at a Time. **9**(1): 19-25: 19.

[4] Bird, S. (1996: 20).

[5] Bird, S. (1996: 20).

[6] Bird, S. (1996: 21).

[7] Maintenance Management maintains an overview of the maintenance program and coordinates the roles of each of the following sub-committees: Landscaping, Roofs and Structural, Building Skin and Porches, Utilities, Common House, Shop and Tools, Outdoor Walks and Equipment.

[8] 'Standing aside' in a consensus process is somewhat equivalent to abstaining from a vote, although there are many subtle differences, the description of which are beyond the scope of this chapter.

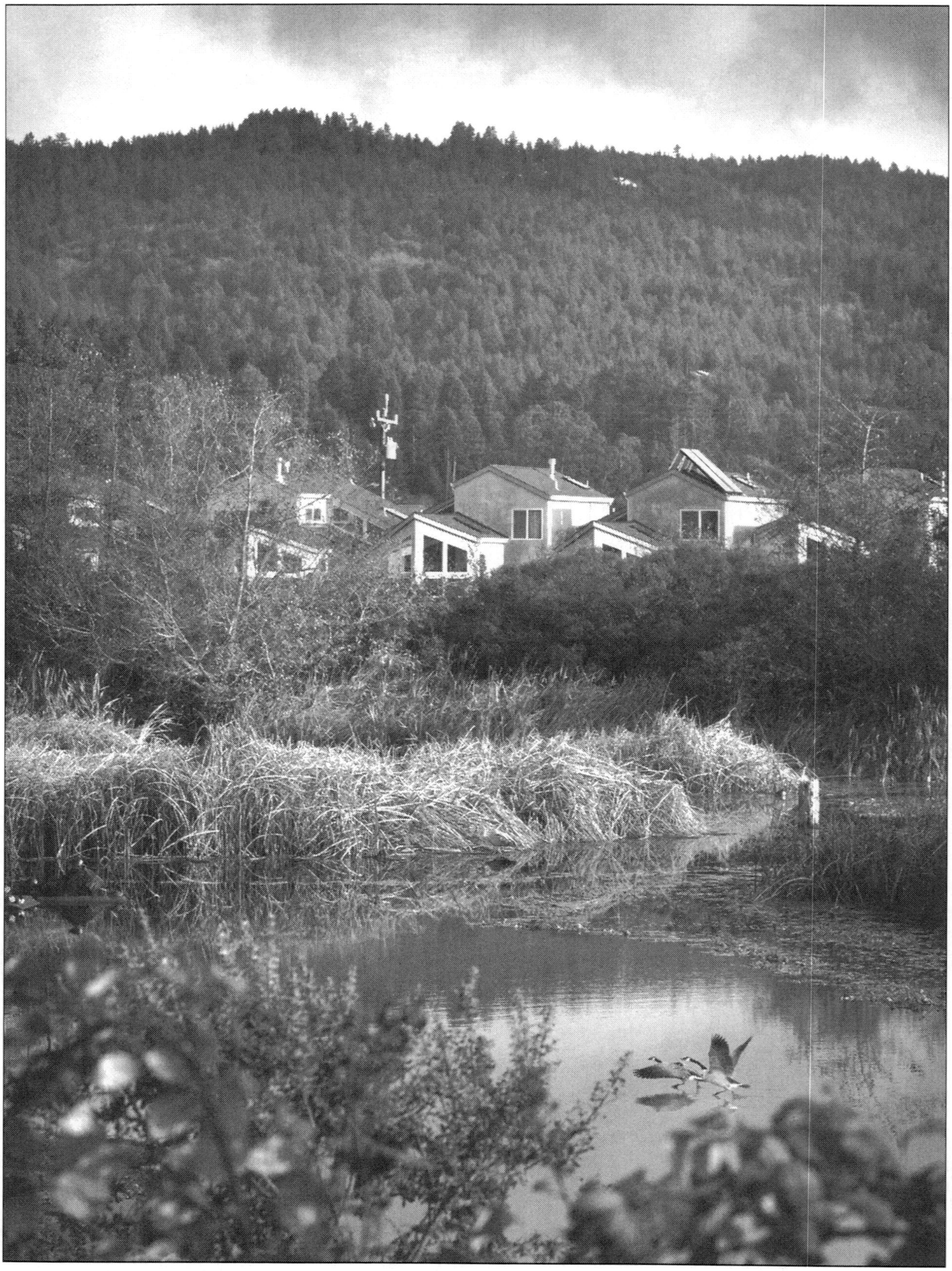

6 Marsh Commons Cohousing

The story of Marsh Commons…is one of the most amazing tales of persistence and tenacity in the annals of cohousing.[1]

Name	Marsh Commons Cohousing		
Address	101 South G St, Arcata, CA 95521		
Context	At the edge of a marsh on the outskirts of a small town.		
Households	17 (3 Studios, 1x1bd, 7x2bd, 3x3bd, 3x4bd)		
Adults	23	Children (under 18 yrs)	12
Renters	9	Working from home	7
Developed	April 1990 – January 2000		
Developers	The residents as the Marsh Commons Joint Venture.		
Designer	Joyce Plath of Eco Lodging		
Funding	Loans from Coast Central Credit Union and the Six Rivers Bank.		
Site area	0.61 hectares / 1.5 acres		
Common house.	418 m² / 4,500 ft²		
Ave. dwelling	105 m² / 1,125 ft²		
Project cost	US$2,540,000		

Table 6.1: Community Data.

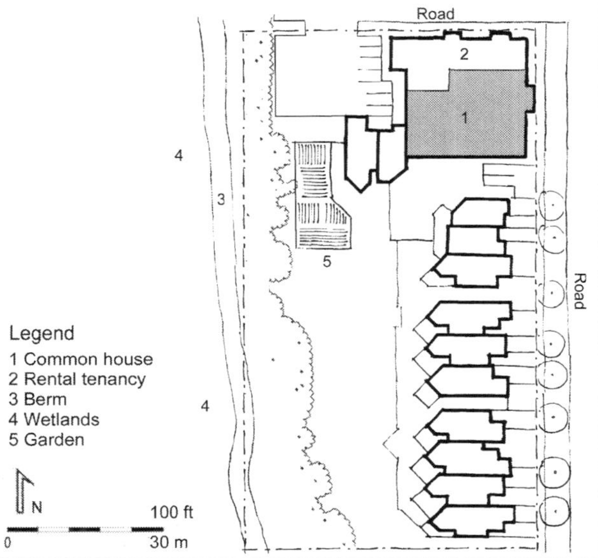

Figure 6.1: Site plan.

Legend
1 Common house
2 Rental tenancy
3 Berm
4 Wetlands
5 Garden

Arcata is a small, post-industrial university town in the very north of California. Once the domain of a rapacious lumber industry, Arcata is now celebrated for its innovative, pro-environmental policies and practices. The Council, business leaders and the populace appear united in their commitment to the environment. Appropriately then, this was the setting for *the* most epic environmental struggle in the short history of North American cohousing.

Marsh Commons Cohousing is located at the edge of the *Arcata Marsh and Wildlife Sanctuary*, part of a world-famous wastewater treatment and reclamation initiative. As recently as the late 1970s this was a blighted industrial and landfill site. Utilising only local expertise and technologies, the City pioneered the development of an aquaculture-based, sewerage treatment system. Now, 150 acres of fresh and saltwater marshes, mudflats and grasslands (Figure 6.2) are home to over 200 species of birds. Countless ducks and waterfowl drop in on their annual migration. Hundreds more stay to breed in the fecund wetlands. Each year, thousands of birdwatchers and nature lovers enjoy purpose-built trails and observation platforms provided by the City.[2]

The transformation from wasteland to wetlands has an uncanny parallel in the development of the cohousing project. It too, required the rehabilitation of a blighted, industrial site. Group members purchased the property in 1993. Just five blocks from the centre of town, it comprised an operating truck stop and motor vehicle workshop. In January 1995 they commenced renovating the 7000 ft² workshop. It is rare for cohousing groups to construct their common house before the dwellings, but in this instance, an existing building large enough to also include lettable commercial space provided the impetus.

Recycling the 50-year-old structure presented the first of many challenges to come. The discovery of major structural damage raised the renovation costs by approximately US$40,000. Undeterred, group members salvaged what they could of the building's frame and fabric in order that lumber from endangered old-growth forests would not be sacrificed for the project. They demolished an old barn in the neighbourhood, recycling its now-precious redwood as wall lining for the dining room. A member wrote at the time, "It is good knowing that old…lumber has been given a new life in our floors, walls, and ceilings".[3] Within six months, the building was complete. Long-term tenants were quickly found, providing sufficient cash flow to cover all building costs including mortgage payments, insurances and maintenance.[4]

The decision to take a separate construction loan and mortgage for the common house soon proved critical when finance was sought for the dwellings. With a contractor ready to start and the rainy season fast approaching, the million-dollar plus construction loan promised by a local bank suddenly fell through. Using "threats, brinkmanship and creativity", financing was renegotiated, but this time, separately by each household rather than by the group as a whole.[5] This was made possible by a previously agreed *Town House* tenure arrangement whereby householders technically own the land under their dwelling.[6] However, it required a deposit of US$50,000 from each household and for the whole group to meet with the bank for some hours to impart 136 notarised signatures.

Another crisis loomed when it was realised that construction would cost US$70,000 more than previously estimated. The requirements of a *Town House* development are more stringent than those of a condominium, particularly in terms of fire separation between dwellings and the routing of services. Undeterred, the group scraped together contributions from members already pushed to their financial limit, a private loan from a friend of cohousing and another (unsecured) loan from the bank. Euphoria accompanied the start of construction. "The groundbreaking was beautiful," a members recalls. "We invited the bankers, the city manager, the local newspaper, and the whole cohousing community. We were in seventh heaven".[7]

The next crisis arrived some days later. This time, however, it was truly catastrophic. Excavation of a three-foot deep "football field-sized hole" for the purpose of seismic compaction of the subsoil revealed sufficient toxic contamination to attract an immediate stop-work order. It was almost too much for the group to bear. "We were in shock. We thought we had done our homework," recalls one member. And, indeed, they had. Before buying the property the group had sought expert advice in the form of an environmental report that deemed the site "sufficiently clean for residential construction".[8]

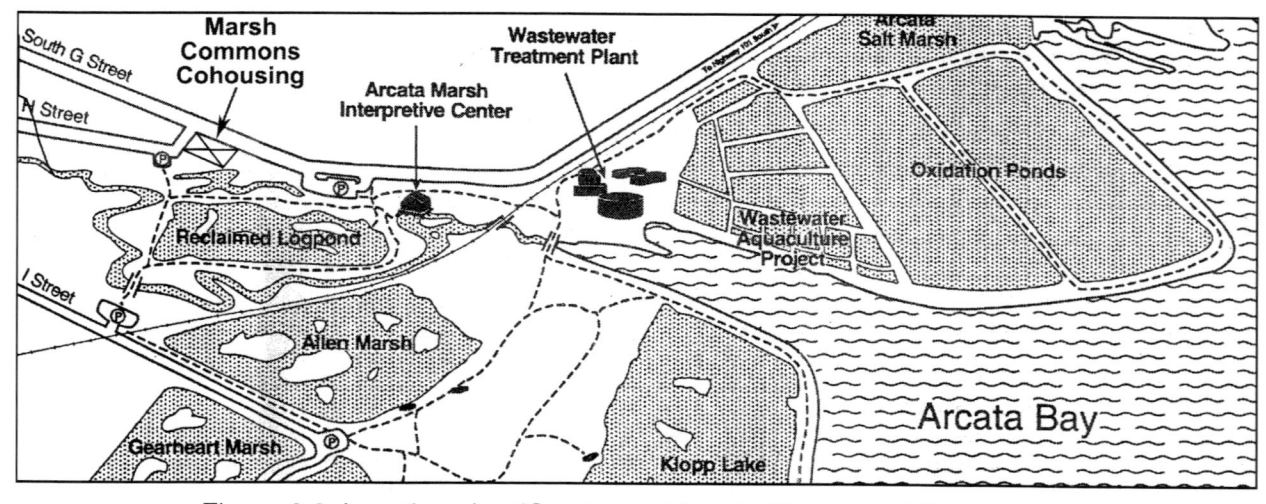

Figure 6.2: Location plan (Courtesy of Arcata Chamber of Commerce).

Months passed whilst an assessment was made. With the help of a US$15,000 emergency loan from the City, the group hired a "hot-shot" environmental lawyer and an environmental private eye named *Douglas Fir*. Fir located photographs of the site dating back to the 1960s that revealed a leaking diesel tank located directly over the worst of the contamination – a so-called 'hotspot'. Fortunately, the deposit was old and free from modern chemical additives. Nonetheless, a geotechnical report revealed that further excavation of the hot-spot would be required and that none of the removed soil was clean enough to return to the pit.

"We wanted to get out," recalls one member. "It was desperate and we were panicky, angry with the gods, each other, the City, the State, and the previous owners".[9] Yet there was no way out. The group, together with previous owners, was being held responsible for the cleanup. Bids were sought for remediation of the site. Options included: bio-remediation using fungi, vegetation and micro-organisms; thermal desorption; trucking the soil 150 miles to a certified waste disposal site; and several other technically complex and very expensive strategies. None, it seemed, would cost less than US$300,000. A member recalls the group's desperation:

> We owned 200-300 large dump truck loads of dirty dirt plus further undetermined 'hot spot' excavation and it was winter and cold and dreary. We almost lost our civility. By this time we had spent more than $100,000 for attorneys, soil consultants, engineers, laboratory work, and additional site excavation and maintenance. Our meetings were dismal and chaotic, and the consensus process had completely deteriorated.[10]

Into this abyss of panic and fear arrived, as if descended from heaven, a pair of 'guardian angels' in the form of Stuart and Lynette Staniford-Chen. Previously from N Street Cohousing (see Chapter 7), they had recently moved to Arcata for career-based reasons. Stuart had expertise in meetings facilitation and Lynette, an attorney, offered the group *pro bono* legal advice.

Photo 6.2: Community meeting being held in the common house.

Chapter 6: Marsh Commons Cohousing

Photo 6.3: Joyce Plath, a resident and the project's designer, preparing a common meal.

Photo 6.4: Marsh Commons is probably the only cohousing community with a kids' room big enough to accommodate a half basketball court.

Eight months of negotiation followed, involving countless meetings between lawyers representing the cohousing group, the City, previous owners and the engineering firm that originally approved the site for residential development. Finally, a prior owner with eleven acres of nearby land agreed to take the contaminated soil whilst another with a trucking firm agreed to deliver it there. The City of Arcata, also once an owner, agreed to dig out the hotspot and load the trucks. Furthermore, it agreed to forgive the $15,000 loan and provide a further redevelopment loan to cover the group's accumulated debts and the cost of clean replacement soil.

However, the group was still not free from crisis. Their building permit was about to expire. If it had, recently amended building regulations would have necessitated revised structural engineering and a fresh building application. A last minute extension was granted, but only after members somehow raised the $6,000 fee. Similarly, the construction loan(s) had expired and the bank was threatening withdrawal. Only the good faith of a single senior bank official enabled an extension of the loan. Approaching winter rains were threatening to delay construction for six more months. In the event, the rains held off long enough to allow excavation and transportation of the contaminated soil, delivery and compaction of the replacement soil, and construction work to begin. The first homes were completed one year later but construction continued until January 2000, five years after it had first started (i.e. on the common house). It had been ten years since the group first met.

The resultant development has many unique attributes. The residents have dramatically rehabilitated a severely contaminated post-industrial site. They have immediate access to, and sweeping views of, a magnificent wildlife sanctuary and yet are within fifteen minutes walk of downtown Arcata. Their homes are robust; that is, they can be adapted to suit different and changing lifestyles. The twelve original units now accommodate seventeen households; such is their potential for spatial subdivision.

Many residents work from home, some specifically because the homes were wired for intranet and broadband services. Some dwellings have recycled wooden floors. Others have certified sustainably harvested flooring known as *Smart Wood*. Sixty percent of the framing lumber is also *Smart Wood*. Three of the houses utilise solar hot water whilst all are plumbed for the purpose. Natural light is maximised in all the dwellings through the careful positioning of skylights. One dwelling utilises photovoltaic power.

The common house is equally robust, with large, easily adaptable spaces that will meet the community's needs long into the future. Perhaps uniquely, it contains a recreation room large enough to accommodate a half-basketball court (Photo 6.4). The fixtures, fittings and finishes in the common house appear to be of the finest quality, and yet, much of the fit-out (and of course the building itself) is of recycled materials. The carpets, insulation and paint are recycled. Compact fluorescent lighting is used throughout the common house. The pantry is a *California Cooler*, chilled with air piped from the building's exterior.

Not surprisingly, given the project's history, the residents of Marsh Commons have a total aversion to petrochemical-based products. Wet area floors are covered with *Marmoleum* made from flax or linseed rather than petrochemical-based ingredients. The garden and landscaping are 100% organic, as they must be, given the adjacency of the nature reserve. Residents steward a berm that separates their site from the wetlands despite it being located on Council land. "The three 'F's – fragrance, flowers, and fruit – guide us in bringing back a piece of paradise," they suggest.[11] In order to protect wildlife, pet cats are kept inside and dogs must be on a lead.

During the worst moments of crisis when trust and civility were all but lost, emotional if not cathartic expressions of fear and recrimination were commonplace. As a consequence, the ongoing social dynamics at Marsh Commons are still, two years after move-in, somewhat fractious or abrasive. The wounds are not yet entirely healed. Residual hurt and mistrust remains. Emotional outbursts can still occur both in and out of meetings. Yet, suggests one member, "the challenges we faced may have been of great benefit to us. It gave us an opportunity to express and bring to the surface all our pent up neuroses, frustrations, and ill-conceive thoughts". As a result of the experience, relations within the group now exhibit an uncommon authenticity. In cohousing generally, social interaction is somewhat muted by middle-class reserve and deference; not so at Marsh Commons.

Common meals, held three times per week, are universally popular. The rostering system is simple, relaxed and efficient. Full attendance of the residents (plus three associate members) is assumed unless prior notice is given. A committee of two unilaterally draws up the roster, nominating teams of two who do all the work: determine the menu; purchase the ingredients; prepare the meal; and clean up afterwards. Menus are not published in advance, but there are always dietary alternatives.

The cooks receive credit for their expenditure and $4 is debited against those who attend. The accounting is mostly on paper and only occasionally reconciled. The after-meals clean up is quite relaxed, since income from the rental tenancies funds a commercial cleaning service once every week. This, in turn, enables regular renting of the common house to university groups, the Green Party and others.

This dynamic interplay of economic, recreational, social and cultural dimensions of community life, together with the convenient location and pro-environmental features of the project, renders Marsh Commons an example of 'best practice' sustainable development – one that genuinely encourages residents to 'work, live and play' within their neighbourhood. "We have it all here," remarks one proud and appreciative founding member, "we really have".

Photo 6.6: Residence entrance.

Photo 6.7: Residence living area.

Photo 6.5: South facing windows provide stunning views of the marshland.

Notes:

[1] Editorial comment by Don Lindermann in <u>CoHousing: Journal of the CoHousing Network</u>, Spring 1998, **11**(3): 19.

[2] Van Wert, K. (1995). Birds of Arcata Marsh and Wildlife Sanctuary. Arcata, The Friends of Arcata Marsh (FOAM).

[3] http://www.marshcommons.org/ (1996). Building for the Environment, Marsh Commons Cohousing Group. Sept, 2002.

[4] Starr, S., P. Starr, et al. (1998). "Paradise at Last: Arcata Group Overcomes 6 Years of Challenges". <u>CoHousing: Journal of the CoHousing Network</u> **11**(3): 19-21.

[5] Starr et al. (1998: 19).

[6] It is much more common for cohousing groups to take a condominium legal structure which gives householders ownership of the space enclosed within the dwelling, not the land on which it stands.

[7] Starr et al. (1998: 20).

[8] Starr et al. (1998: 20).

[9] Starr et al. (1998: 20).

[10] Starr et al. (1998: 20).

[11] http://www.marshcommons.org/ (1996). Building for the Environment, Marsh Commons Cohousing Group. Sept, 2002.

Photo 7.1 (above): Christmas stockings, one per household, hang in the common house, symbolically representing the community as a 'family'.

Photo 7.2 (left): An anonymous gift giving ritual that occurs at N St every Christmas.

Photo 7.3 (below): An attractive tiling detail at the entrance to one of the dwellings (see also Photo 7.7).

7 N Street Cohousing

Today when people ask me about starting a retrofit cohousing community, I tell them to find a block of houses they like, rent or buy two and share meals at least once a week. Most importantly, invite friends and other prospective members to those meals. By sharing food and dreams, a community grows.[1]

Name	N Street Cohousing		
Address	724 N-Street, Davis, CA 95616		
Context	College town, suburban setting.		
Households	17 (1x2bed, 9x3bed, 7x4bed)		
Adults	39	Children (under 18 yrs)	19
Renters	26	Working from home	6
Developed	June 1886 – present day		
Developers	Residents themselves		
Architect	None		
Funding	Member equity, assorted loans.		
Site area	0.92 hectares / 2.27 acres		
Common house.	93 m^2 / 1000 ft^2		
Ave. dwelling	110 m^2 / 1180 ft^2		
Project cost	US$1,960,000		

Table 7.1: Community Data.

Figure 7.1: Site plan.

N Street Cohousing is an example (indeed, the prime example) of *retrofit* cohousing; i.e. cohousing that *evolves* within an already existing residential setting. It is not, like other projects, purpose built. Rather, pre-existing buildings and adjacent open space is adapted to suit cohousing principles and practices. The creation of retrofit cohousing is therefore environmentally neutral because no new land or buildings are required. It is more affordable than conventional cohousing since it can begin with as little investment as the sweat equity involved in removing a fence between two dwellings. For these reasons, some argue that retrofit cohousing is the most promising avenue for the widespread development of sustainable urban communities.

N Street, Davis is located within a large tract of single-family housing built in 1955 (Figure 7.2). Though modest, the dwellings epitomise the privatised suburban culture of the post-war period. Once identical, these cheap fibro[2]-clad bungalows with driveways to the front door have living spaces facing into private backyards surrounded by six foot high fences that prevent any possible social interaction between neighbours. However, they are affordable and close to the University of California campus so have always been popular with students.

In 1979, five students established a shared house at 716 N Street (Figure 7.3).[3] The dwelling had previously been enlarged from three to five bedrooms with the addition of a second storey. The group was politically progressive and socially ambitions. With an emphasis on shared meals, social interaction and good communication, they successfully established a cohousing-like culture years before the word, cohousing, was even invented.

> If they didn't know how to cook before moving in, they certainly did by the time they left. ...Five nights a week one of us cooked for the others. This simple practice was critical to binding us together as a household. Meals at N Street were fun. The conversations were memorably irreverent and stimulating.[4]

One of the residents, Kevin Wolf, bought the property in 1984 but changed none of the fundamentals of this fledgling community. Over the years, the group had transformed their suburban backyard into a flourishing garden of edible delights. Davis, after all, is located in California's Central Valley, one of the great 'fruit bowls' of the world. The group had often speculated about the possibility of expanding the garden, so when an adjacent property to the North (724 N Street) came onto the market Wolf's partner, Linda Cloud, purchased it with a view to removing the side fence and expanding the garden, and the community. The act of tearing down the fence, it could be said, signified the birth of the cohousing community.

Out of enthusiasm for their shared vision of an ever-expanding community, the group spoke to owners and renters of surrounding properties with a view to inducting new members and securing new properties. One of these approaches resulted in the acquisition of a third house, one that shared its back fence with 724 N Street. Another quickly followed when Wolf and Cloud purchased an option on 732 N Street.

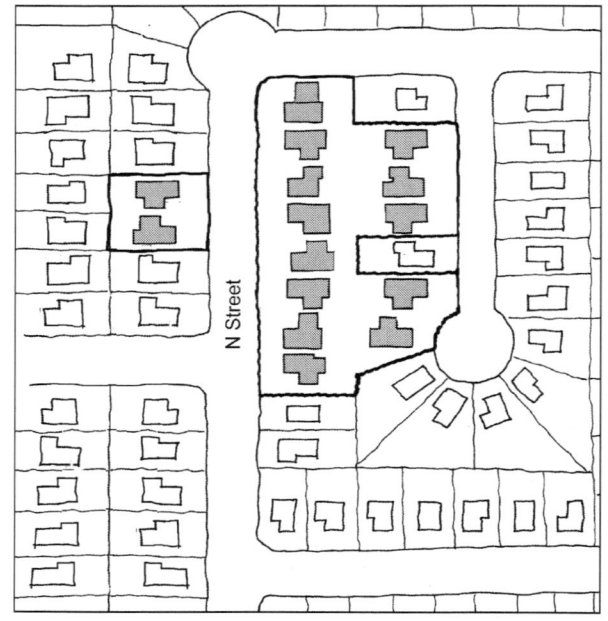

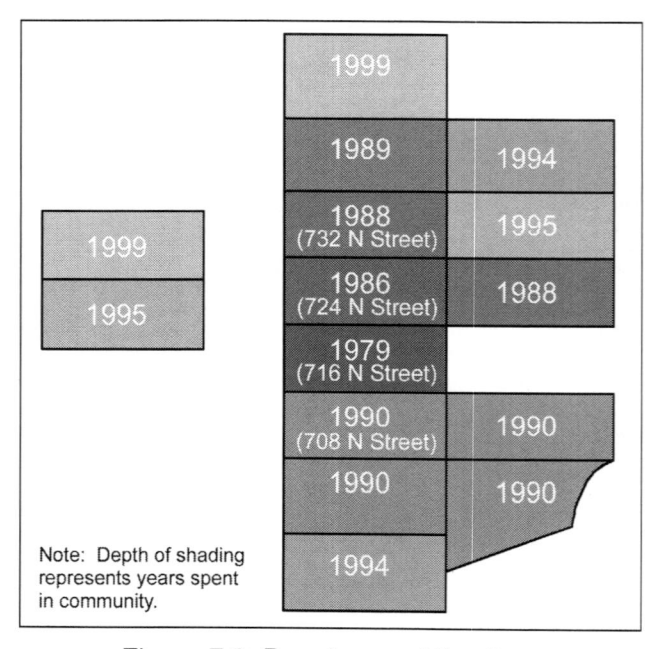

Figure 7.2: Location plan (after Smith 1998)[5].

Figure 7.3: Development timeline.

At about this time, in late 1988, Cloud read the recently published book by McCamant and Durrett, *CoHousing: A Contemporary Approach to Housing Ourselves*. The cohousing concept provided a 'container' for all the ideas, values and aspirations of the group. It gave their particular kind of communalism a name. "In naming something, you give it power," notes Wolf, "because you are able to identify it, envision it better [and] name it to other people in a single word".[6] Furthermore, the book presented previously unthought of ideas and strategies that provoked a reassessment of the community's long-term goals. The idea of a common house intrigued the group, but was problematic. The advent of a common house would be expensive and require greater commitment from members. It would signify a "more serious form of community".[7]

In the meantime, more houses were being added and more fences torn down. In late 1989, 708 N Street came onto the market. A consortium of associates of the community (mostly unknown to each other) formed a unique ownership scheme, the *708 Partnership*. None could afford to buy a home in their own right, yet between them, they could raise the down payment. Nine members each

Photos 7.4 and 7.5: Homes and gardens at N St.

contributed what they had – their investments ranging from $500 to $7,000. "[They] designed an ownership arrangement unlike any that exist[ed]," another researcher has written. "The purchase of 708 N Street represented the power that can be achieved through cooperation".[8] It was to become an important precedent.

Further households were incorporated under long-term leases signed with sympathetic absentee landlords. Known as 'Master Leases,' these permitted adaptation of properties to suit cohousing principles and practices, including the demolition of fences. Others joined after first observing the activities of the cohousing community from over the fence. They liked what they saw and felt compelled to join in.

An ongoing discussion about the feasibility of a common house had polarised the community. Many members were keen to establish one, whilst others were satisfied with the status quo. The original two-storey dwelling at 716 N Street was the obvious candidate for adaptation since it was larger than the others and centrally located. Its tenants, however, were not enamoured of the idea. They were already enjoying nightly common meals and cohesive social relations. Ultimately, agreement was reached and a date was set for the start of renovations (September, 1991) which gave occupants unwilling to participate a year to find alternative accommodation.

Through the '90s, N Street Cohousing continued to expand. In 1999, the community successfully applied to the City for a zoning change from *Residential-1* to *Planned Development*. This set an important precedent for retrofit cohousing. It recognized the development as a single legal entity and significantly loosened regulations governing further expansion. Attached 'granny flats', for example, were allowed to be larger than normal. Under this guideline, the northernmost house in the community has been remodelled as a duplex with the cost of the land being shared by the two owners, both single women (Photo 7.6). It seems unlikely that the rezoning will ever be reversed, as it would require massive physical changes to the property and the full agreement of owners. Rather, the community looks forward to a future of unfettered growth and development. "We believe we have in place the legal, social…and cultural components that will allow N Street Cohousing to flourish as long as Davis is a city in the Sacramento Valley of Northern California", quips Wolf.[9]

Typically in cohousing, the common house contains most shared facilities. At N Street however, through choice and circumstance, shared infrastructure and amenities have always been dispersed. This encourages movement to all parts of the site and diversifies opportunities for social interaction. The common house contains only the kitchen, dining and living rooms plus facilities including a TV/VCR, small library, bulletin boards and pigeonholes for each household. An adjoining patio provides a venue for outdoor common meals in summer. Elsewhere, there are two laundries, tool sheds, children's play facilities, a hot tub, sauna, chicken coop and numerous outdoor settings for social exchange or quiet contemplation. All households and common facilities are linked with a flagstone path that meanders throughout a lush permaculture of groundcover, flowers, vegetables, shrubs and trees. The pathway, built with sweat equity in 1993 and extended since as necessary, is a physical and symbolic reminder of the bonds of community, "tying us all together in practical ways; aesthetic ways; perceptual, emotional ways; and in creating a real sense of flow and open connection between us all," suggests one member.[10]

The sense of community at N Street is as palpable as in any purpose built cohousing project where residents have a greater 'investment' of time, energy and capital. The high proportion of renters (two thirds of adults) and high turnover appears not to diminish social cohesion. Indeed, the opposite is true, as Kevin Wolf reports: "Every year we have a turnover of around 4-5 renters in the community with the new ones almost always adding a wonderful addition of energy to our meals, work, social life, discussions and fun".[11] Renters can, and do, become homeowners. Houses that become available for sale are invariably purchased by already renting members of the community. "That's what makes us so strong," suggests one owner occupant. "Almost everyone here starts as a renter. So home buyers know exactly what they're in for. They already know the people and all about the community. "That's *why* they buy the house". This is a significant departure from the cohousing norm where houses can sell on the open market to people with little knowledge or experience of community life.

The social and cultural aspects of life at N Street are rich and varied. There are games nights, full moon dances, parties and celebrations. Nobody's birthday goes unnoticed, as each appears on a community calendar, circulated monthly. As in most cohousing communities, members collectively observe traditions such as Halloween, Thanksgiving and Christmas. Christmas is celebrated early, so those who wish can be with family on Christmas day. In the common house, 17 stockings, one for each household, symbolically hang over the fireplace (Photo 7.1). The main event is an anonymous *used* gift giving ceremony (Photo 7.2). Participants each contribute a single gift. Most have little monetary value, but are imbued with humorous, symbolic or esoteric meaning. In turn, by lots drawn from a hat, participants select a gift from the pile – their choice being intuitive or based upon size, shape or wrapping. They may keep their 'prize,' or exchange it for an already opened, more appealing gift (although no one gift can be so claimed more than three times). Greatest anticipation and hilarity accompanies the unwrapping of the perpetual booby prize, a long-playing album by Lonnie Donigan. This somewhat oddball event is high-spirited, irreverent and wholesome.

Photo 7.6: A duplex developed by two single women.
Photo 7.7: Barbara, one of the proud first home owners.

Chapter 7: N Street Cohousing 65

The community has similarly adopted and adapted other, less well-known traditions. 'Coming of age', for example, is celebrated whenever a child of the community turns sixteen. A unique event is planned in consultation with the debutante – a celebration that most appropriately honours and celebrates his or her arrival into adulthood. The community has also fashioned its own 'Day of the Dead' traditions involving a masked procession to the local cemetery and back (Photo 7.8).[12] Around fifty participants, including some who spontaneously join the parade as it passes, gather at the cemetery to light candles and evoke the names of departed loved ones. Back at N Street, over dinner, they share stories about past relationships: of family life, their parents, lost friendships, favourite pets – the gamut of meaningful human association. In the experience, the bonds between them are reinforced and their appreciation of the cycle of life and death, deepened. Such is the potential of a close, trustful community for a shared spirituality of its own making.

N Street exemplifies retrofit cohousing on many levels. It demonstrates an affordable development strategy, one that evolves at an unforced pace and permits members to remain within their neighbourhood. The apparently simple act of 'tearing down the fences' (the community's catch-cry) raises collective, shared values above individualistic, privatised ones. N Street has evolved into one of the most socially cohesive, politically progressive and culturally innovative of all cohousing communities. In exploring and exploiting the nexus between owners and renters, it's a kind of living dialectic. N Street personifies anti-fashion, anti-consumerist and pro-environmental values and practices. As such, it is a critically important social change model.

Photo 7.8: N-Street founder, Kevin Wolf, participating in the annual "Day of the Dead' procession.

The N Street ethos may well have been inspired by the dwellings themselves. They are modest in the extreme. Said to be "ugly" by many residents, their small rooms, poor spatial qualities and cheap materials negate the popular notion of 'home as castle.' Whilst most are now refurbished, improvements have mostly been limited to the removal of asbestos, addition of insulation and introduction of double-glazing.[13] The very genesis of the project, the amalgamation of private yards into a single shared space, has always been the focus of upgrading. Yet the intent, established in the early '80s when the community comprised a single shared house, has never been the making of a large, manicured, suburban backyard. Rather, an unplanned, integrated, 'natural' landscaping has been the objective.

> [We] scattered seeds of edible plants across the entire lot. Plants would come up, some would be thinned, mulch would be added, harvest would occur but always, some plants were allowed to go to seed. As a result Miner's lettuce is harvested all winter…Magenta-headed amaranth provides summer greens and beauty throughout summer. Cherry tomatoes come up any and everywhere as kids graze, spill and smash their sweet fruits as they wander through the yards. Potatoes never are completely harvested and continue to pop up year after year. Garlic heads are forgotten, and sprout by the fist full.[14]

Much of the harvest is served in common meals, which are usually vegetarian with a vegan option. Bought produce is almost always organic due to its excellent availability from both the Davis Co-op and a weekly Farmers Market. The community is acutely aware of the issue of embodied energy so strive to shop locally for locally produced goods. Kitchen scraps from the common house are fed to common chickens, which lay common eggs in return. At N Street, food procurement is part of a 'system' characterised by such qualities as integration, observation, and nurture. These are passive, 'female' kinds of qualities, which, according to Wolf, are also the essentials of community itself. He offers the following advice for those wishing to instigate retrofit cohousing:

> [B]e generous, patient, sincere…and somewhat humble. And have a vision [you] keep alive by sharing and growing it as others join in. …Make the journey the destination, have a lot of fun, experience and learn much, and share the wonders of community with others whom you will grow to love and appreciate.[15]

Notes:

[1] Wolf, K. (2003). *N-Street Cohousing*, in <u>Another kind of space: creating ecological dwellings and environments</u>. A. Dearling and G. Meltzer. Lyme Regis, Enabler Press:129-133:129.

[2] "Fibro" is an Australian colloquialism meaning fibre cement sheeting (of the type available in the US from Hardies Pty Ltd) once ubiquitously used to clad cheap homes and beach houses in Australia.

[3] 'Shared house' is Australian parlance for what is known in America as a 'cooperative house.'

[4] Wolf, K. (2003:130).

[5] Smith, K. F. (1998). <u>Retrofit Cohousing: Redesigning Existing Neighborhoods to Meet the Changing Needs of Today's Society</u>. Masters Thesis; University of California, Berkeley

[6] Jeffreys-Renault, T. (1989). Tearing Down Fences. <u>Farmer Bob's Sometimes News & Local Review</u>. Davis: 11, 13.

[7] Smith, K. F. (1998: 21).

[8] Spreitzer, D. (1992). <u>Living in My Thesis: Cohousing in Davis, California</u>, Masters Thesis; School for International Training, Vermont.

[9] Wolf, K. (2003:133).

[10] Quoted in Smith, K. F. (1998: 54).

[11] Smith, K. F. (1998).

[12] This ancient festival originated in prehispanic Mexico but has been much transformed since. It's an occasion for remembering and honouring deceased loved ones and, in the process, celebrating the continuity of life.

[13] Two or three houses have been completely remodelled as much more liveable and attractive, but still relatively small, dwellings.

[14] Wolf, K. (2003:132).

[15] Wolf, K. (2003:133).

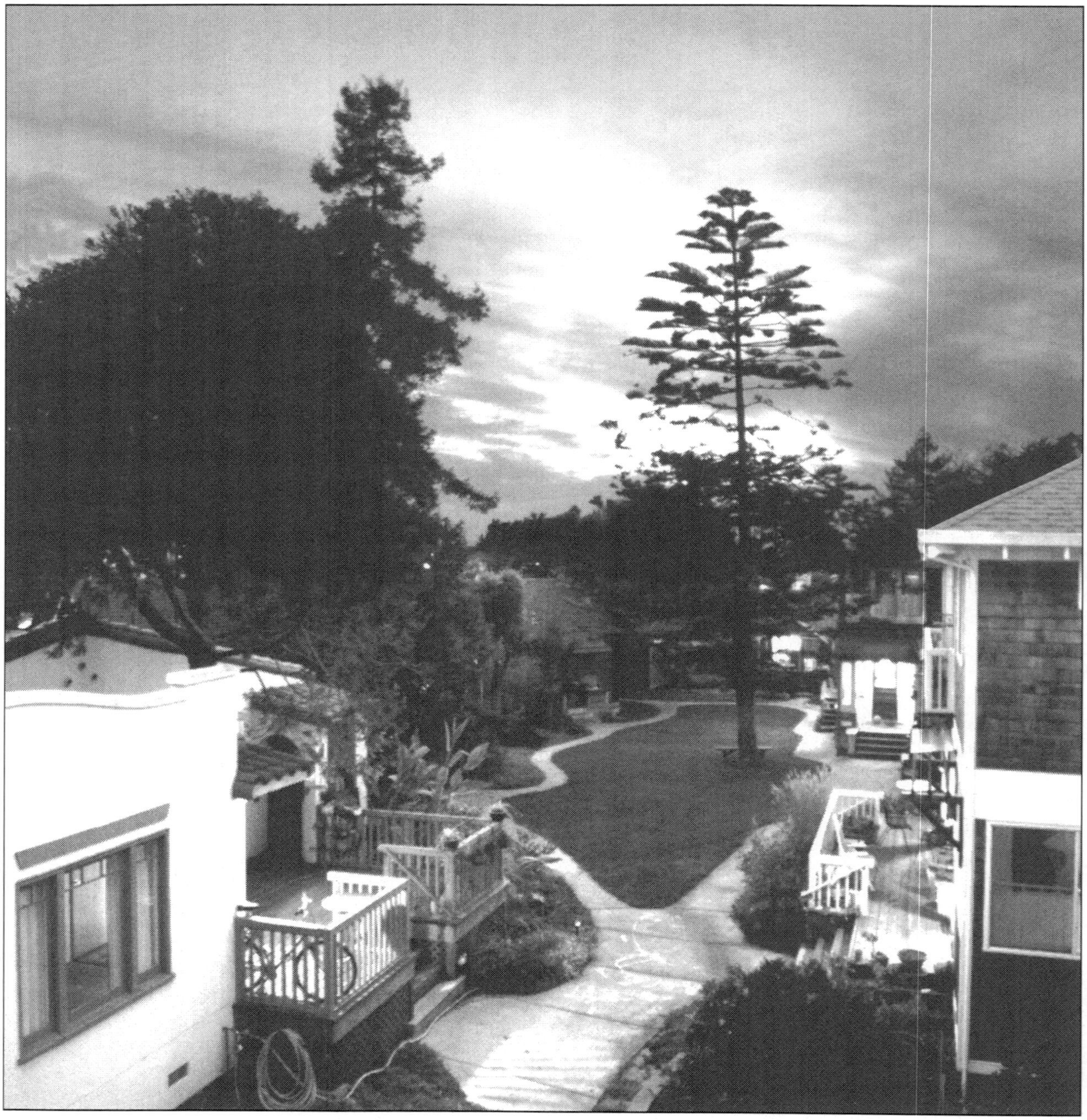

8 Berkeley Cohousing

Do you want to improve the environmental impact of your project? You can do far better than standard practice without going broke, but you will have to work for it. With persistence, your efforts will be rewarded with a project that is much more friendly to the environment. Perhaps even more important, you will have educated your architect, contractor, subs and suppliers, making it that much easier for the next person [or cohousing group] to do the right thing.[1]

Name	Berkeley Cohousing	
Address	2220 Sacramento St, Berkeley, CA	
Context	Suburban – urban infill	
Households	14 (5x1bd, 8x2bd, 1x3bd) +1 assoc.	
Adults	20	Children (under 18 yrs)	6
Renters	2	Working from home	2
Developed	October 1989 – June 1997	
Developers	Members themselves	
Architect	The Cohousing Company	
Funding	25% member equity, 75% loan from First Federal Savings Bank	
Site area	0.31 hectares / 0.76 acres	
Common house.	150 m^2 / 1,622 ft^2	
Ave. dwelling	87 m^2 / 939 ft^2	
Project cost	US$2,580,000	

Table 8.1: Community Data.

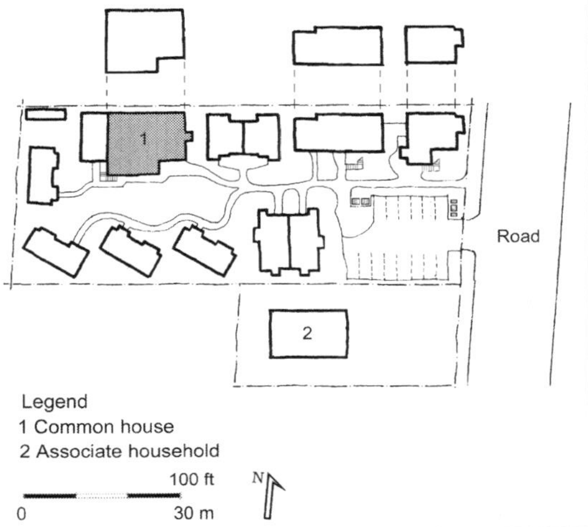

Figure 8.1: Site plan.

Berkeley Cohousing is located on a busy thoroughfare in the heart of the city, within walking distance from the University and countless commercial, recreational and cultural opportunities. It's a prime example of infill urban renewal. The residents acting as their own developer spent five years transforming several dilapidated buildings and a derelict site into a delightful ensemble of fourteen homes and a common house surrounding intimately scaled shared lawns and gardens. The architecture is eclectic in the manner of Berkeley housing generally, incorporating elements of Spanish, Shingle and California Bungalow styles. "The group didn't have a lot of money", notes their architect, Chuck Durrett, "but they did have a lot of discernment. Every little piece of the project was considered and reconsidered".[2]

The process was far from straightforward. The group had no previous real estate development experience and most members were first homebuyers. Although the buildings had been vacant for years, Council was reluctant to approve private development because it was previously a rental property. In Berkeley, very strong protection is provided to rental housing stock, requiring a special ordinance to be written for redevelopment to take place. Approval was finally granted provided half the dwellings were made 'affordable' and their resale values linked to the cost of living (rather than real estate market value).[3] This enforced affordability placed considerable pressure on the construction budget, as did the cost of refurbishing existing dwellings, their limited reproducibility, and the pro-environmental construction strategies sought by the group (see page 70). With the emergence of cost overruns, relations between the group and the contractor soured. Ultimately, a court case ensued, resulting in considerable extra financial cost to the community.

The houses are amongst the smallest in cohousing, ranging in size from a cottage of 53 m² (570 ft²) to a three-bedroom apartment of 104 m² (1118 ft²). In one household, a family of three including two teenagers occupy a 65 m² (700 ft²) cottage. As developers, the group minimized the size of their homes to facilitate affordability but also, to allow for extensive common facilities. The 150 m² (1600 ft²) common house incorporates a kitchen and dining area, sitting room, guest room cum library, children's play room, office and laundry. The common house interiors retain the pre-war character and charm of the original 'big house' on the property (Photo 8.6).

From the outset, the group sought to create a "model of sustainable redevelopment,"[4] starting with the choice of an urban location to minimise vehicle usage. In addition, they:
- extensively reused existing building stock;
- contoured the site to optimise stormwater soakage and reduce run-off;
- relocated well-established, large trees to minimise needless destruction;
- recycled demolition material, construction waste and building product packaging;
- substituted a percentage of (energy-intensive) cement with fly-ash, a waste product;
- used relatively benign ACQ instead of copper-arsenate wood preservatives;
- implemented a range of strategies in respect of sustainable timber usage;
- used relatively benign fibreglass composite roofing shingles in preference to asphalt;
- selected many products for lower environmental impact and minimal toxicity;
- specified insulation levels and window efficiencies beyond the requirements of codes; and
- installed energy and water conserving fixtures and fittings. [5]

Much of the credit for these innovations goes to a particularly dedicated member, Tom Lent, who spent considerable time and effort researching strategies, locating sources of alternative building materials and monitoring the construction process. His contribution was critical in enabling the cohousing group to assess the environmental consequences of their choices. The group was committed to an ecologically benign outcome and was undaunted by the complexities and contradictions inherent in collective decision-making by consensus. Project Manager, Katie McCamant, observes, "It took a group of people with a long-term commitment to creating a great place to live to make the time and financial investments that made this project possible".[6] The project has won several accolades including an *Award for Building Innovation for Homeownership* from the US Department of Housing and Urban Development (HUD).

Photo 8.2: View showing the proximity of a major urban thoroughfare to the residences.

Photo 8.3: A building refurbished as the common house (downstairs) and an apartment (upstairs).

Photo 8.4: Two tiny, attractive pre-existing bungalows, refurbished as residences.

Chapter 8: Berkeley Cohousing 71

Berkeley Cohousing typifies cohousing groups that are pro-active, socially and politically, within the surrounding neighbourhood. The community has hosted numerous neighbourhood events and instigated earthquake preparedness and neighbourhood safety programs. In this respect, Berkeley Cohousing follows a precedent set by several predecessor groups including Doyle Street (nearby, in Emeryville) and Southside Park (in Sacramento).[7] Such groups have profoundly strengthened neighbourhood ties and provided a catalyst for change and renewal.

However, the community's most poignant and inspiring collective act was an internal and very personal matter. It involved the decline in health and passing away due to cancer of long-term member, Donna Dobkin. Donna died at home in the presence of her lifetime partner David and in the midst of a community that had selflessly supported them both during Donna's decline. Their story is told here to illustrate the love and support a community can garner at times of critical need.

In the summer of 1999, Donna Dobkin was first hospitalised in Sacramento, California, about eighty miles from Berkeley. "Two or three people would commute to Sacramento every day," recalls her husband.[8] "Friends surrounded us while Donna made the [post operative] transition from bed to ambulation. Did she get enough rest with all those visitors? She needed the companionship more than the rest".[9] Within a week, David and Donna returned to Berkeley and a welcome home ceremony arranged by the community. "Neither of us could stop crying, we were so touched by the reception," David recounts.[10] A year passed, during which Donna regained her strength and returned to normal life. The cancer was seemingly in remission following chemotherapy.

A year later, however, Donna's blood count rose sufficiently rapidly to force a resumption of chemotherapy. During treatment, Donna suffered a further serious setback – a severe stroke. She was once again, hospitalised, then later, moved to a residential facility for rehabilitation of lost speech and ambulation. Donna was determined to come home, however, and after some weeks she was again able to spend nights at home.

> She so loved being with her community, and she improved. She went from being unable to walk to being able to get around pretty well with a walker. Her speech improved from twenty percent intelligibility to eighty percent. At that point in was deemed that she could continue her rehabilitation at home.[11]

As is common in cohousing when such a need arises, a core group of community members was formed to attend to Donna's care and to provide David with practical and moral support. The laundry would magically be taken care of, as were their pets' needs and shopping. David describes the day-to-day effort of the group during January and February of 2001.

> Alisa would arrive at 6:30 AM on Monday, Wednesday and Friday so that I could go swimming. Nina would relieve her at 7:30 AM and stay until I got home around 9:00 AM. And then someone else would come around 10:00 AM and people would fill in during the day around the core daytime caregivers. Alisa would do all the scheduling, arranging friends to come for two-hour shifts to relieve the core group. This coverage kept Donna occupied and allowed me, a sole proprietor to keep the business from falling apart. Even treading water under such circumstances is a miracle that could not have been accomplished without the team.[12]

Financial pressures increased however, until one member put out a call for help on the national cohousing email list and raised a $15,000 support fund from the cohousing fraternity. Yet for David, the committee's greatest contribution lay in its collective decision-making. "I had never had to make life altering decisions before," he says. "I had no experience of the situation…but others had plenty".[13] The decision to cease treatment and enter palliative care was the toughest. Fortunately, the support fund provided for daytime professional care-givers to relieve the core group, who after

Photo 8.4 (left): A Resident paints colour swatches on the side of the building shown below so that the community might reach consensus on the most appropriate colour.

Photo 8.5: A pre-existing building refurbished as a duplex of eclectic style and character.

Chapter 8: Berkeley Cohousing

some months were feeling the strain. It meant that Donna could remain at home and not have to enter a hospice.

In the previous year, two babies had been born into the community. Their arrival and presence during her final passage was particularly meaningful to Donna and the group. David comments, "she took great pleasure in their visits, knowing as she held them, that they were the continuation of the cycle of life".[14]

Donna died at home in the early morning on May 11th, 2001. Shortly afterward, David rang the common house bell to communicate (by pre-arrangement) the news to the community. "By the time I got back to our house," he recalls, "I was surrounded by people streaming out of their homes in bathrobes, pyjamas etc…Pretty soon our front deck was overflowing with people eating, crying, hugging, reassuring and telling stories".[15] Throughout the day David was surrounded and supported by the community and numerous visiting friends and relatives. Donna's body was lovingly bathed and dressed by three women of the core group. Around noon, the local minister summoned the Dobkins' extended family into their house to bid Donna farewell. "Forty of us crammed into a small room, holding hands and wishing, each of us in our own way, good-bye to our dearest Donna".[16]

In the months following the passing of his spouse, the community naturally and appropriately continued to look after David. "I know that I am loved and never alone" he reports, "There is always someone I can talk with should I need to".[17] David and Donna Dobkin's story is not unique, but one that has recurred in traditional communities for millennia, and in modern-day cohousing many times already. It demonstrates the capacity of a community to support members in need and

Photo 8.6: Residents enjoying a common meal in their 100 year old, Redwood-lined dinning room.

to embrace, not shy away from, the difficulties of illness and death. Don Lindemann, a neighbour and close friend of the Dobkins, adds,

> Normally in our culture, death is so incredibly detached and removed from normal life, happening out of sight and out of mind in a hospital or nursing home. That Donna died at home, amongst her extended 'family' made it so much more acceptable and humane.[18]

Notes:

[1] Lent, T. (1999). "Sustainable, Low Toxic Materials Use and Design in Berkeley Cohousing: Successes and failures, lessons learned". Tom Lent's Information Center: http://tlent.home.igc.org.

[2] Personal communication.

[3] These dwellings had to be available to households on 80% of medium income for the area. However, by national (or even State) standards, the purchase prices were still high.

[4] McCamant, K. (1999). "Cohousing Communities: A Model for Reinvigorating Urban Neighborhoods". New Village: Building Sustainable Cultures 1(1): http://www.newvillage.net.

[5] Lent, T. (1999).

[6] McCamant, K. (1999). "Cohousing Communities: A Model for Reinvigorating Urban Neighborhoods". New Village: Building Sustainable Cultures 1(1): http://www.newvillage.net.

[7] See McCamant, K. and C. Durrett (1994). CoHousing: A Contemporary Approach to Housing Ourselves. Berkeley, Habitat Press.

[8] Personal communication.

[9] Dobkin, D. (2001). "Final Passage in Cohousing". CoHousing Journal 14/1(Fall): 15-19:15

[10] Dobkin, D. (2001:16).

[11] Dobkin, D. (2001:16).

[12] Dobkin, D. (2001:17).

[13] Personal communication.

[14] Dobkin, D. (2001). "Final Passage in Cohousing". CoHousing Journal 14/1(Fall): 15-19:15

[15] Dobkin, D. (2001:18).

[16] Dobkin, D. (2001:19).

[17] Dobkin, D. (2001:19).

[18] Personal communication

Photo 9.1 (above left): A weekly farmers market held outside the historic Swan's Market Building.
Photo 9.2 (above right): Ceramic medallions adorn the building exterior (see top of Photo 9.1).
Photo 9.3 (below): The cohousing community's garden featuring a mural painted by the kids.

9 Swan's Market Cohousing

Swan's Market is a public place, a community space and the center of a re-emerging neighbourhood. It is a place that provides ample opportunities for interaction between many different people, a place that supports and encourages relationship building across traditional barriers, a place where neighbours meet and new acquaintances are made.[1]

Name	Swan's Market Cohousing
Address	930 Clay Street, Oakland, CA
Context	Downtown, urban
Households	20 (3 x studio, 5 x 1bd, 12 x 2bd)
Adults	30	Children (under 18 yrs)	5
Renters	1	Working from home	5
Developed	November 1994 – May 2000
Developers	East Bay Asian Local Development Corporation (a non-profit)
Architect	Peter Waller of Pyatock & Associates.
Funding	Land donated by the City, loan from Wells Fargo Bank & member equity.
Site area	0.1 hectares / 0.25 acres
Common house.	465 m² / 5,000 ft²
Ave. dwelling	95 m² / 1020 ft²
Project cost	US$5,260,000

Table 9.1: Community Data.

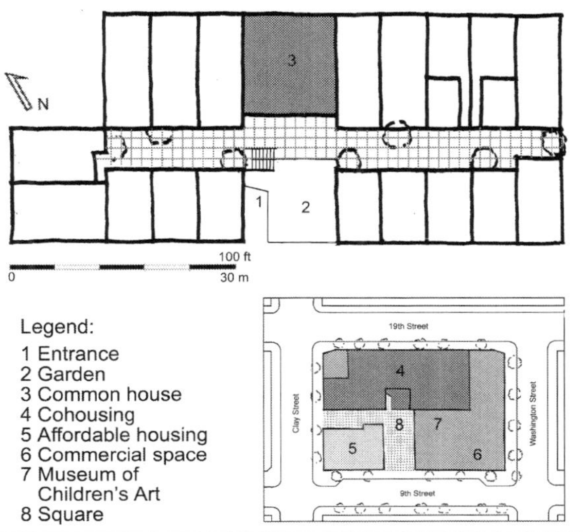

Legend:
1 Entrance
2 Garden
3 Common house
4 Cohousing
5 Affordable housing
6 Commercial space
7 Museum of Children's Art
8 Square

Figure 9.1: Site & location plans.

Swan's Market Cohousing is located in downtown Oakland, CA, just across the Bay from San Francisco (Photo 9.4). It was built as part of a larger redevelopment, the adaptive reuse of a historic building known as Swan's Marketplace. Apart from cohousing, the complex includes:
- eighteen one and two bedroom units for low-income households;[2]
- four units for people living with AIDS;[3]
- an historic (95 year-old) fresh food market;
- retail outlets including a café, Japanese restaurant, flower shop and clothing stores;
- several art and craft galleries, including the very popular Museum of Children's Art; and
- commercial space leased by an architectural firm, a TV Channel and community organisations.

The original market hall was constructed in stages between 1917 and 1940. Ultimately, it occupied an entire city block. Between the wars the population of downtown Oakland swelled with workers from southern states. Swan's became a social hub for Chinese and African American residents. Following WWII, as supermarkets gradually supplanted traditional market halls, Swan's prevailed due to its diversified service and loyal customer base. Ultimately (in 1984) it closed, but not before "it had become a landmark fondly remembered by two generations of East Bay residents for whom it was a major shopping destination".[4] For the next ten years the derelict building served as a stark reminder of the process of urban blight.

> The boarded-up eyesore was a constant reminder of a once thriving heart of downtown that now lay abandoned and in decay. It served as an embarrassment and a symbol of the decline of the city and the loss of a way of life. …The vacant lots

Photo 9.4: Oakland at dusk – Swan's Market in the foreground, San Francisco in the distance.
Photo 9.5: Village Square (front) cohousing and shops (beyond) and affordable housing (left).

and lack of housing in this downtown neighbourhood contributed to this sense of abandonment. The streets...were often dark, lifeless and scary. This site, perhaps more than others in Oakland, represented the hopelessness, neglect and abandonment of the American city.[5]

In 1994, as part of a strategy of urban renewal initiated by Mayor Jerry Brown, the City of Oakland invited tenders for the redevelopment of three adjacent city blocks including Swan's. The only submission proposing to retain and recycle the market hall came from the non-profit developer, *East Coast Bay Asian Development Corporation* (EBALDC). EBALDC was clearly motivated by the cultural heritage of the building, but was no doubt cognisant of the US$1m in tax credits available for saving the market hall. Its bid offered support for community organisations, small, local and minority businesses and included considerable affordable housing, which indeed, is EBALDC's primary mission. The City Council decided to split the project, granting the Swan's redevelopment to EBALDC and the remaining two blocks to private developers.

In the meantime, a nascent cohousing group was developing a separate vision. Its members aspired to living a collaborative, urban lifestyle in or near the fast gentrifying, historic precinct of Old Oakland. For the social advantages of cohousing and the attractions of urban life, particular members were prepared to move from 300 m² family homes in the forested Oakland-Berkeley Hills into 100 m² downtown apartments.

> What we had going for us was the incredible convenience of downtown living – 'walking distance' to just about everything (restaurants, museums, theatres, entertainment centres, work places, galleries, shopping, Chinatown), the availability of extensive public transport, lively city life all around, and, at least for some, the challenges and pleasures of being pioneers.[6]

On learning of the proposed Swan's redevelopment, the group sought involvement in the project. EBALDC had no experience of, nor interest in, developing market rate housing, however, the cohousing group offered partial funding for, and guaranteed sales of, the cohousing units. Their involvement improved the feasibility of the project as a whole and the affordable housing, in particular. The unique design features of the cohousing scheme were well understood by EBALDC since its project manager, Josh Simon, was a resident of nearby Doyle Street Cohousing. A complex community design process ensued, involving the developers, architects *Michael Pyatock & Associates*, the cohousing group and their consultants, heritage groups, local businesses and arts organisations. The final design, suggest the architects, was "shaped by community input and the fiscal constraints of a very expensive adaptive reuse of the structure".[7]

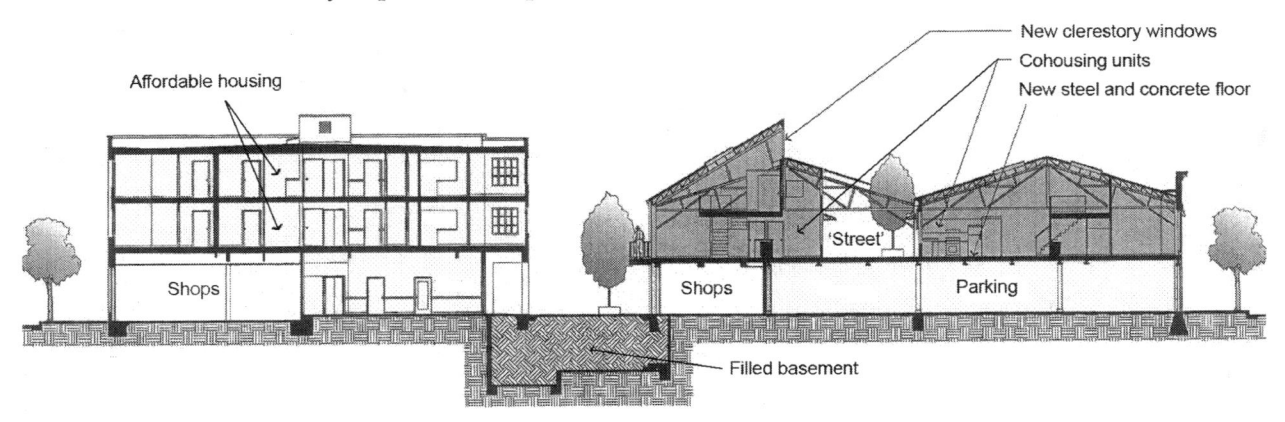

Figure 9.2: Site section (Drawing by architects, Pyatock and Assoc.).

Chapter 9: Swan's Market Cohousing

The resultant development comprises an ensemble of separate yet contiguous parts (Figures 9.1 and 9.2). Public access is available into the heart of the site where a 'village square' has become a venue for music, entertainment, gatherings and informal interaction (Photo 9.5). The affordable housing occupies the upper two levels of a new building in the south-western corner of the site. At ground level, shops and lettable space are accessible from the street and the pedestrianised route through the site. The resurrected fresh food market is located in the south-eastern corner of the site, along with shops and restaurants. Above them, is the Museum of Children's Art and lettable commercial space.

The cohousing units, mostly two-storey townhouses, are located along the building's northern edge, one level above the street. Although there are twenty units, there are fifteen different variations. They face into a shared pedestrianised 'street' typical of many cohousing projects (Photo 9.6). The centrally located common house comprises: kitchen, dining, living and kids rooms at the level of the units; laundry, guest room, exercise room, workshop and parking at street level; and extensive storage space in the basement. The retention of the original roof structure brings to the architecture the funky character and spaciousness of loft living (Photo 9.7).

Since its completion in 2000, Swan's Market has had a major social impact on the locality. It has added 38 housing units to a previously lifeless part of town, provided 2,800 m^2 (30,000 ft^2) of retail space, been the catalyst for numerous new restaurants and shops in the area, increased day and night-time pedestrian activity, reduced crime in the area by 18%,[8] directly created 150 new jobs (including a number of entry level jobs for disadvantaged individuals) and provided vitally needed food and supplies for low-income households.[9]

Photo 9.6: The pedestrian 'street'.

Photo 9.7: Common dining room.

In social and economic terms, the Swan's redevelopment provides a model for a mixed use, diversely occupied, "elegantly dense"[10] transformation of an historic quarter. Furthermore, it can be seen as a microcosm. The same development model could conceivably be applied to the changing needs of a larger precinct, suburb or region. Whilst this may seem self-evident to most readers of this book, in truth, the essential characteristics of Swan's are anathema to most development agencies. Evidence for this abounds in the sprawling, homogeneous, single-use, class and race-segregated, low-density developments that are such a ubiquitous feature of American and, for that matter, Australian cities. The fundamental differences between these two models are those between an ecological and an economically rational worldview: integration versus separation, inclusion versus segregation, and a generous, optimistic motivation rather than a cynical, expedient one. One cohousing resident observes:

> The project is a good fit with the existing neighbourhood. The affordable housing accommodates households that have relocated from Chinatown, the Market Hall continues to serve the African American residents. The resulting mosaic of communities is something that no for-profit developer would have accepted.[11]

The thinking of the cohousing group in relation to their particular aspirations was similarly ecological. Members were motivated by "minimising the duplication of resources, the sharing of meals and facilities such as a laundry and guest quarters, making best use of the available land, and dedicating least possible space to the automobile".[12] The group was anxious to connect with neighbours. They originally intended that the affordable housing would be directly linked to the cohousing so as to further increase opportunities for interaction within a more diverse community.

Photo 9.8: Living room of a private residence.

Chapter 9: Swan's Market Cohousing

Photo 9.9: Teenager's bedroom – space efficient and funky.

Ultimately, this aspiration went unrealised. But the group did manage to achieve most of their other pro-environmental goals including: making good use of the existing building; creating modestly sized, energy efficient dwellings; and providing sufficient garden space to be able to produce reasonable quantities of organic food (Photo 9.3).

It is too early to comment on the success or otherwise of the cohousing project in terms of its social cohesion, relationship building, trust and accord. But for this particular group more than most cohousing communities, this is a critical concern. The feature that motivated many residents to join the community, namely its downtown location, is paradoxically the greatest threat to its social cohesion. "I don't see many people here with a deep commitment to cooperative living," observes one member. "Rather, the attraction for many residents is the location". [13] Another believes that "people are busy with their own lives and they don't have the energy to put into the cohousing project".[14]

A level of distraction from the essential cohousing social aspirations of the community is not unique to Swan's or urban projects, generally. Indeed, because cohousing is a mainstream phenomenon, it is common to almost all cohousing groups. And the perception of a general lack of commitment is prevalent in most new projects. There is inevitably an initial period (typically between two and four years) of settling-in, recovery from an exhausting development phase, getting to know one's new neighbours, fine-tuning management systems and developing cultural and social pursuits. Even so, there are few, if any, other cohousing groups that have as much on their collective doorstep to attract members away from internal 'affairs of State'. It will be fascinating to watch this pioneering community evolve in the years to come.

Notes:

[1] Mark Beratta of the Oakland Redevelopment Agency quoted in Pyatock & Assoc (2001) Submission to the Rudy Bruner Award for Urban Excellence.

[2] Low-income is considered to be 60% of AMI (Area Median Income).

[3] Members of these households live on approximately 20% of AMI.

[4] Pyatock & Assoc (2001) Submission to the Rudy Bruner Award for Urban Excellence.

[5] Pyatock & Assoc (2001).

[6] From the cohousing group's web site, http://www.Swan'sway.com/, June, 2003.

[7] Pyatock & Assoc (2001).

[8] According to Alex Greenwood of the Oakland Redevelopment Agency in Pyatock & Assoc (2001).

[9] Mark Beratta in Pyatock & Assoc (2001).

[10] Major Jerry Brown's words, characterising his vision of urban consolidation.

[11] Michael Schaffer, a founding member, comments in Pyatock & Assoc (2001).

[12] Pyatock & Assoc (2001).

[13] Personal communication.

[14] Personal communication.

Photos 10.1 and 10.2: The environmentally responsive houses (mostly duplexes) at New Zealand's first cohousing project, Earthsong Eco-Neighbourhood. It has solar hot water heaters on every roof.

10 Earthsong Eco-Neighbourhood

Our vision is to establish a cohousing neighbourhood based on the principles of permaculture that will serve as a model of a socially and environmentally sustainable community.[1]

Name	Earthsong Eco-Neighbourhood
Address	449-457 Swanson Rd, Ranui, Auckland, NZ.
Context	Suburban, rural edge.
Households	17 (8x2bed, 6x3bed, 3x4bed)
Adults	29
Children (under 18 yrs)	11
Renters	13
Working from home	7
Developed	July 1995 – June 2002 (Stage 1 only)
Developers	Cohousing NZ Ltd, the residents.
Architect	William F Algie
Funding	Member equity (25%), National Bank of NZ (70%), Prometheus, an ethical fund (5%.)
Site area	1.67 hectares / 4.13 acres
Common house	Unbuilt, planned for Stage Two.
Ave. dwelling	92 m² / 990 ft²
Project cost	NZ$4,200,000 / US$2,400,000

Table 10.1: Community Data.

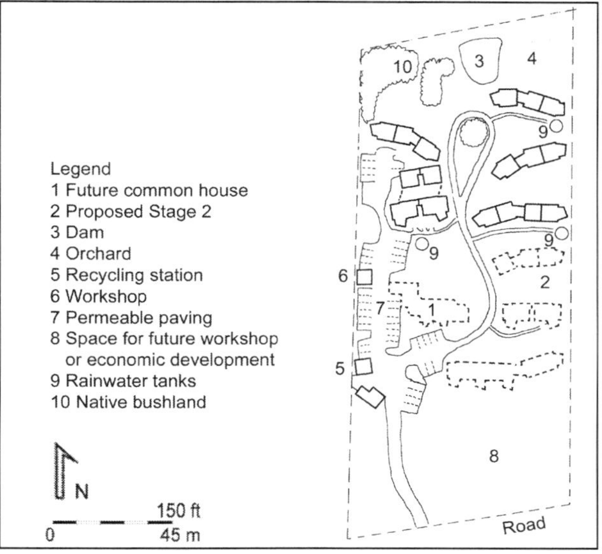

Legend
1 Future common house
2 Proposed Stage 2
3 Dam
4 Orchard
5 Recycling station
6 Workshop
7 Permeable paving
8 Space for future workshop or economic development
9 Rainwater tanks
10 Native bushland

Figure 10.1: Site plan.

Of all the communities included in this series of case studies, Earthsong Eco-Neighbourhood has perhaps the most ambitious vision. The simple, pithy statement above encompasses (but also conceals) a hugely rich and complex social and environmental agenda. In terms of its social aspirations alone, the group is not unique. Such ambition is common in cohousing. However, the environmentally sustainable technologies of this project are amongst the most comprehensive in cohousing and undoubtedly the best documented.[2]

Initially, founders of the project envisioned an ecovillage. Later, the vision changed to incorporate certain cohousing concepts. Amongst these was the notion that the project should be within a walk of commercial and community facilities and within easy reach of Auckland city by public transportation.[3] Striving for integration and connectivity (as opposed to autonomy and self-sufficiency) but without the use of private transportation is a fundamental *ecological* strategy. Implicitly, it requires an urban or suburban location. Aptly and symbolically, at the time of this shift in emphasis the name of the project was changed to that of an eco-*neighbourhood*, rather than an eco-*village*.

Ultimately, the site selected was further from central Auckland than anticipated. However, it met most of the group's other requirements. It was within 500m of shops and facilities, had a gentle north-facing slope, was large enough to accommodate the project whilst retaining existing trees and native bush and had room for future expansion of an economic, live/work nature. As a bonus, the land had previously been in the caring hands of two generations of organic orchardists.

From its inception, the group had adopted permaculture as its primary set of site planning principles. In further developing its goals for the site, the group creatively melded permaculture with: the needs of a diverse yet socially cohesive community; environmental and economic good sense; and necessary budgetary considerations. The full list of site planning strategies, forming only a small part of the complete design brief, is much too comprehensive to include here.[4] Most notably, it incorporated: people centeredness; a balance between public and private; security and safety; and integration with the wider community. This tripartite fusion of environmental, social and economic concerns is considered by many theorists to be a necessary underpinning of sustainability.

The group's desire to develop a "diverse intergenerational village" required that the architectural brief include a range of household types and meet the different needs of children, teens, parents, singles, the disabled and the elderly. A further aspiration – to *demonstrate* (in the layout, buildings and services) the "highest possible standards of sustainable human settlement" – mandated energy efficiency, natural climate control, passive solar design and importantly, the demonstration and monitoring of appropriate technologies.

The technologies specified in the design brief included rainwater collection, solar hot water, renewable energy use, on-site stormwater, grey water and sewerage treatment (if permissible) as well as comprehensive recycling and compost systems with the potential to achieve "zero waste". It called for an architecture of clustered buildings with significant space between the clusters (i.e. a neighbourhood of neighbourhoods), natural materials, easy indoor–outdoor accessibility, and transition between private and community space via a 'soft edge' of verandas, decks and screens.

Given the demands of the brief, the complexity of the project and the necessity for an ongoing community design process, architect Bill Algie might have joined the project with some trepidation. Yet, Algie had previously designed projects of somewhat similar scale and complexity (schools and retirement villages) and had experience with design for community groups. The group itself was well versed in consensus decision-making, having already invested considerable time and energy in refining their processes. They had benefited from a preliminary design workshop with Katie McCamant and years of discussion of permaculture and cohousing principles. The conditions were in place for something quite special to emerge.

Figure 10.2: Proposed common house (Drawing by W Algie, Architect).

The reality of Earthsong Eco-Neighbourhood, at the time of writing in late 2004, is still some distance from the vision. Stage One of the project, the first seventeen dwellings, is complete. However, the common house portrayed in Figure 10.2 is not yet built. It will be part of Stage Two, being constructed in 2004-5. Two years following move in, the landscaping is beginning to take hold but will require years more growth before it becomes the mature permaculture envisaged.

The housing layout is unconventional for a cohousing project (Figure 10.1). It represents a marriage of cohousing and passive solar design principles. Buildings line up in loose rows, facing north for maximum solar exposure, but also face each other across open space so as to maximise the opportunities for chance social interaction. Some dwellings therefore 'face' south. Access is to the rear, or southern side, of the dwellings to leave the front or northern edge fully available as a permaculture belt. The houses have generous north facing glazing and are largely constructed of rammed earth, which provides the requisite high thermal mass. All construction materials were assessed for toxicity, 'breathability', natural durability and level of embodied energy. The exterior cladding is of sustainably harvested, untreated Macrocarpa. The homes have beautiful interior qualities of space, light, colour, texture and solidity as well as something else quite intangible; they really 'feel' good (Photos 10.4-7). It is perhaps an *organic* quality in the sense that Frank Lloyd Wright used the word to mean 'growing from, or rooted in, the site'. This is easy to understand given that the earth used in the construction was, indeed, excavated from the site.

Photo 10.3: Rammed earth walls under construction.

The technological systems at Earthsong Eco-neighbourhood are comprehensive. It happens that the project is located in Waitakere, New Zealand's first designated *Eco City*. The Waitakere City Council (WCC) is one of the few to have adopted the principles of Agenda 21.[5] The Council has taken a life-cycle view of energy, resources and waste; seeking to "assist individuals and business to adopt a holistic approach to resource use which results in using less energy, generating energy from renewable resources, using resources more wisely and producing less waste".[6] The concurrence of a supportive Council, the aspirations of the group and the determined efforts of particular members has produced a comprehensive and integrated response to resource use.

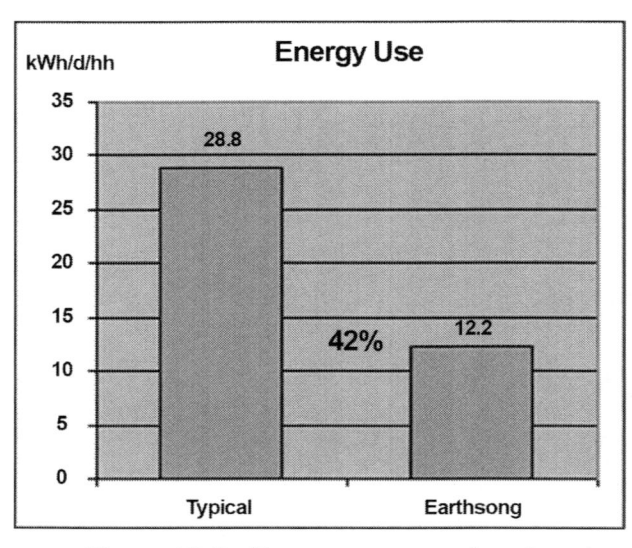

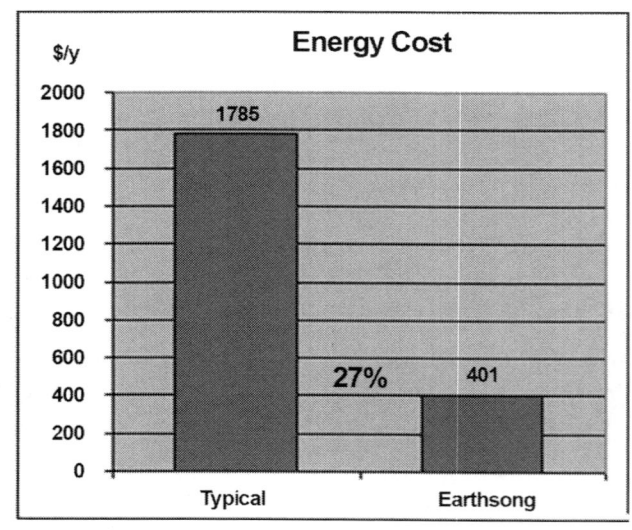

Figure 10.3: Energy usage and cost savings at Earthsong (Data analysis by Peter Scott).

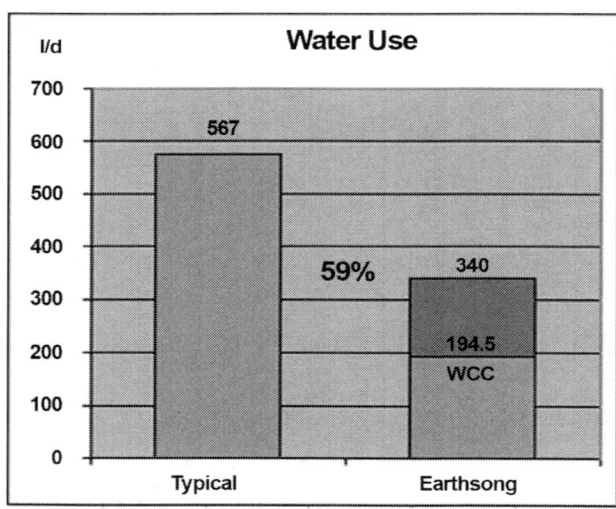

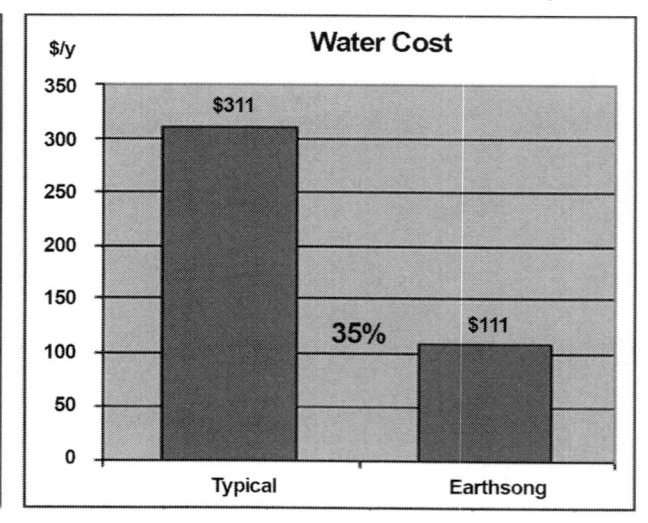

Figure 10.4: Water usage and cost savings (Data analysis by Peter Scott).

Solar energy is utilised to significantly reduce the energy consumed in space and water heating. Passive solar design ensures that the homes are warm in winter and cool in summer. All the units have solar hot water collectors on the roof (Photos 10.1 and 10.2). Data collected in the first twelve months of occupation reveal that the dwellings used only 42% of the energy typically consumed by homes in New Zealand. This is, of course, a multi-factorial comparison, involving behavioural differences as well as technological ones. It should also be noted that New Zealand households consume only a modest amount of energy compared with other developed countries – 10, 500 kWh annually, compared with Australia (16,000 kWh) and the US (27,000 kWh).[7] Due to their energy conservation measures and the opportunity to purchase power at bulk rates, electricity bills at Earthsong Eco-neighbourhood will most likely cost about a quarter of the 'normal' outlay (Figure 10.3).[8]

Despite (or perhaps, because of) New Zealand's notoriously high rainfall, water conservation is taken equally seriously at Earthsong Eco-neighbourhood. Having a critical mass of cooperative households has enabled the group to install a rainwater collection system that is both efficient and cost effective. Above ground 30,000 litre tanks collect rainfall from each cluster of six or seven households (Figure 10.1). This supply, together with technological and behavioural (consumption) measures, is expected to reduce water consumption to about half that of conventional homes in the region. Reliance on the City water supply (i.e. from WCC) is ultimately expected to be around 15% of the norm.[9] (Note that until Stage Two is built and the common areas are all plumbed for rainwater the WCC supply will constitute more than that.)

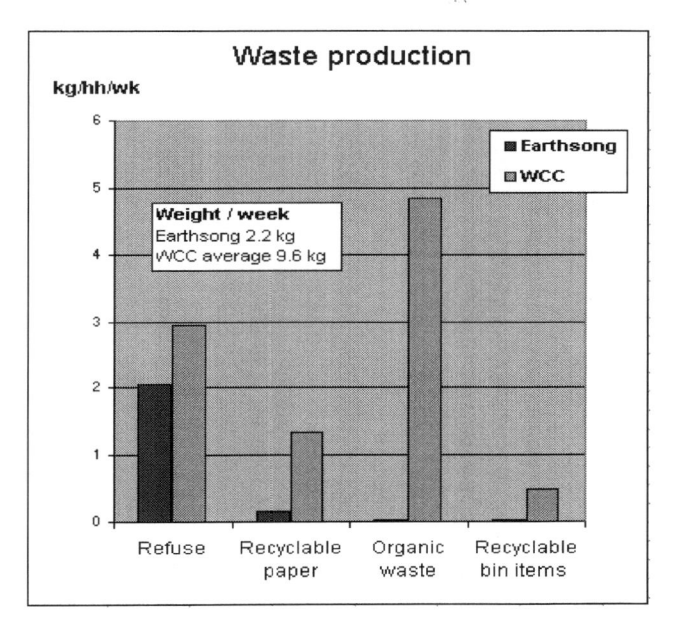

Figure 10.5: Household waste production compared with the WCC norm[10] (Peter Scott).

The stormwater management strategy at Earthsong recognises the deleterious effects of impervious surfaces such as roads, driveways, carparks and roofs without rainwater collection devices. Vegetated swales ensure that stormwater is absorbed back into the ground and/or directed toward a detention pond used for irrigation and serving as a wildlife habitat (Photo 10.2). In the process, airborne pollutants are filtered and neutralised. The car parking is permeably paved, except for limited hard paving provided for delivery and emergency vehicles. The value of these measures goes far beyond their contribution to water quality in the wider catchment. By serving as a demonstration project that has already attracted considerable publicity, the Earthsong precedent has created confidence and offered inspiration to other individuals and groups considering similar measures.

Wastewater treatment is the notable omission from an inventory of Earthsong's technological systems. The group had long aspired to on-site treatment of wastewater, including sewerage. Two separate feasibility studies have confirmed its cost effectiveness and the site's suitability. Notwithstanding the considerable benefits, legal advice suggested that the Auckland Metropolitan Drainage Act 1960 precluded on-site treatment. In 1999, the group sought an exemption, but was denied. Without the resources to mount a challenge to the law, they proceeded with a conventional wastewater reticulation system. However, it has been designed to allow easy modification to an on-site solution in the future.

In April 2003, rubbish (i.e. solid waste or garbage) collected by WCC from Earthsong was audited to determine what improvements to their recycling practices might be effected through education of the residents. The overall results of this snapshot analysis were very good. They indicated that the recycling of organic waste was being adequately handled on site and that accurate recycling utilising Council bins and its paper collection was already occurring (Figure 10.5).

Photos 10.4-7: Earthsong interiors have excellent qualities of light, colour and materiality.

Taken separately, Earthsong's pro-environmental measures are far from unique. It is the holistic, comprehensive and life-cycle approaches to sustainable technologies that distinguishes this project. The long-term perspective of the group is well illustrated in Table 10.2. It shows the projected savings over twenty years that the application of these technologies will achieve for each household. The final comment in the last line of the table – that the buildings at Earthsong Eco-neighbourhood are expected to last 100 years – encapsulates the fundamental sustainability of this ambitious project.

Activity	Annual savings (NZ$)	Savings over 20 years (NZ$)	Comments
Water savings	265	5,290	Water efficient fittings. Tanks. Pressure reduction valves.
Wastewater savings	345	6,900	Based on WCC transition to user-pays in two years time.
Electricity savings	975	19,500	Solar space heating. Solar hot water.
Rubbish savings	55	1,100	Rubbish is cheap in our society! Compost separated on site
Maintenance savings	1,550	31,000	Minimal paintwork. Avoidance of carpets. Durable materials
Due to co-ownership	467	9,330	Common laundry. Shared garden and office equipment.
Through cooperation	1,065	21,300	Child minding, bulk food purchase, car pooling etc.
Total for 1 unit	4,721	94,420	This is just the first twenty years. Houses are projected to
Total for 32 units	151,072	3,021,440	last in excess of 100 years.

Table 10.2: Projected average household cost savings (Prepared by Peter Scott).

Notes:

[1] Part of the group's vision statement from a brochure, *Earthsong Eco-Neighbourhood*.

[2] Most of the documentation is available online at http://www.ecohousing.pl.net/.

[3] Site selection criteria also included: having enough land for growing food; open space; good earth energies; a supportive council and neighbours; and a benevolent and patient vendor. See http://www.ecohousing.pl.net/design/sitecriteria.html.

[4] See http://www.ecohousing.pl.net/design/design_brief.html. This is a fully comprehensive brief (perhaps frighteningly so for consultants) that the group is happy to share with others.

[5] Agenda 21 is the comprehensive and complex document that resulted from the 1992 Earth Summit in Brazil. It was a commitment by world leaders to strive to achieve sustainability in the 21st C. WCC adopted it as policy in 1993.

[6] From the Council's *Greenprint* (ie. it's policy adapted from the principles of Agenda 21) available on its web site: http://www.waitakere.govt.nz/AbtCit/ec/greenprnt.asp.

[7] See the NZ Government EECA (Energy Efficiency and Conservation Act) Web site: http://www.eeca.govt.nz/.

[8] The data used for 'usual' consumption is based on the BRANZ's (Building Research Association of New Zealand) HEEP (Home Energy End-Use Project), which takes data from 100 randomly selected houses.

[9] Note that these are projections. Currently, insufficient metering has been installed to be able to calculate savings.

[10] Based on Council's own analysis of 300 households in September 2002.

Photos 11.1 and 11.2: The common house at Cohousing Cooperative.

11 Cohousing Cooperative

> Based on the belief that humans are social beings, we are attempting to extend the physical and social boundaries which presently surround Australia's nuclear family homes. Our community will improve the social standard of living of our members and will benefit Australia by providing a cooperative housing model which can potentially reduce government physical and human service costs.[1]

Name	Cohousing Cooperative		
Address	201 Strickland Ave, Cascades, Hobart		
Context	Suburban but close to bush.		
Households	11 (1x1bd, 3x2bd, 4x3bd, 2x4bd, 1x5bd)		
Adults	14	Children (under 18 yrs)	16
Renters	all	Working from home	2
Developed	March 1989 – March 2000		
Developers	Cohousing Cooperative Society Ltd, the resident, together with the Tasmanian Department of Community and Health Services.		
Architect	James Morrison and Yvette Breytenbach of Morrison & Breytenbach Architects.		
Funding	$1m Federal/State Government grant under the Community Housing Program.		
Site area	1.21 hectares / 3 acres		
Common house.	130 m² / 1400 ft²		
Ave. dwelling	100 m² / 1076 ft²		
Project cost	A$1,142,000 / US$720,000[2]		

Table 11.1: Community Data.

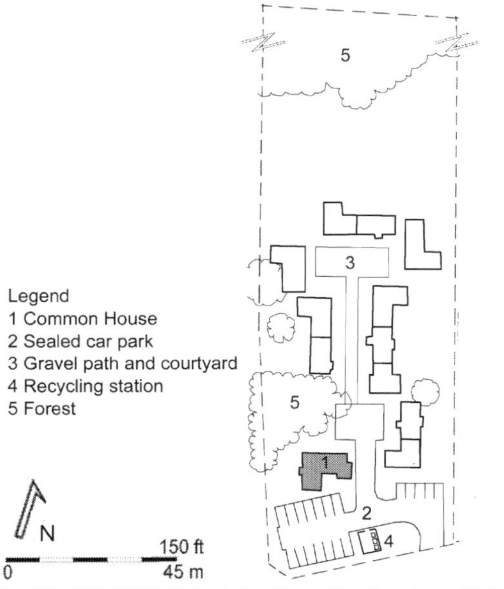

Legend
1 Common House
2 Sealed car park
3 Gravel path and courtyard
4 Recycling station
5 Forest

Figure 11.1: Site plan.

Cohousing Cooperative is located in Hobart, Tasmania – Australia's 'Deep South'. There are only three cohousing projects built in Australia. Another, Cascade Cohousing, happens to be just a block away (see Chapter 12). The third, Pinakarri Cohousing, is in Fremantle, Western Australia. Though limited in number, Australian cohousing projects have made an important contribution to the furthering of cohousing development practice. In different ways, each project has successfully addressed the need for cohousing to be more affordable and, therefore, accessible. Cohousing Cooperative is a publicly funded project for low-income households. Cascade Cohousing, financed by the residents, has implemented significant sweat equity to greatly reduce the cost of membership. Pinakarri creatively integrates equity and non-equity housing and has a purpose built home for one severely intellectually and physically disadvantaged resident.

Cohousing Cooperative, as the name implies, is a legally constituted Cooperative Society. The principle purpose of a Housing Cooperative is to secure housing for low-income households. In Australia and elsewhere, such an organisation can apply for Government funding to house eligible families and individuals. Cooperative ownership is rare amongst non-Scandinavian cohousing. In almost all of the cohousing in Britain, Australia, New Zealand and the US, residents own their dwellings outright. In a Housing Co-op, on the other hand, land and buildings belong to the Cooperative, which in turn rents the dwellings to its members. Rent is set at 25% of household income and tenure is guaranteed even if that income increases significantly.

Members of Cohousing Cooperative become eligible for accommodation according to a calculation that takes into account (in addition to income) the extent of their participation in Co-op activities, the level of their interest in cohousing, the duration of their membership as well as family size and circumstance. Single parents, for example, have an increased priority. Tenants are a mix of mostly single mothers, couples with young children, people with disabilities and students. Prior to joining, Co-op members were living in scattered and cheap rental housing without the extra cost savings available in cohousing. A mother of five explains:

> The private rental market is very limited and the quality of accommodation in the price bracket we could afford was not very good. Cohousing allows us to have good accommodation, while making many savings on areas such as electricity and the costs of garden equipment and maintenance.[3]

Photos 11.3 and 11.4: Two meals being prepared in the common house, one, an Aussie barbeque.

Cohousing Cooperative formed in 1991 and successfully sought funding from Government Departments of Housing through the early nineties. The total budget was set in 1994 with the expectation of housing twelve adults and twelve children. The project was finally built in 1999-2000 to house fifteen adults and sixteen children, but without an increase in budget.[4] Cost cutting was achieved through the substitution of alternative building materials, downgrading of appliances and the introduction of sweat equity. During construction they installed an intranet that electronically links the dwellings and enables the cost of Internet broadband to be shared. Using their combined purchasing power, residents bought power tools and hardware at trade prices and garden materials in bulk. They painted their own dwellings and were responsible for the landscaping. Since moving in, the group has further used its economy of scale to purchase bread and dairy products at bulk rates and there is frequent informal sharing of household goods and gardening equipment.

The project occupies a superb site in the foothills of Mt. Wellington, a landmark mountain with spectacular rock formations within view of the cohousing (Photo 11.6). The architecture of two-storey row housing has a crisp, contemporary character. Its deep red concrete block base supports an upper level clad in striking, grey-blue corrugated metal sheeting. The project has a 'classical' cohousing layout. The dwellings face into and across a pedestrian 'street' linking courtyards at each end. It is affectionately known as 'Corrugation Street' due to the high level of social interaction that occurs there.[5] The common house lies between the car park and the dwellings; residents returning home can easily check in to collect their mail or their children, or see what's for dinner.

Figure 11.2: Eastern elevation of Cohousing Cooperative (Morrison & Breytenbach Architects).

Photos 11.5 and 11.6: The corrugated cladding reflects the form of the mountain beyond.

To the outside observer, the project appears to be a community of, and for, the children. They dominate in terms of their numbers and their presence. Toys and bikes are liberally and randomly distributed throughout the common areas, conveying a strong visual message about priority of usage. The kids 'hang out' together in typical cohousing style, as one of the parents explains:

> When we moved in...most of the households with children had a trampoline. And for a couple of years these trampolines sat at the rear of their houses, and were bounced on occasionally. And then someone put one trampoline next to another trampoline. Once the children had bounced away in a roughly synchronised way it

occurred to them to bring together all the trampolines from all the houses' backyards. And so this spring, wet as it is, sees children bouncing, lounging, lying, sleeping, talking and just hanging out, on five trampolines, the biggest in the middle, under a grand old white gum in view of the mountain.[6]

For the safety of children at play, vehicles are not welcome in the courtyards or connecting 'street', although these do provide access for service and emergency vehicles. The courtyards are obvious venues for ball games, albeit a source of some angst for residents and gardeners in the vicinity (Photo 11.7). Perhaps the quite 'thin' soft edge between the dwellings and the public domain means that visual and aural privacy is difficult to establish within the dwellings.

The Co-op's management structure is defined by rules prescribed in law under the Cooperatives Act. All residents participate in management decisions using a consensus process set out in the rules. Site Meetings of the residents are held fortnightly and Board Meetings involving five members are held monthly. There is also an AGM at which Board members are elected. However, all members are able to participate at all meetings. Consensus is said to be working well but there is a shortage of good facilitators. The group has held, and will continue to run, workshops in meetings facilitation, consensus decision-making and conflict resolution. Skills development has also occurred in the areas of record keeping, financial management, cooperative law, project development, responsible leadership and land management.

Within the management structure is a Property Committee that works with members to develop a maintenance and upgrading program. Each building (of two or three dwellings) receives regular maintenance attention, supervised by the committee. In addition, each household presents a prioritised list of proposed upgrades to the committee. These measures are progressively implemented as the budget allows. The process is fully documented, accessible and transparent.

Levels of social support run high at Cohousing Cooperative. The 'Parents' committee provides practical and emotional support for families. The children are taken to school and picked up according to a roster administered by the committee. After school childcare is similarly rostered (Table 11.3). Another committee, the Heart Group, organises regular and spontaneous social and recreational events. Christmas dinners and Easter egg painting (introduced by a German member) have already become regular traditions. In winter, snow is brought down off the mountain in the back of a ute[7] for the kids to make snowmen and ice skating excursions are organised for the whole community. The committee also arranges occasional events such as yoga workshops and craft nights.

Goulburn St School Transport Roster and after school care (3-5pm weekdays) FEB 2001					
	Monday	Tuesday	Wednesday	Thursday	Friday
Taking Kids to school	Frank Jim, Zorro and Mitzi & Ben every second week Alexandra Jilly, Asa, Loui, Paul	Frank Jim, Zorro, Mitzi & Ben Alexandra Jilly, Asa, Loui, Paul	Anna Mitzi, Ben Jilly & Loui Delta Paul, Asa & Jim	Delta Paul, Asa, Loui, Holly & Jim	Anna Mitzi, Ben, Jilly & Loui Delta Paul, Asa & Jim
Picking Kids up from school	Frank Jim, Zorro, Mitzi & Ben Alexandra Asa, Loui, Jilly, Paul	Anna Mitzi, Ben Jim & Zorro Delta Paul, Asa, Loui & Jilly	Alexandra Asa, Loui, Jilly Delta Paul & Jim	Frank & Alexandra (week about) Jim, Jilly, Mitzi & Ben	Frank Loui & Jim Anna Jilly, Mitzi Ben & Asa
Parent responsible for after school care and kids potentially attending	Alexandra Mitzi, Ben, Jim, Zorro, Paul, Asa, Loui, Jilly.	Anna Mitzi, Ben, Jim, Zorro, Paul, Asa, Loui, Jilly, Jaffa, Oprah	Delta Asa, Loui, Jilly, Paul, Jim, Zorro, Jaffa & Oprah	Kathy Jim, Jilly, Mitzi, Ben Jaffa & Oprah	Frank Jim, Zorro, Jaffa Oprah Paul, Asa, Jilly, Loui (maybe Mitzi & Ben every second week)

Table 11.2: Rostered car pooling and childcare arrangements.

Photo 11.7: Car park being used for an impromptu game of cricket.

Photo 11.8: Hard landscaping – the quintessential sweat equity project.

It is not surprising, given the background of many members, that this community has a progressive – perhaps even radical – socio-political worldview. There is considerable ideological commitment amongst the group to grassroots accessibility, equal opportunity and social change. This manifests in small and large ways. A garden gate was moved to make welcome neighbours and encourage the public to walk through the site. This is a declaration of openness; making the point that theirs is not a gated community or an enclave. There is a prevailing feminist sentiment that ensures support is provided for disadvantaged women, including single mothers, within the community and without.

Members of Cohousing Cooperative appreciate the rewards and benefits that their efforts have delivered and feel a responsibility to assist other groups with similar aspirations. The common house is made available to such groups for meetings. The South Hobart Progress Association, for example, occasionally meets there. The Coop is in the process of seeding, sponsoring and mentoring another cooperatively owned cohousing project. Furthermore, the project has attracted widespread interest in Australia and provided considerable inspiration to housing and community activists. Cohousing Cooperative importantly offers a precedent and suggests an approach to achieving a much more affordable and accessible cohousing.

Notes:

[1] From the Preamble to the Rules of Cohousing Cooperative Society Inc.

[2] Currency conversion is based on relative values at the time of construction (in 1999-2000).

[3] Grube, K. (2001). New neighbours get close for comfort. The Saturday Mercury. February 3, 2001. Hobart: 32-33.

[4] 2000 National Awards for Excellence in Community Housing Report. See http://www.nchf.org.au/abcriteria8.htm.

[5] 'Corrugation Street' is a double pun. It refers to both the cladding material of the dwellings (corrugated metal sheeting) and the long-running British TV serial, Coronation Street, which portrays daily life in a close-knit urban community.

[6] Personal communication.

[7] Ute is a colloquial Australian shortening of 'utility vehicle' - called a 'pick up' in the US.

Photos 12.1 and 12.2: Cascade Cohousing situated in the bush-clad foothills of Mt Wellington.

12 Cascade Cohousing

...the parties [to this agreement] hereto have expressed desire to engender a sense of community through the design of the development and the regular sharing of meals in the common house...and a common intention to build energy efficient houses and to consider the environmental impact of all aspects of building design and construction.[1]

Name	Cascade Cohousing
Address	12 Saunders Crescent, South Hobart.
Context	Suburban with access to open space.
Households	15 (3x1 bd, 8x2 bd, 4x3 bd)
Adults 20	Children (under 18 yrs) 8
Renters 4	Working from home 0
Developed	November 1989 – June 2001
Developers	The residents themselves.
Architect	Detlev Geard
Funding	Individual mortgages and sweat equity.
Site area	0.86 hectares / 2.13 acres
Common house.	280 m² / 3,080 ft²
Ave. dwelling	101 m² / 1,087 ft²
Project cost	Approx A$2,000,000 / US$1,500,000

Table 12.1: Community Data.

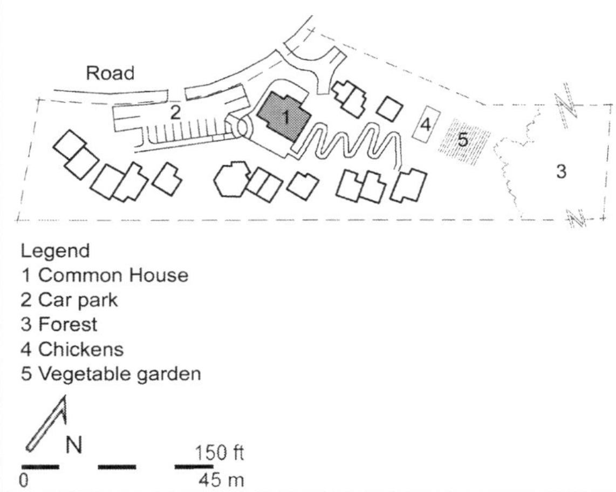

Legend
1 Common House
2 Car park
3 Forest
4 Chickens
5 Vegetable garden

Figure 12.1: Site plan.

Cascade Cohousing, like Cohousing Cooperative (see Chapter 11), is located in Hobart, Tasmania. It too, is situated high in the foothills of Mount Wellington. The narrow site falls steeply to the east, offering views of a bright blue Derwent River and downtown Hobart in the distance. Close-packed houses 'cascade' down the hill (Figure 12.2). They have a striking consistency of form, materials and colour, but with variations that reflect the creative input of individuals and households. Their steep roofs and flared eaves are perhaps reminiscent of Bavarian farmhouses. A large common house, different in form to the dwellings, occupies the centre of the site. Pathways and flights of stairs link the buildings and create outdoor seating places. The landscaping is informal – bordering on messy.

Cascade was the first cohousing project in Australia. Its founder, Ian Higginbottom, has been referred to as the father of Australian cohousing. Ian read McCamant and Durrett's book in the late 1980s and was so inspired he undertook a private study tour of Denmark to see cohousing for himself. On his return, he gathered together a core group of six committed individuals to search for suitable land. Although it was not made explicit in a mission statement, the group aspired to a socially progressive and environmentally responsive cohousing project. Their single most important site selection criterion was that the land be within a twenty-minute bicycle ride of downtown Hobart. "Since commuting is the greatest single use of energy for most households, reducing car use results in real benefits for the environment", suggested their literature of the time.[2]

In 1991, the group purchased five contiguous house blocks that were close to town, opposite a bus stop, had good solar exposure and wonderful views. Unfortunately the land had been so brutally cleared that even the topsoil was removed. They engaged an architect specialising in passive solar design, and together they developed a site plan and a series of options for small, passive solar homes. They eschewed classic cohousing site strategies in favour of maximising solar exposure for

Chapter 12: Cascade Cohousing 99

the dwellings. As a result, the project is much less internalised than most cohousing and without a pedestrian street or courtyard to act as a principle social hub. Perhaps this was never a possibility given the steep slope of the site. Instead, residents gather as a community in and around the common house.

Construction began in 1992 and the first three households took up residence in April 1993. A year later, five more homes were completed. Residents chose one of the original house options or, together with the architect, designed something else. In such cases, environmentally responsive guidelines governing the choice of form, materials and finishes were applied. A resident describes the conflicts inherent in such a process:

> The choice of building materials was difficult for us all. Building is not an ecological process [fundamentally]. All one can do is try to make it the least damaging possible. We all had to make our own decisions but generally opted for smaller than usual houses and to use materials and finishes that were the least damaging biologically.[3]

All homes have large north facing windows, thermal mass and environmentally benign materials and finishes. Aerated concrete (Hebel) blocks have been used in most homes due to their insulation value and ease of assembly.[4]

In those early days, residents were effectively living in a building site (Photo 12.3). Hobart's high rainfall ensured that thick mud was a constant companion. Most were working on their own dwellings, the landscaping had not yet been established and there was no common house. Weekly common meals were held in yet unfinished homes. It is perhaps a reflection of the tough conditions and pioneering spirit of the time that five of the eight households comprised single people without children, three women and two men. One of the women, 70-year-old Mary Jenkins describes the satisfaction and rewards inherent in the building process:

> My neighbour and I shared our finances and energies to build together on one site and, for me, it was a most rewarding and learning experience. My 50m² home [Figure 12.2] has a mezzanine bedroom, a small downstairs bedroom-study with adjoining bathroom, and French windows which open onto a small deck which has enough space for an outdoor table and benches. My living room-kitchen also has French windows which open onto an outdoor sitting area and garden. Views from all of my windows show native vegetation or fruit trees. A skylight in the mezzanine gives me much valued extra light and a view of trees, sky and stars.[5]

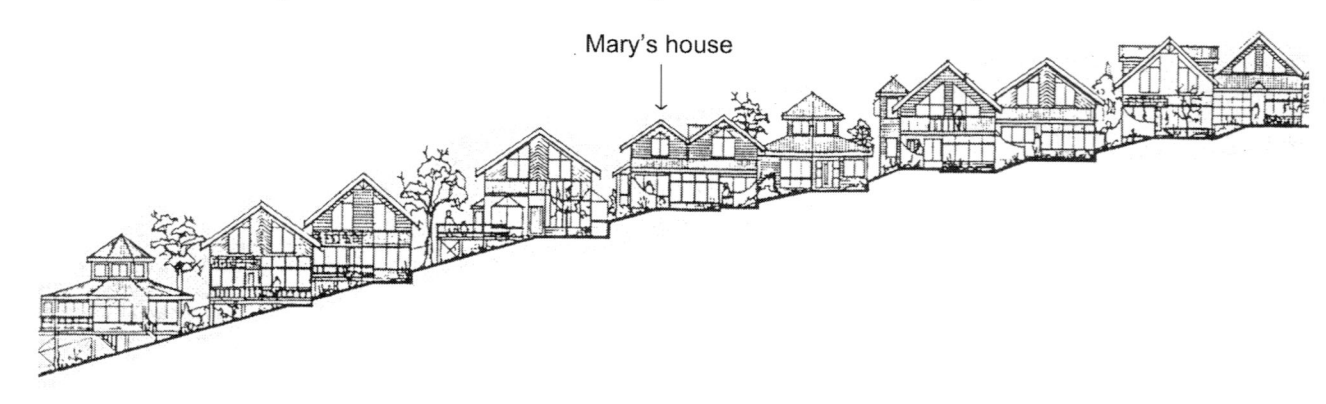

Figure 12.2: Northern elevation of the dwellings
(drawn by architect, Detlev Gnaulk).

From the outset, sweat equity was considered a fundamental strategy in achieving *affordable* cohousing. Members could decide themselves how much 'sweat' they would invest in their own dwellings, but the landscaping and common house were always going to be constructed by the residents. A 1993 brochure promoting the project stated: "All residents who are able will need to contribute some labour to the construction of the common house. This could be anything from laying bricks to sewing curtains, depending on residents' skills and inclination. Tree planting and path building will also be tasks undertaken by residents".

Photo 12.3: Landscaping under construction. Photo 12.4: Landscaping completed.
Photo 12.5: Sweat equity provides opportunity for cost savings, collaboration and learning.

Chapter 12: Cascade Cohousing 101

Photo 2.6 (top): Common meals are sometimes held outside the common house in summer.
Photo 2.7 (bottom): The shared bulk food storage system in the common house kitchen.

The common house was built over an extended period in 1994-5. It is large, comprising a single, 100m² space containing a kitchen, dining area and lounge (a 'Great Room' in American parlance) plus a guest room, kid's room, multipurpose room (for TV, library, meetings etc), laundry and workshop. "Construction involved a far greater time commitment than any of us quite realised when we decided to do it," notes Ian Higginbottom.[6] However, their contribution of time and labour has imbued members with a profound appreciation of the building that now provides a spacious and well-appointed setting for a rich program of social and recreational activity. "There are lots of things we do together with great gusto," explains one enthusiastic member. "Our...Christmas party must have rocked Lenah Valley".[7] Christmas and the midwinter solstice celebrations have already become much anticipated traditions. The community also celebrates birthdays, achievements, departures and homecomings. Musical performances, children's plays and poetry readings are regular events. The common house has been used for yoga, exercise classes, mothers' groups and spiritual gatherings. A writing group meets for readings and discussion.

Common meals are held on Tuesdays, Thursdays and Sundays. Numbers attending vary between fifteen and twenty-five. Meals are mostly vegetarian but occasionally fish is served. In summer, the community often eats outdoors and lingers on until late in the extended southern twilight (Photo 12.3). The details of the cooking system are worth reporting here, particularly because common meals are so successful. The system is probably the most unusual in cohousing, perhaps even unique. Residents can partake of common meals as often or as seldom as they like, yet there is no record kept of participation nor is there any monetary accounting. *No money ever changes hands*. The system encourages members to attend common meals three times per week for a cooking commitment of once in approximately seventeen meals. It is premised on the adage, "what goes around, comes around". It is simple, trusting and casual – a quintessentially Australian innovation, perhaps.

CASCADE COHOUSING COOKING SYSTEM

- A cooking sign-up chart is posted every four months.
- It is suggested that members should offer to cook:
  - once if they like to eat common meals less often than weekly,
  - twice if they like to eat common meals one or two times per week,
  - three times if they like to eat common meals twice or more each week,
  - four times if they like cooking an awful lot or feel guilty for previously not signing up often enough.
- The cook is responsible for the menu, shopping and all costs as well as food preparation and clean up, although there are always willing hands to assist with washing up.
- Signing up for meals is appreciated but not expected. Cooks cater for 20 and hope for the best, relying on improvisation if the numbers vary greatly.
- No record is kept of attendance.
- No costs are levied.
- Guests' costs are absorbed.

Twice a year there are 'Kids' Meals' which an adult member, Angie, organises *in lieu* of her cooking commitment. Four to six kids participate, sometimes with the involvement of a neighbouring playmate. They first meet to discuss the menu, delegate responsibilities and devise a shopping list. Then they all go shopping with Angie. Apparently they have always been disciplined in shopping only for items on the list. Meals are generally quite sophisticated and the children apply a lot of effort to presentation – making individual salads, for example. Quality has come a long way since the inaugural Kids' Meal, when the discussion of the menu went something like this:

Angie:	Well, what do you think we should cook?
Kids (in unison):	Pasta and cheese!
Angie:	Ooookkay. But might we provide an alternative...for a bit of variety?
Kids:	OK. That could be...[pause]...spaghetti and cheese!!
Angie:	Sure. But what else?
Kids:	Pasta and Parmesan!!!

Chewing gum was the suggested desert. These days deserts are more likely to comprise cake or chocolate mouse but still include a couple of bowls of lollies ... and chewing gum.

The children also hold a 'Kids' Club' at occasional common meals, when they sell various crafted items: drawings (such as those in Figure 12.3, which cost the author 20c each), cards, simple clay sculpted hearts etc. Previously they have saved the $10 or so made at each event until $100 was accumulated, with which they bought a tent used for sleeping out and camping trips. It appears that in cohousing, kids are learning to be entrepreneurial as well as cooperative and creative.

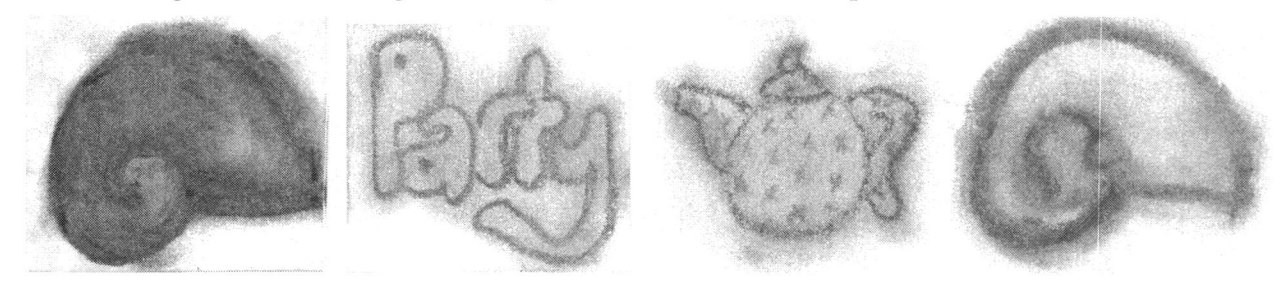

Figure 12.3: Drawings available for sale at the 'Kids' Club'.

Levels of social support run high at Cascade. "It's always interesting for me to return from a trip", comments one member, "glad that, always, someone is prepared to do the airport run [and] to take care of plants...and to feel so secure about my home and friends".[8] Childcare is not formalised as it is at neighbouring Cohousing Cooperative, but then the numbers of children there and their ages are quite different. However, informal childcare is ever available and the community maintains a fund from which childcare is paid to ensure that parents can attend meetings and other important events. Another fund is kept for the purchase of birthday presents and flowers if, for example, a member falls ill. Informal sharing is prevalent, as it is in cohousing generally. Cars for example, are liberally shared; to the extent that one couple managed without a vehicle for seven years because there was always one to borrow. As trust has deepened, so communication has improved. Mary Jenkins once wrote in a community newsletter:

> Our abilities to deal with problems have matured as we have got to know each other and become able to express – most of the time – likes and dislikes without offence to the individuals concerned. Recognising ourselves as a group of diverse individuals, we have really worked on conflict management to achieve this with a special fund for this purpose. This has become the most important learning process for me. Never in my life have I felt that I had such good neighbours.[9]

Given such high levels of agreement and cooperation, it is worth asking whether the community *as a collective* has been able to achieve its pro-environmental aspirations. An environmental audit conducted in 1996 revealed the following statistics.[10] The passive solar homes are indeed energy efficient, using less than 50% of the electricity consumed by typical Hobart homes of a similar size. The proximity to town and availability of an excellent bus service has ensured that about 30% of residents cycle to work and 45% take the bus. Overall, Cascade members use their vehicles about 25% less often than other Taswegians (i.e. residents of Tasmania) and about 35% less often than other Australians. It must be noted, however, that because they live in Tasmania and need regularly to visit the mainland, members fly three times more often than Australians generally.

There is no grey water or black water (sewerage) recycling at Cascade. However, recycling of solids is done well. The community recycles 84% of its waste paper (compared with 39% in Tasmania, generally), 100% of its glass (to 46%), and 84% of its plastic (to 30%). Larger unwanted items are delivered to the local Tip Shop, a commercial recycling depot down the road. Clothes are enthusiastically recycled within the community. Kitchen waste invariably finds its way into the compost heap, worm farm or chicken coop, all of which are collective enterprises. With the ready availability of compost and worms, it is not surprising that, at time of writing, the gardens are maturing well – the site having recovered from the traumatic clearing a decade before. Numerous fruit trees produce copious amounts of fruit in summer. There is a steady supply of organic free-range eggs. The bulk food buying program that services both common meals and private needs is one of the most comprehensive in cohousing (Photo 12.7).

The most impressive feature of the environmentalism at Cascade Cohousing is not any one or more of their particularly effective practices. It is the *raft* of practices as a whole, and the manner in which they have been integrated into daily life. Although the group was 'green' to begin with, significant additional behavioural change has occurred because relationships are close-knit and the community is socially cohesive. Mary Jenkins explains: "Many of our practices have become ecological habits as we reuse, recycle, and reduce by sharing clothes, cars and equipment".[11] The three Rs (reuse, recycle and reduce) are cornerstones of the pro-environmental ethos at Cascade Cohousing. Theirs is an anti-consumerist stance that recognises the need – if not the imperative – for middle class consumers to live more simply and with less. Mary continues:

> Because I have built such a small home, storage is limited. Sometimes I think of adding storage space but then I remind myself of the third 'R', 'reducing', which is more difficult than 'reusing' and 'recycling' – and a clearout starts again.[12]

Notes:

[1] The Cascade CoHousing Legal Agreement (1994)

[2] Cascade Cohousing: Project Summary; August, 1993.

[3] Jenkins, M. (2003). *Living Small and in Community in Tasmania* in Another Kind of Space: creating ecological dwellings and environments. A. Dearling and G. Meltzer. Lyme Regis, Enabler Publications: 147-149: 148.

[4] Concrete blocks that can be 'glued' together, rather than cemented in place, are easier for non-professional builders to lay.

[5] Jenkins, M. (2003:148)

[6] Personal communication.

[7] Roberts, J. (1997). Sunny village, sunny future. The Sunday Tasmanian. Hobart: 50-51: 51

[8] Jenkins, M (2003:149)

[9] Personal communication.

[10] Gibbs, P., R. Warman, et al. (1996). Environmental Audit for Cascade Cohousing. Hobart, University of Tasmania.

[11] Jenkins, M (2003:148)

[12] Jenkins, M (2003: 149)

Figure 13.1: Utilising existing and introduced vegetation to create an effective micro-climate.
Photo 13.1: Concrete framed building with trellises attached (Images courtesy of Tetsuro Kai).

13 Kyōdō no mori Cohousing

これまでのコーポラティブ事業と対比して今回のプロジェクトがユニークな点は、環境共生という明確なコンセプトを打ち出し、いわばそのコンセプトを実現させるための手段として、コーポラティブの手法が選ばれているということである。

[Translation of the above text:] The uniqueness of *Kyōdō no mori*, as compared to past cooperative projects, is the way in which collaboration was used as a tool in achieving integrated community living within an urban biotope.[1]

Name	Kyōdō no mori (Forest of Kyōdō)	
Address	Setagaya-ku, Tokyo	
Context	Urban (dense low rise residential)	
Households	12	
Adults	23	Children (under 18 yrs)	3
Renters	2	Working from home	3
Developed	December 1997 – March 2000	
Developer	Tetsuro Kai of TeamNet	
Architect	U Architects, in conjunction with Atelier HOR and AB Design.	
Funding	Tsukuba method (see below).	
Site area	0.08 hectares / 0.19 acres	
Common house.	None	
Ave. dwelling	90 sq m. / 969 sq ft.	
Project cost	616,340,000 Yen / US$5,500,000[2]	

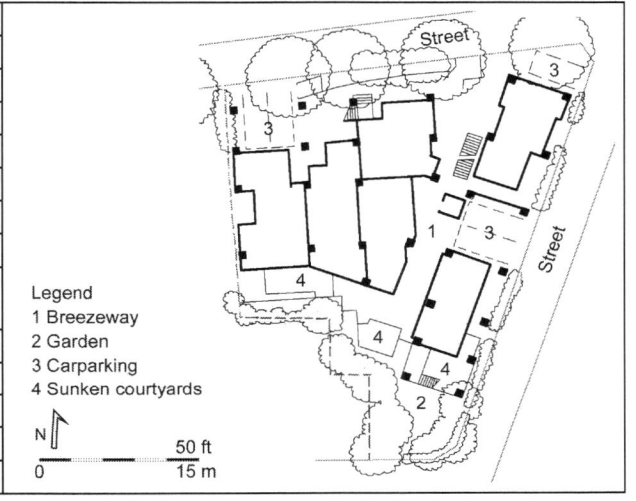

Table 13.1: Community Data.

Figure 13.2: Site plan (ground floor).

Legend
1 Breezeway
2 Garden
3 Carparking
4 Sunken courtyards

Tokyo is a rare city. It has no historical or business centre, is not zoned by socio-economic function and has no prevailing urban morphology.[3] There is no discernable master plan or urban design intervention. High-rise towers, architectural follies, sinuous expressways, neon signage, billboards, power poles and a lattice of overhead cables are superimposed on an historic (medieval) fabric of close-packed, ramshackle wooden dwellings, temples and market buildings. The conjunction is utterly chaotic. As a city with no centre, no cohesion and no order, Tokyo's sole *raison d'étre* appears to be unfettered growth and development.

The city has been reconstructed three times in the last century: following the earthquake of 1923, the firebombing of World War II and prior to the 1964 Olympics. Several construction booms since have further transformed a city where the only constant seems to be change itself. Buildings, like fashion, seldom last. Many are demolished before their time. Some are designed for disassembly and let by landowners waiting for the already high land values to rise even further. The high density wrought by inflated property values pushes buildings up against their neighbours and the street.

A question that has long preoccupied architects working in Tokyo, of which there are many foreign notables, is how should buildings respond to both the physical context and the prevailing economic imperative?

In 1960, an architectural movement known as Metabolism was launched by progenitor, Kenzo Tange. The conceptual basis of Metabolism was change itself. Rather than see architecture in terms of fixed form and function as Modernism had done, Metabolists saw buildings (and by extension, the city itself) as an assemblage of component parts that could be upgraded over time. Metabolism's technological underpinning required advocates to adopt varieties of hierarchical superstructure (spine, core, frame etc.), and indeed, megastructure, for which they were roundly criticised in Christopher Alexander's essay, *A City is Not a Tree*.

The environmental wakeup call, progressive social values and economic slowdown of the 1970s forced a reassessment of the benefits of technology in Japan, as elsewhere. Post-Metabolists were less concerned with reshaping the city – instead, taking a more pragmatic approach based on insertion and infill within the existing urban fabric. For Tadao Ando, for example, this meant adopting a defensive and privatised response to hostile and chaotic surroundings. His mostly small projects turned their backs on the city, 'offering' featureless concrete walls to the street but extremely poetic and psychically nurturing spaces within.

In the 1980s, around the world, Post-Modernist thinking offered a more generous reading of late Twentieth Century urbanism. Rather than retreat from urban chaos, architects drew inspiration from its dynamism and vitality. In Japan, under the added influence of advanced electronics technology and an accelerated urban culture, architects like Toyo Ito experimented with qualities of lightness, translucency and the ephemeral. Using lightweight materials, screens and layers, they saw their architecture as contributing to a volatile, quixotic, media-mad culture.

It is against this rich background that the cohousing project described here can best be understood. And there is another ubiquitous cultural phenomenon that was also a prime influence. Throughout Tokyo, along the streets and narrow alleyways, residents adorn the street facade of their dwellings with potted plants of all kinds. The practice can ostensibly be read as practical, productive urban agriculture and a contribution to the public realm. But more fundamentally, it's an expression of a profound and ancient connection with nature borne of the Shinto belief system. The cohousing project known as *Kyōdō no mori*, or Forest of Kyōdō, exemplifies this relationship.

Photo 13.2: Creating a micro-climate with shade cloth and vines climbing on twine.

The site in low-rise, but extremely dense, Setagaya district had been stewarded by a single family for 300 years. An organic farm for all but the last two decades, the most recent owner had let it revert to natural woodland. Along its northern boundary, five enormous 120-year-old native *Zelkova* trees offer valuable shade in summer and provide a windbreak in winter. The combination of all these factors (i.e. background, context, site history and land features) gave rise to a metaphorical design concept, best translated as 'creating an urban biotope', comprising three basic tenets: capturing and enhancing nature's offerings; imitating nature's laws in architecture and; applying nature's lessons in life. All three strategies were deemed more achievable through collaboration - in other words, "the intelligent utilisation of the power of community makes it possible to create value that cannot be realised by individuals working alone".[4] Such was the uncharacteristic genesis of this atypical cohousing project.

The participatory design process was fully comprehensive. This is especially remarkable since the project was the first cohousing development in Japan and so was without a wellspring of local experience from which to draw. Furthermore, the residents had no prior knowledge of cohousing. They came together to expedite the design and development of the project, not to build community, as is generally the case in cohousing. And yet, a community was built in the process.

The consultation process was instigated by project developer and intending resident, Tetsuro Kai. It involved four levels of negotiation, represented graphically in Figure 13.1:
1. Meetings between the architect and each household to discuss their personal requirements.
2. Meetings of the developer, architect and other consultants to discuss building technology.
3. Meetings of a steering committee comprising the developer and three households randomly rotated according to availability (Photo 13.3 shows an example).
4. Meetings of the whole community i.e. all the householders including the developer-resident.

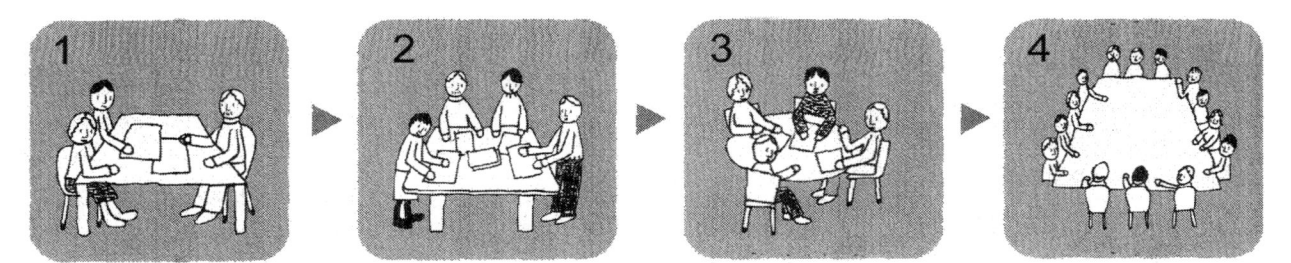

Figure 13.1: Community design consultation stages (Graphic courtesy of Tetsuro Kai).

Meetings were conducted according to a strict etiquette comprising four principles:
- A problem or concern for any one household is an issue for the whole community.
- Solutions to problems should be generic (i.e. generally applicable) not unique.
- No one person or household can be singled out for criticism or censure.
- Personal issues should not be brought to meetings.

Photo 13.3: Steering committee (Photo by Tetsuro Kai).

Chapter 13: Kyōdō no mori Cohousing

At first glance, these agreements might indicate high levels of cohesion and commitment. But perhaps they simply reflect Japanese corporate culture in which the aspirations of individuals are often forsaken for the good of the organisation. Consensus decision-making was utilised in all four forums. However, when agreement could not be reached within a predetermined timeframe, a secret ballot was utilised to break the deadlock. This is rare in cohousing and, again, could be interpreted as a characteristically Japanese contrivance to prevent personal embarrassment or 'losing face'. In any case, the consultation process had to be efficient in order to deal with the complex implications of a project development model known as *Tsukuba*.

The *Tsukuba* method has evolved in Japan as a means of dealing with a severe inheritance tax imposed on successive generations of landowners. Given its size, the owner of this particular property would be required to pay about 775 million Yen (about US$7.5 million or A$10 million) should the property be sold. Known in Australia as leasehold, *Tsukuba* is an arrangement whereby the land remains the property of the owner but is leased to others to utilise. In Japan, a lease on residential property typically runs for thirty years, at which point it's renegotiated, which usually results in building demolition. In this instance, however, all parties (landowner, developer and residents), being motivated by ecological considerations, sought a more enduring architecture. The resolution, seemingly derived from Metabolism, comprised a concrete structural frame with a hundred-year lifespan and infill panels (walls, floors and ceilings) with a lifespan of thirty years.

The agreed construction system, which arose from legal and technological considerations, offered intriguing unforeseen possibilities. The positioning of walls, floors and ceilings, being entirely flexible, became a giant 3D jigsaw puzzle to be solved collaboratively through the participatory design process. Dwelling cost was measured in terms of three dimensional space, rather than floor area, as neighbours set about trading horizontal *and* vertical space.

Photo 13.4: An attractive internal stair.[5]

Photo 13.5: Shared outdoor space.

The outcome was extremely complex architecturally, but one that optimised the spatial needs of each household and produced some intricately crafted dwellings with exquisite, Ando-esque architectural qualities of space, light, colour and materiality (Photo 13.4).

Residents were also thoroughly involved in the construction process. Some of the rich one-metre-deep topsoil excavated from the site was set aside for a roof garden and the remainder given to elderly neighbours and a local school. They potted and later replanted site vegetation and were responsible for all the new landscaping. Significant trees were milled and recycled as bench tops, doors and windows, whilst waste timber became firewood. Residents were even involved in the production of the infill panels – literally 'getting their hands dirty' with a natural, plankton-based render applied to wall panels. Participation in design and construction ensured that residents gained commitment to the ongoing management of the project, upon which the building's operable environmental systems now depend.

In spring, residents conjure a fine lattice of twine stretching upward over three floors of the southern façade (Photo 13.2). Permanent bamboo trellises attach to the eastern and western facades (Photo 13.1). Throughout summer, a vertical landscape of vines grow up the building, thus 'creating an urban biotope' which is the ethos of the project. Figure 13.1, a north-south section through the building, illustrates this principle. The huge trees to the north, vegetation on the roof and vines to the south envelop the building in a canopy of green. Cool air is drawn into the building at or below ground level by a solar chimney effect created by voids within. Passive solar design ensures year-round comfort despite the extremes of Tokyo's climate. The building envelope is thoroughly insulated and double-glazing is installed throughout. Wood stoves provide a small amount of supplementary heating in winter. A grey water system filters and purifies wastewater using water plants and then circulates it throughout the building with pumps powered by photovoltaic cells.

Photo 13.6: Solar powered grey water system.

Photo 13.7: Shared roof garden.

Chapter 13: Kyōdō no mori Cohousing

Opportunities for cohousing-like space sharing at *Kyōdō no mori* have been severely limited by Tokyo's unreal property values. A dedicated common house was just not feasible. However, the community does have a common dining facility. A traditional wood fired barbeque on the roof, set within a conversation pit and surrounded by shared vegetable and flower gardens, provides an attractive setting for social interaction (Photo 13.8). In the absence of a common house, social and cultural occasions occur mostly within private dwellings as residents open their homes to the community for spontaneous events including traditional tea ceremonies and dramatic performance (Photo 13.9). Shared open space is limited and private exterior space is only available in the form of sunken courtyards or balconies.

Photo 13.8: The common dining area – a traditional barbeque pit on the roof.

Photo 13.9: A community event being held in a private home.

Tokyo's first cohousing project demonstrates just how robust is the cohousing model. Because cohousing is founded on common human (indeed, tribal) needs such as sharing, collaboration and social support and is free of any ideological or political agenda, it has universal appeal. Further, its essential simplicity ensures it can be adapted to suit particular geographical, climatic and cultural conditions. There is fast growing interest in cohousing in Asia and an awareness of it in Africa (see Chapter 1). Cohousing is becoming a truly global phenomenon.

Notes:

[1] Tetsuro Kai (2000), Case study: Kyōdō no mori, JT: 87-111: 87

[2] Currency conversion based on relative values at the time of construction (in 1999-2000).

[3] In architectural and planning terms, 'morphology' refers to a coherence of grain, structure or form across a part or a whole city or village.

[4] Satagaya Town Planning Centre (2000) Mori wo Tsukuru Sumai Zukuri: 49.

[5] Photo courtesy of Tetsuro Kai.

Part Two

Part One presented 'portraits' or 'snapshots' of twelve cohousing communities. Each 'portrait' took a different emphasis, in order to accentuate the differences between the communities and illustrate their uniqueness – of people, place and culture. The material or data presented was almost entirely *qualitative*, based as it was on interviews, community literature, photographs etc, and my personal observations and impressions. Little cross-community comparison was attempted which, in any case, is problematic with qualitative data alone. Part Two introduces a great deal more material. This new data is predominantly *quantitative*, being mostly derived from two surveys conducted in each community (and several others which do not feature in Part One). The survey data is more suited to cross-community comparison since numbers can be compared more objectively than impressions, anecdotes and photographs.

The first four chapters of Part Two offer comparative analysis based on survey and other data. The analysis is themed; each chapter focuses on a different domain (or aspect) of community life. The reasons for choosing particular themes and not others is a complex matter of methodology not detailed here. Interested readers should refer to the author's PhD dissertation or a journal article published in 2000.[1] Suffice to say that the domains considered (circumstance, interaction, relationship and engagement) were nominated by the survey respondents themselves as those which most significantly influenced their environmental attitudes, values and practices.[2] The purpose of the analysis in Part Two is to establish *why*, *how* and *by how much*.

The final two chapters of Part Two take the analysis one or two steps further. Chapter 18 introduces the notion of empowerment and uses that construct to tie together threads of the analysis previously considered separately. This is done with the assistance of a conceptual model, the Community Empowerment Model (CEM). Finally, Chapter 19 broadens the discussion. It speculates (on the basis of the preceding analysis) about the form and organization of a future sustainable society.

Clearly, Part Two is considerably more serious in its intent than Part One (which exists to 'set the scene' for the more substantive analytical material to come). The reader should not be discouraged however. If you have made it to the end of this introduction then it should not be too challenging. So please read on…this is where things get *really* interesting!

GM

Notes:

[1] See Meltzer, G. (2000). Cohousing: Toward Social and Environmental Sustainability. PhD Thesis, Brisbane, The University of Queensland or Meltzer, G. (2000). "Cohousing: Verifying the importance of community in the application of environmentalism." Journal of Architectural and Planning Research 17(2): 110-132.

[2] Residents were asked the following open-ended question: "In your own words, briefly jot down how you think living in cohousing influences (if at all) your household's ecological attitudes and practices". Categorisation of their responses revealed the domains utilised in the analysis. Typical responses to the question are included (as illustrations of the concept) in grey boxes at the beginning of each section.

Photos 14.1 and 14.2: The importance placed on location, site planning and architecture in cohousing is epitomised in these images of Jackson Place Cohousing (top) and Duwamish Cohousing in Seattle.

14 Circumstance: physical setting and managed systems

Circumstance is defined in The New Shorter Oxford English Dictionary as "external conditions affecting or that might affect action". For cohousing residents, their circumstance, so defined, comprises the *setting* (location, site planning and architecture) of their project and its collectively managed *systems* such as composting and recycling. These are the most tangible features of cohousing and those that most overtly impact on the daily lives of residents. 'Circumstance' can both set obstacles and offer conveniences that significantly affect pro-environmental practices.

Setting: location, site planning and architecture

> "We drive more because our cohousing community is located further from shops and activities than our last place".
>
> "More social activities at the community has reduced driving to visit friends".
>
> "Smaller, more energy efficient houses are the big difference".
>
> "Our houses are built with energy efficiency as a high priority".
>
> "No garages and smaller houses keeps people from buying too much stuff"
>
> "Lack of storage space highlights the tendency to accumulate things".[1]

The physical and spatial attributes of a cohousing project are the most immutable. Its location, site planning and architecture affect patterns of behaviour for the life of the community and will, therefore, significantly determine its long-term environmental impact. For all but a few cohousing groups, choice of location, site planning strategies and the architectural brief are determined during a long and arduous participatory process. Inevitably, members come and go from the group during the development period and occasionally an irreconcilable split may develop. Eventually, after a period of member self-selection and seemingly interminable discussion, criteria are established that guide site selection and planning, the architectural design and landscaping. Sometimes members are also involved in the construction process.

Location

For many groups, choice of location is their single most important decision (or at least it seems to be at the time). Location fixes proximity to commercial and service facilities, schools and places of employment. It effectively determines the need for travel, although public transport, home or community schooling, telecommuting and home-businesses all mitigate automobile dependence. Location sets the context for participation in a local community. Some cohousing residents develop local trading and consulting services operating from within the community. Particular cohousing communities have contributed to urban revitalisation and instigated class action to protect the quality of their neighbourhood.

Given the impact of location on vehicle dependence, it is instructive to look at the relocation of cohousing households from their previous residence. Have they moved closer to, or further away from shops, schools and employment, for example? Households reported their change of location as follows (see Table 14.1).[2] Of the 278 households surveyed,[3] 20 had lived in rural locations before moving into cohousing. Of those 20, seven had moved to a different rural location, nine had moved to a small town and four had moved to a suburban location. Similarly, of the 58 households that previously lived in small towns, four moved to less dense rural locations, 30 moved into cohousing in the same or another small town and 24 moved to a suburban location...and so on. Table 14.1 reveals that prior to moving into cohousing, respondents predominantly lived in urban and suburban locations (72%). In cohousing they are mostly located in suburbs and small towns (79%). The overall drift, then, is toward less dense locations and presumably further away from shops, schools and workplaces. Increased driving might therefore be expected unless residents are somehow able to reduce their automobile dependence.

Prior Location			Current (cohousing) location			
	#	%	Rural	Small Town	Suburban	Urban
Rural	20	(7%)	7	9	4	0
Small Town	58	(21%)	4	30	24	0
Suburban	90	(32%)	12	24	47	7
Urban	110	(40%)	10	21	60	19
Totals	278		33 (12%)	84 (30%)	135 (49%)	26 (9%)

Table 14.1: Prior and current locations of cohousing households (N=278).

To measure any such changes in driving behaviour since members moved into cohousing, each household was asked three questions:
- To what extent do licensed members bike or walk moderate distances rather than drive?
- To what extent do they minimise driving by car-pooling or coordinating trips with others?
- To what extent are your social and recreational needs met within a walk or a bike ride from home?

Respondents answered each question for both their pre-cohousing and current cohousing situation (according to a standard five point *Likert* scale ranging from 'never' to 'always'). Differentials between prior and current tendencies were calculated and averaged to produce a multi-factorial indication of driving modification for each household and each community. In *every* community, members reported reduced driving as well as increased biking and walking behaviour. The average reported change across the whole cohousing population was a reduction in the extent of driving by approximately 9%.

So despite the majority of cohousing residents moving to areas of lower density, they seem to have addressed the stereotype of the vehicle-dependent commuter. In most communities the use of public transport is considered a prime virtue. Indeed, many groups base their site selection *primarily* on the proximity and ease of public transport. A very recent project, for example, Jackson Place Cohousing, has been built close to the centre of Seattle expressly for the purpose of reducing vehicle dependence (Photo 14.1). At Quayside Village Cohousing, six households manage without a car because they can walk or take public transport in meeting their general needs. Should they need a vehicle for special purposes, there will almost certainly be one they can borrow from a neighbour.

All cohousing groups share cars albeit mostly informally. In a few cases, two or more households co-own a vehicle. Some communities formalise car-pooling, such as Cohousing Cooperative with its School Transport Roster. However, the data shows that cohousing residents are mostly able to reduce their driving due to two further factors: casual trips (to the local store or the post office, for example) are invariably coordinated with others; and, most importantly of all, their community offers vocational, social and recreational opportunities *at home*.

Cohousing residents accordingly own (marginally) fewer vehicles and more bicycles than they did before moving into cohousing (Table 14.2). Residents reported owning a total of 450 vehicles, down 18 or a modest 4% fewer than the number owned prior to moving into cohousing. The proportions of one-car and two-car households were 47% and 45% respectively, whereas prior to moving into cohousing they were 41% and 51% respectively.

	\multicolumn{9}{c}{Change in the number owned per household}	Net change
	4 fewer	3 fewer	2 fewer	1 fewer	nil	1 more	2 more	3 more	4 more	
Vehicles	1	1	6	37	199	34	2	-	-	-18
Bicycles	2	2	9	41	168	40	13	2	3	+11

Table 14.2: Reported changed ownership of vehicles and bicycles.

Site planning

Site planning is one of the most distinctive physical characteristics of cohousing. As previously illustrated, and repeated here for convenience, McCamant and Durrett identified four generic configurations of low-rise or medium density buildings that suited the special needs and aspirations of cohousing communities (Figure 14.1). Dwellings are organised along or around: (a) a pedestrian street, (b) a courtyard, (c) a pedestrian street with activity nodes, or (d) a glass-roofed atrium. These planning strategies are said to offer the following advantages:
- they use land, materials and energy economically and efficiently;
- they offer safe and varied outdoor environments for families with children;
- they offer privacy to individual households and their separate rear gardens; and
- they promote community interaction provided the open space and spaces between buildings are carefully designed for the purpose.

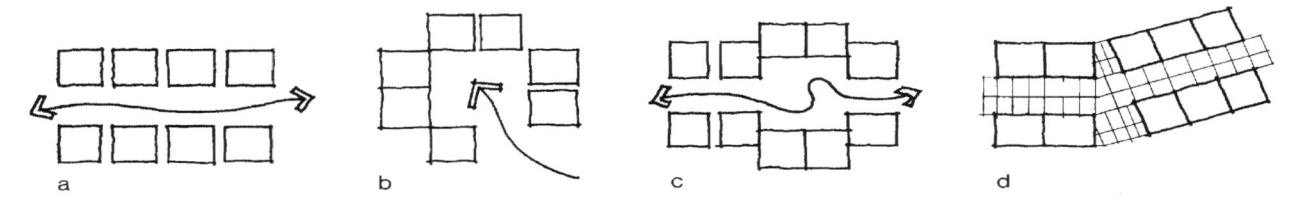

Figure 14.1: Four generic cohousing site plans (drawing by McCamant & Durrett).

Most North American and Australasian cohousing projects conform to one or other of these four generic layouts. This is no doubt due, in part, to the influence that McCamant and Durrett have exerted on the evolution of cohousing both through the success of their book and their consulting as architectural practitioners. Of the projects featured in this book, only Marsh Commons and Cascade Cohousing do not conform to any of the McCamant and Durrett types. Whilst exhibiting some of the attributes of the pedestrian street type, these groups have chosen to line up the dwellings in a *single* row due to site constraints and in order to maximise solar access.

Unlike 'classic' cohousing, many of the projects featured in this book do not provide each dwelling with a separate private backyard remote from the 'public realm'. This applies to Quayside Village, Songaia, Marsh Commons, Berkeley, Swan's Market and Kyōdō no mori. It appears that this particular site planning feature is considered a lesser priority in the latest generation of cohousing projects. Perhaps this should not be too surprising given the author's observation that private back yards in cohousing generally are decidedly underutilised.

On the other hand, the corralling of vehicles at the edge of the site appears to have consolidated as a fundamental site planning strategy. Quayside Village, WindSong, Puget Ridge, Swan's Market and Kyōdō no mori all have basement parking, which ensures that vehicles are almost entirely absent from the site. It seems likely that this particular trend will gain further momentum in line with an increased willingness amongst the general population to rethink personal transportation priorities.

Stewardship

Because cohousing residents comprise a consensual intentional community rather than a neighbourhood of independent households, aspects of land-use, housing density, infrastructure and landscaping can be rationalised and integrated to a greater extent than in conventional residential developments.

Typically, cohousing communities adopt a 'stewardship' role in relation to their site, clustering buildings and limiting vehicle access so as to increase efficiencies, maximise open space and preserve valuable features and qualities of the property. Rural and semi-rural cohousing groups such as Songaia and WindSong are pro-active in the stewardship of their considerable open space.

Other cohousing groups have broadened their stewardship – instigating protest action against environmentally damaging development in their region. Members of Highline Crossing Cohousing (near Denver, Colorado), for example, were pivotally involved in protest action against a proposed freeway development that threatened wildlife in their neighbourhood (Figure 14.2).

Figure 14.2: A notice on the common house noticeboard at Highline Crossing Cohousing.

Density

A widely held perception in both the US and Australia is that more compact housing forms and their associated higher residential densities contribute to protection of the environment. This certainly applies in cohousing, but evidence is largely anecdotal. What might a more quantitative analysis reveal?

Statistical analysis of density in the cohousing projects featured in this book reveals considerable variation. Two fundamental measures of density are used (Table 14.3). Gross Household Density (GHD) is the number of dwellings per hectare (d/h) of the property as a whole. Net Household Density (NHD) is the number of dwellings per hectare of *developed area* only, including roads, parking, cultivation, landscaping and playing fields. Since some communities have large areas of undeveloped land, it is more useful when discussing density in social terms to use Net Household Density.

The only rural community, Songaia, has by far the lowest NHD at 6 d/h. This is not in itself surprising but the figure is somewhat exaggerated because their developed area includes a very large vegetable garden and stormwater detention pond. The three urban communities – Swan's, Quayside and Kyōdō no mori Cohousing – predictably have very high NHDs. All the rest, which could be said to be more typical of cohousing projects generally, have a NHD lying between 21 and 45 d/h. These projects are considered suburban, since that is their context, but in fact many of them have immediate access to undeveloped open space and in that sense, are semi-rural.

	Households	Residents	Persons per household	Site area (hectares)	Developed area (hectares)	GHD (du/h)	NHD (du/h)	NPD (p/h)
Swan's Market Cohousing	20	35	1.75	0.10	0.10	200	200	350
Quayside Village Cohousing	19	34	1.79	0.10	0.10	190	190	340
Kyōdō no mori Cohousing	12	26	2.17	0.08	0.08	150	150	325
WindSong Cohousing	34	97	2.85	2.39	0.83	14	41	117
Berkeley Cohousing	14	26	1.86	0.31	0.31	45	45	84
Cohousing Cooperative	11	30	2.73	1.21	0.40	9	28	75
Puget Ridge Cohousing	23	53	2.30	0.98	0.80	23	29	66
N Street Cohousing	17	58	3.41	0.92	0.92	18	18	63
Marsh Commons Cohousing	17	35	2.06	0.61	0.61	28	28	57
Cascade Cohousing	15	28	1.87	0.86	0.55	17	27	51
Earthsong Eco-Neighbourhood	17	40	2.35	1.67	0.80	10	21	50
Songaia Cohousing	13	36	2.77	4.25	2.02	3	6	18
Mean	18	42	2.33	1.12	0.63	63	69	142

Table 14.3: Density analysis.

Comparison of the density of these 'suburban' projects with that of conventional suburbia is tempting yet problematic, given (a) the unusual site development features in cohousing, and (b) the minefield of definitions and meanings associated with various (often deficient) measures of suburban density.[4] So a further two sets of figures have been included for the purpose – the average number of persons per household in each community and, derived from that, the Net Person Density (NPD) or *persons per hectare* of developed land. This measure is likely to be a more reliable vehicle for such a comparison.[5]

The NPD of conventional suburban developments in Australia and the US is about 30 persons per hectare although it can be up to one and a half times higher where small-lot 'strategies' apply. Table 14.3 shows that the NPD of the 'suburban' cohousing varies between 50 p/h and 117 p/h, with a mean of 64 p/h or more than twice that of conventional suburban developments. Suburban cohousing, in fact, matches the density of many tract housing developments of more recent times, in which increasingly larger houses are built on ever shrinking lots. However, they demonstrate vastly improved land-use efficiency through clustering buildings and limiting vehicular access to accommodate vocational, social, and recreational activity within a walk of members' homes.

The variability of these density measures across the twelve cohousing projects is quite striking and, perhaps, unexpected. That there is such a wide range of Gross Household Density is not so surprising given that cohousing is found on both tight urban sites and large rural properties. However, the variability of Net Household Density and Net Person Density is genuinely surprising. If Songaia is excluded due to the above-mentioned anomaly, then there is a ten-fold difference between the least and greatest NHD measure, and a seven-fold difference in NPD.

E. R. Alexander suggests that *perceived* density or the *experience* of density in any given built environment is dependent upon much more than quantitatively measured density as outlined above.[6] He suggests that at least three other factors are involved:
- qualitative physical factors such as the effect of form, scale and detail of buildings;
- individual cognitive factors – one's perception of privacy, comfort, control etc; and
- socio-cultural factors such as prevailing norms of space usage and social interaction.

He represents these factors in the model shown in Figure 14.3. Alexander's model proves to be a useful construct for the purpose of discussing cohousing density.

"Qualitative physical factors" are an important, if not symbolic dimension of cohousing site planning and architecture. Site planning for social purposes around positively formed outdoor spaces can bring clarity to the site plan by employing a balance of solid and void, openness and closure, hard and soft landscaping.

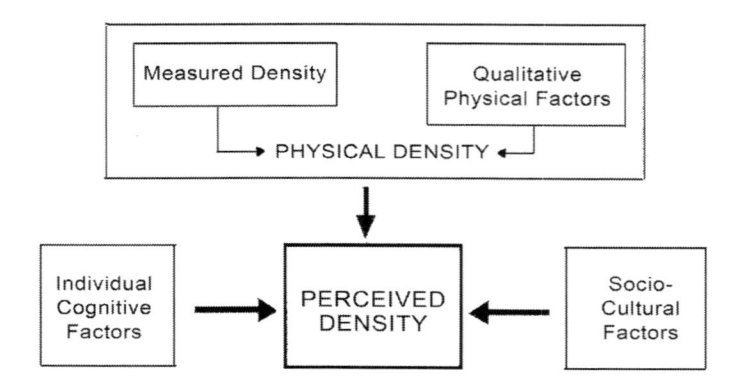

Figure 14.3: Alexander's model of perceived density.

The consistency of height, well considered massing and juxtaposition of buildings in most cohousing projects delivers a coherence that enables easier navigation by residents and speedier familiarisation by visitors. Irrespective of comments in the next section about neo-vernacular architectural 'style' in cohousing, the consistency it brings (of character, detail, colour etc.) contributes to a comfortable experience of place. These attributes may well enable cohousing groups to live at higher densities than might otherwise be possible.

"Individual cognitive factors" such as the need for control and sufficient privacy to induce a balance between public and private are fundamental considerations of cohousing site design. In well-designed cohousing, a fine-grained privacy gradient is established whereby residents can control their exposure and accessibility to others. This is known as an 'intimacy gradient' whereby "the spaces in a building are arranged in a sequence which corresponds to their degrees of privateness".[7] This is critical in cohousing where a rich and intimate 'public' life can only be sustained if it is complemented with privacy over which members have complete control. In most projects, the provision of a front porch or deck enables members to read a paper or take tea within the public realm. The rooms in the house become increasingly private from front to back and a secluded backyard for private use is usually provided.

However, it's the "socio-cultural factors" of cohousing that are perhaps the most effective in reducing perceived density. The group's intentionality and main purpose for being – the building of close-knit social relationships – will clearly allow a higher perceived density (and therefore measured density) than would be tolerated by a group of uninvolved neighbours in similar circumstance.

Figure 14.4 shows the close quarters tolerated by Puget Ridge residents whereby living rooms on the 'pedestrian street' face each other across six metres of public realm. It is difficult to imagine how they could live in such propinquity if it were not for the socio-cultural norms that are unique to cohousing.

Figure 14.4: Close living at Puget Ridge Cohousing (Drawing by Lagergquist and Morris Architects).

Finally, the surroundings of any residential precinct, can also affect perceived density.[8] If adjacent open space is available for recreational use or if the housing development has permeability that allows easy access to open space beyond, then the negative psychological effects of high measured density will be ameliorated.[9] These characteristics are prevalent in cohousing. It is common for development groups to deliberately seek a site with adjacent recreational open space.

Architectural form

A feature of the projects investigated in Part One is the diversity of their architectural form and character. This is largely a reflection of their diversity of location in five different countries. They echo unique regional styles developed in response to local culture, landform, climate and available materials i.e. the vernacular building form of their region. The cohousing projects of the Pacific Northwest, for example (WindSong, Songaia and Puget Ridge), all have basements, clapboard siding and steep roofs – traditional in a region of long snowy winters and high rainfall.

This begs the question, however, of the relevance of neo-vernacular 'style' (whether in cohousing or more generally) given that contemporary building procurement and modern lifestyles are so different from their traditional counterparts. Historically and regionally referenced domestic architecture is, of course, ubiquitous in the West where popular preference and the dictates of the marketplace have limited the development of more innovative housing solutions that might better suit contemporary domestic life.

In cohousing, however, there are additional arguments for a unique and contemporary architecture. Given the potential of the collaborative design process, one might expect cohousing groups to better express their progressive social values and collective identity through their architecture. That they generally do not is clearly a complex matter in which levels of personal and group commitment as well as the skills and experience of the architect play a role. Members will be concerned about the perceptions of outsiders and resale value. For a few, this will be the first or the last opportunity to build their 'dream home' and, deliberately or subconsciously, they will resist subjugation of their personal aspirations to those of the group.

Dwelling size

It is widely held that cohousing residents occupy less built space than conventional households, and indeed, this is borne out by the data. Table 14.4 offers a breakdown of the number and average size of the dwellings in each of the twelve communities studied. The average dwelling size ranges from 79 m² (650 ft²) to 127 m² (1,367 ft²) with the overall average being 100 m² (or 1,076 ft²). In the United States, a typical single-family house built in 1993 – about the same time the cohousing discussed here was being designed – was reported to occupy 2175 ft² (202 m²).[10] And indeed, since then, Americans have constructed *increasingly* larger houses.[11] In America then, cohousing dwellings are about half the size of typical new-built houses.[12]

In large part, cohousing residents are willing to live in smaller dwellings because they can utilise a range of common facilities. They will usually not need or want their own laundry, rumpus room or home office if these facilities are available in the common house. Nor will each household need a 'spare room' for visitors if one or two shared guest rooms are provided in the common house. Chuck Durrett agrees that a viable, generous common house is the key to minimising the size of private dwellings but only, he adds, *if it works*!

> Make sure there are commodious guest rooms in the common house. Make sure that the kids' room really, really works so that adults can feel relaxed in the dining room. First and foremost, the common house has to be somewhere that the residents want to be. Otherwise you might as well not have it.[13]

	Studios		1 bedroom		2 bedroom		3 bedroom		4 bedroom		Mean
	No.	Size	No.	Size	No.	Size	No.	Size	No.	Size	Size
Quayside Village Cohousing	1	45	8	65	5	82	5	105			79
Berkeley Cohousing			5	70	8	95	2	111			87
Kyōdō no mori Cohousing			5	75	4	94	3	107			90
Earthsong Eco-Neighbourhood					8	82	6	102	1	118	92
Swan's Market Cohousing	3	70	5	70	12	111					95
Puget Ridge Cohousing			3	63	11	88	7	109	2	130	95
Cascade Cohousing			3	80	8	100	4	120			101
Marsh Commons	3	37	1	42	7	93	3	158	3	167	105
Cohousing Coop			1	70	3	95	4	110	3	130	108
N Street Cohousing					1	84	9	102	7	125	110
WindSong Cohousing			6	62	1	88	19	111	8	167	115
Songaia Cohousing			2	79	3	93	8	152			127
Mean size (m^2)				52		68		94		115	145	100

Table 14.4: Dwelling size (in m^2) by numbers of bedrooms.

In addition to living in smaller dwellings, cohousing residents are prepared to live in more compact building *types* than they did previously – contrary to an overwhelming national preference for detached family dwellings.[14] Table 14.5 reveals that while 70% of households lived previously in detached family homes, in cohousing 84% live in attached dwelling types.[15]

Previous dwelling			Cohousing dwelling			
	#		Detached House	Duplex	Town House	Apartment
Detached house	187	(70%)	32	72	74	9
Duplex	30	(11%)	6	13	9	2
Town House	14	(5%)	1	2	9	2
Apartment	39	(14%)	5	17	14	3
Totals	270		44 (16%)	104 (39%)	106 (39%)	16 (6%)

Table 14.5: Cohousing households' current and prior dwelling type.

Building Technology

Specialist cohousing architect, Bruce Coldham, argues that the 'scale of organisation' of cohousing could be its "principle contribution to a [future] sustainable society".[16] He explains with the help of the diagram shown in Figure 14.5 that various technologies operate most efficiently and are most appropriate at a particular scale. Photovoltaic conversion, for example, operates best at domestic scale whereas wind turbines (larger devices of greater technological sophistication) operate best at the scale of towns or regions.

HOUSEHOLD
Efficient, durable construction
Photovoltaic conversion
Solar water heating
"Source" separation

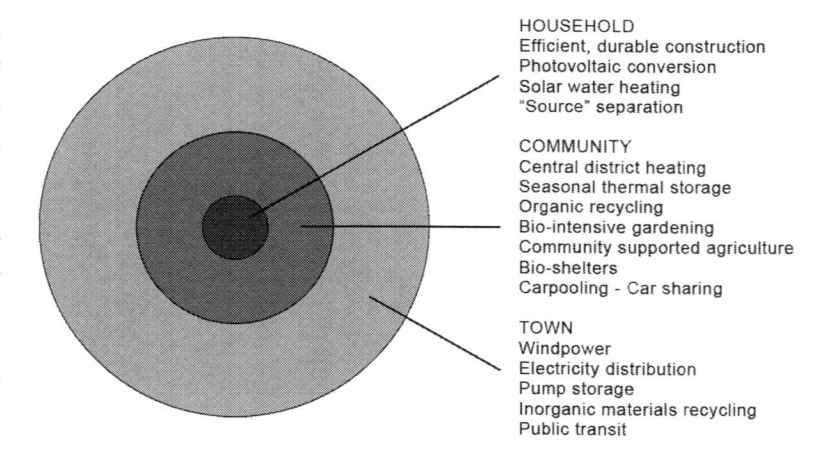

COMMUNITY
Central district heating
Seasonal thermal storage
Organic recycling
Bio-intensive gardening
Community supported agriculture
Bio-shelters
Carpooling - Car sharing

TOWN
Windpower
Electricity distribution
Pump storage
Inorganic materials recycling
Public transit

Figure 14.5: Scales of technological efficiency (Diagram by Bruce Coldham).

Cohousing, being a small community type with social ties that enable it to act as a single entity, provides a rare opportunity to optimise technologies such as centralised heating, thermal storage, biomass processing and on-site sewerage disposal. Yet, despite the generally compact architectural form of most American cohousing projects (Table 14.5) and each group's commitment to sharing, minimal coordination of mechanical services or infrastructure has occurred.

In Coldham's own community (Pine Street Cohousing in Amherst, Massachusetts), a geothermal heat pump has been installed that delivers air at subterranean temperatures to the dwellings. In some communities, Quayside Village and Puget Ridge for example, domestic mechanical services (i.e. space and water heating plant) have been located in shared utility spaces. And Quayside, of course, has its centralised grey water system. In general, however, the inherent potential of small-scale, socially cohesive communities for the centralisation of infrastructure and mechanical services has not yet been realised in cohousing.

Effective passive solar design is evident in only a few schemes (Earthsong, Cascade and perhaps Marsh Commons). Water conservation technology is even less common, with Quayside, Earthsong and *Kyōdō no mori* being the obvious exceptions, although a number of communities utilise landscape technologies (i.e. swales, pervious paving, detention ponds etc.) to ameliorate stormwater damage. To their credit, a number of communities have addressed resource consumption and waste reduction by successfully refurbishing existing buildings (N Street, Puget Ridge, Marsh Commons, Berkeley and Swan's) and recycling demolition and waste building materials.

Construction materials

The selection of construction materials and methods is a vexed matter. Many groups set out to select materials on the basis of their environmental impact. Most are guided by their architect, but sometimes a committee of members is appointed to undertake the research, analyse the data and recommend options to the group. However, analysis of the environmental impact of materials is extremely complex and difficult. There is disagreement, even amongst experts, over the intrinsic merits of particular construction materials. Calculation of their embodied energy and life-cycle environmental impact involves complex computer modelling beyond the capacity of most consultants let alone an *ad hoc* cohousing committee. Like many players involved in building procurement generally, cohousing groups often settle for token analysis and ill-informed decision-making.

The choice of siding, or cladding, offers a good example of this kind of quandary. In the US, a cement product called *Hardiplank* (recently introduced from Australia) is claimed by many to be an 'environmentally responsible' material, if not a panacea. The same advocates usually suggest that 'wood' is not. This is often based on a romanticised interpretation of timber conservation principles and does not consider the pros and cons of different wood species, old-growth forest versus new-growth or plantation timbers, embodied energy due to transportation from different locations or the locking up of carbon. Hardiplank is often recommended without consideration of the environmental impact of cement extraction, its high energy manufacturing process, or the embodied energy implications of its transportation as a very heavy material. This kind of dilemma lurks behind the purchase of almost all building products.

Architectural qualities

Beyond technological matters, the *qualities* of a building have additional environmental importance. Spatial qualities, the availability of natural light and ventilation, thermal comfort and indoor air quality all contribute to user health and well-being as well as the desirability, and therefore the frequency, of building use. As mentioned above, if the common house is to successfully contribute to a group's social cohesion and facilitate sharing and cooperation, then it needs to be inviting, robust and pleasant in order to encourage and optimise usage. If the cohousing emphasis on striking a balance between community and privacy is to be represented architecturally, then the dwellings also need to provide equivalent levels of domestic comfort and solace. With one or two exceptions, all the communities included here have succeeded in creating private and shared spaces of high quality. A few offer spaces and places that are absolutely gorgeous!

However, the question of indoor air quality (IAQ) and acceptable toxicity levels – also a matter of environmental quality – does not appear to be a high priority for most cohousing communities. Groups generally leave IAQ to the discretion of each household. In some projects, particular households have gone to considerable lengths to reduce toxicity in their homes using extra fans and vents, low-toxicity paints and sealers, natural carpets and flooring etc. However, in cohousing such commitment is an exception rather than the rule.

In conclusion, this investigation of cohousing location, site planning and architecture suggests that in only some cases have groups realised their aspiration for genuinely low-impact architecture. Founding residents of *every* group verified that 'building lightly on the earth' had been an early ambition even if it did not appear in their vision or mission statement. Many groups reported being restricted by the requirements of regulatory and financial bodies. Resistant contractors and the cost premium they applied to non-standard products and processes frustrated others. Most groups found that research of the environmental impact of materials and methods required too much time, given the already very demanding nature of the development process. There are exceptions however. Quayside, Marsh Commons, Earthsong and Cascade stand out in terms of their low-energy construction and mechanical services. Berkeley, too, has been highly successful in the utilisation of low-impact materials and methods.[17] Given the strength of communication that exists across the cohousing network it is likely that these communities will have alleviated, by their example, the difficulties of those that follow.

Systems: the management of inputs and outputs

> "Living in cohousing has made ecological practices easier and more accessible".
>
> "It's easy to recycle as a community".
>
> "In cohousing, the economy of scale can be captured and utilised".
>
> "Our community compost heap started us composting".
>
> "I compost because someone else maintains the compost pile".
>
> "Common meals are prepared with more organic ingredients than we have in our own meals".

The cohousing *systems* that reportedly improve the environmental practices of members include *waste management* (i.e. recycling, composting, repair and reuse), *food procurement* processes and the provision of *common meals*. It's generally the case that individuals or committees coordinate these processes on behalf of the whole community.

Waste management

Typically in cohousing, residents separate their waste for recycling according to an agreed protocol (Table 14.6) and then take the material to a centralised depot. A designated individual or a committee will then fine-tune the separation and deliver bins to the curb for pick-up or to the nearest appropriate public depot in the area. A similar arrangement applies to composting. Residents take kitchen and garden waste to a central composting station. Usually, a gardening or landscape committee coordinates the composting process, but some communities appoint a *'Compost Meister'* to layer and turn the compost heap(s).

recycling reference chart

recyclable	NEWSPAPER	PLASTIC	STEEL	CARDBOARD	ALUMINUM	GLASS
MATERIALS	Flyers & inserts are okay.	Plastic bottles with #1 or 2 on the bottom of the container.	Tin, steel, bi-metal and empty aerosol cans.	Corrugated cardboard only. Corrugated means two layers of cardboard with ribs inside.	Aluminum cans, foil and pie pans.	Clear and brown glass food and beverage containers only.
DON'TS	No mail, catalogs, magazines, phone books or plastic bags.	No plastic bags, yogurt or cottage cheese, motor oil or chemical containers	No containers used for paint, flammable or hazardous materials.	No cereal boxes or non-corrugated cardboard.	Don't put anything in the cans.	No green glass. No ceramics, PYREX, light bulbs, flat glass, window panes, glasses or blue glass.
HOW TO PREPARE	Put in paper sack along side of bin. (NOT IN THE BIN.)	Remove tops, rinse and crush or flatten.	Remove food or liquid and rinse.	Flatten and put in paper sack along side of bin. (NOT IN.)	Rinse and flatten.	Remove lids, food, liquid and lead collars on wine bottles.

Table 14.6: A typical cohousing recycling protocol.[18]

Research into recycling amongst the general population has confirmed that commitment to the practice correlates strongly with levels of convenience or inconvenience entailed in the process. A major disincentive, even amongst environmentalists, is the time and trouble involved in preparing, separating, storing and transporting materials. Predictably then, cohousing residents report that the easy availability of a recycling system managed by a few members on behalf of the whole community induced significant improvement in their practices.

In order to quantify such changes in their recycling and composting practices since moving into cohousing, residents were asked to assess (for both their pre-cohousing and current situations):
- the extent that they separated bottles, cans, plastic and paper for recycling; and
- the extent that they composted kitchen scraps and garden waste.

The data (processed similarly to that for driving moderation) revealed that respondents concertedly recycled and composted before moving into cohousing and, yet, a marked improvement of approximately 16% in the extent of their effort had still occurred. Organisation at the community scale clearly encourages individuals and households to recycle more effectively. This is even truer of composting, which requires considerable expertise and physical effort to implement successfully.

Repair and reuse, as strategies to avoid the unnecessary purchase of new items, are variably applied in cohousing. Undoubtedly, the presence of a shared workshop in a community enables members without tools to affect repairs on broken household items. Some communities have a 'free box' in the laundry – a repository where residents deposit clothes and other household items for reuse by others. The internal recycling of clothes, however, whilst ubiquitous in Danish *bofælleskaber* is somewhat less popular in North American and Australasian cohousing.

Food procurement

The size of most cohousing communities (20 – 30 households) offers an economy of scale which might be expected to encourage coordinated fruit and vegetable production and processing.

> It [food production] is an opportunity for more sustainable living that arises from a series of connections – a small community of producer consumers; useful land created from clustering of buildings; recycling organic wastes; facilities for processing and storing food. The opportunity is inherent in the scale of social organisation. The community scale facilitates the transformation of a string of individual backyard avocations into a community enterprise.[19]

A few communities *do* have well-established shared vegetable gardens coordinated by committees or work-groups on behalf of the membership. However, most groups leave vegetable production to individuals to manage in 'private' garden plots or those shared by a small number of households. In some of these communities, a percentage of the produce is then 'tithed' for use in common meals. But, in general, a minority of cohousing households regularly benefit from the availability of fresh, locally grown produce. With the notable exception of Cascade Cohousing, few of the more recently established groups enjoy an abundance of fruit, although there are many orchards planted that are still immature so not yet bearing fruit.

Another potential for community-based food procurement is the bulk purchase and distribution of dried and other foods. In Denmark, communities commonly operate convenience shops where residents can purchase household items and bulk foods at reduced cost. Of the communities included in this book, Quayside, Songaia and Cascade have viable bulk buying enterprises but, in general, groups have yet to implement such arrangements on a community-wide scale. Individuals report purchasing a reasonable amount of food in bulk, but the extent is little different from that of their pre-cohousing practice.

Common meals

Cohousing advocates will say that shared meals are critical to social cohesion and symbolic of community life. Yet the frequency of common meals in the twelve communities studied varies widely. WindSong and Songaia have the greatest number at six and five common meals per week respectively. The remainder have three or fewer.

Furthermore, compared with other group activities (parties, meetings, workshops etc.), common meals are not particularly well attended. Only 58 % of cohousing residents report that they attend common meals "usually" or "always". This is less often than social events (72%), general meetings (79%) and voluntary workdays (65 %) (Table 17.2). This is a complex, multi-factorial matter. The noise level experienced in some common house dining areas is high enough to deter some members from attending. The degree to which common meals are organic varies widely despite general adherence to the principle. Food preferences and allergies are often problematic with vegetarians and those on restricted diets sometimes being poorly catered for. Children also prove difficult to please, as one articulate kid explains:

> I don't really like the Common House dinners because a lot to them have soup and I don't like soup. When they do have kid meals, they usually have like rice with some vegetable like peas and cooked carrots and other sorts of vegetables like squash that I don't like. I would like to congratulate people who make things I like, like white rice, hamburgers, corn bread, salad, bread, pizza, burritos, tacos, self-serve things and hot-dogs that aren't made out of turkey. Of course, I also like

desserts but most meals don't have them. I'd be eating at the Common House a lot more if they had stuff I like.[20]

Particular communities strive to overcome such difficulties. Songaia and Cascade, for example, have innovative relaxed cooking rosters that accommodate the demanding lifestyles of residents and encourage members to attend common meals. In several communities cooks valiantly cater for everyone's needs using a chart of members' allergies and preferences to ensure that alternatives are always available (Table 14.7).

Category	Food	Deb	Andrew	Alison	Bruce	Belida	Cath	Coral	Drew	Edward	Gale	Harry	Ingrid	Joyce	Kelly	Milly	Oprah	Tilly	Una	Zoe	OK Alternatives
Condiments	Salt		A	A															A		
Condiments	Sugar		A		A				A	A	X				A					X	fruit sweetener, reduce quantity
Condiments	Tamari (w/wheat)			X						X										X	wheat free tamari
Condiments	Vinegar			X						X										X	serve dressings on the side
Condiments	Spicy								A					?			A				"
Dairy	Butter		A																		margarine (Sheryl etc)
Dairy	Cow milk & cheese		A	A		A				A	X									X	yogurt, goat milk, hard goat cheese
Dairy	Goat cheese - soft		A	X																	cheddar type, not cream cheese typ
Dairy	Yogurt w/sugar		A						A	A	X				A					X	plain yogurt w/no milk solids
Dairy	Cow ice cream		A	A					A	A	A	X			A					X	sorbet, rice dream, other non dairy ice cream ("Star")
Veggies	Broccoli																X				serve on side
Veggies	Brussel Sprouts																X				serve on side
Veggies	Cauliflower																X				serve on side
Veggies	Onion or leek - cooked												X								large enough pieces to pick out
Veggies	Onion - raw				X					X		X			X						serve on side
Veggies	Sprouts in salad						X														serve on side
Veggies	Spinach (cooked)																X				serve on side or raw
	Mushrooms	X																			out a little mushroom-free

Table 14.7: Part (about a third) of the Food Preferences chart at Berkeley Cohousing.

Notes:

[1] These quotations are selected responses to the survey question: "In your own words, briefly jot down how you think living in cohousing influences (if at all) your ecological attitudes and practices". They illustrate the thinking of cohousing residents in respect of the aspects of community life being discussed in the section.

[2] This particular comparison (and some of those to follow) was only made for households that relocated, more or less intact, from their previous circumstance; that is, except for the loss or addition of single child, elderly relative or unrelated tenant. If households had broken up when relocating or had formed only upon arrival in cohousing, then comparison of locational change would be problematic.

[3] Some of the data presented in this and the following chapters was part of survey conducted in 1996 as part of the author's PhD research of 18 cohousing communities. Participants in the survey comprised

Chapter 14: Circumstance

87% of the North American cohousing population at the time so the results are, statistically speaking, very significant ie. reliable. For more details of the study and its findings see Meltzer, G. (2000). "Cohousing: Verifying the importance of community in the application of environmentalism". Journal of Architectural and Planning Research 17(2): 110-132.

[4] See McLoughlin, B. (1991). "Urban Consolidation and Urban Sprawl: A Question of Density". Urban Policy and Research 9(3): 148 – 156 and Alexander, E. R. (1993). "Density Measures: A Review and Analysis". Journal of Architectural and Planning Research 10(3, Autumn): 181-202.

[5] McLoughlin, B. (1991) argues strongly for a measure of persons per unit area as a less arbitrary measure than one based on households. The NPD presented here is based on his taxonomy. He presents a nested hierarchy of density measures including an NPD based on the land occupied by dwellings plus their access roads, incidental small open spaces, small local shops, local primary schools and half the width of adjoining suburban distributor roads. This is more inclusive, (perhaps by 5%) than the 'developed area' used in this book but is the closest that could be found, and is particularly attractive given McLoughlin's suggestion that it represents the spatial form of "daily, intimate and routinised human activities".

[6] Alexander, E. R. (1993). "Density Measures: A Review and Analysis". Journal of Architectural and Planning Research 10(3, Autumn): 181-202.

[7] Alexander, C., S. Ishikawa, et al. (1977). A Pattern Language. NY, Oxford University Press.

[8] Rapoport, A. (1975). "Towards a Redefinition of Density". Environment and Behavior 7(2): 133-158.

[9] Bamford, G. (1995). Sustainability, Social Organisation and the Australian Suburb. Catalyst '95: Rethinking the Built Environment, Canberra, Faculty of Environmental Design, UC.

[10] Reuer, J.-P. (1995) includes a chart of the sizes of new dwellings across 30 different regions. I have simply averaged those figures.

[11] Burke, T. (1991) reports that the NAHB (National Association of House Builders) found in 1980, that 24% of home buyers sought a bigger house, whilst 22% preferred a smaller one. By 1989, despite an ageing population and decreasing average household size, 59% desired a larger house and only 6% wanted a smaller one.

[12] Note that the inclusion in the data of non-US examples does not distort the comparison.

[13] Personal communication

[14] Burke, T. (1991) quotes a 1988 survey of the American National Association of House Builders (NAHB) which found that only 3% of respondents would prefer to live in a town house and 6% an apartment. "People's longer term aspirations in the US are quite categorically directed at the large detached house" he notes.

[15] In the 1996 survey, residents were asked what type of dwelling were they living in before moving into cohousing. A comparison was then made with the type of dwelling in which they currently live.

[16] Coldham, B. (1992). "A Green Lesson from Europe: Cohousing as an Important Step Toward Sustainable Society". Northeast Cohousing Quarterly 3(2, Winter): 2-4: 2.

[17] Lent, T. (1999). Sustainable, Low Toxic Materials Use and Design in Berkeley Cohousing: Successes and failures, lessons learned., Tom Lent's Information Center: http://tlent.home.igc.org.

[18] From the booklet given to new residents and visitors at Commons on the Alemeda in Santa Fe: *Life at the Commons, It's Uncommonly Good: A Guide to Living at the Commons on the Alameda*.

[19] Coldham, B. (1992:3)

[20] Kolya (1996). "The Trouble with Common House Dinners (and Other Things That Bug Me)". Nyland News: The Call For Whatever(October 1996): 12.

15 Interaction: interpersonal influence and exchange

Interaction can be defined as either "the action or influence of persons…on each other" or "reciprocal action".[1] In the following analysis, the degree of reciprocity will be used to distinguish two types of interaction, *influence* and *exchange*. Cohousing residents with particular expertise exert *influence* on other members of the group *unilaterally* – as do the group's agreements. *Exchange,* on the other hand, is an altogether more subtle and bilateral process involving "reciprocal action". Both types are critical in developing or raising environmental awareness and for spreading knowledge about how to apply environmental values in practice.

Influence: agreements and the role of experts

> "Our mission statement serves as a constant reminder to us of our objectives and our commitment to the environment".
>
> "We were attracted to the project because of the environmental values".
>
> "It's easy here. People pass out fliers on recycling, composting, organic landscaping and vegetarianism. There are classes, a food co-op and much more".
>
> "We have become more aware of the environmental impact of our actions because of daily contact with people with greater environmental awareness".
>
> "Others have expressed concern or taught us about certain aspects which I had little previous knowledge about".
>
> "There are lots of greenies here. Advice is always available".

Some environmental practices, recycling for example, are now so widespread they are no longer mysterious to middle class Westerners. However, this is not the case for lesser-known strategies such as water and energy conservation, selective green consumerism and voluntary simplicity. When people join a cohousing group with little knowledge of such practices they are inevitably influenced by more experienced members and by the group as a whole via its agreements.

Agreements

Cohousing communities always have one or more sets of codes, rules or agreements that affect the behaviour of individual members. When the project is a duly constituted condominium (or a Strata or Community Title in Australasia), as all but a few are, members are legally bound by a set of Codes, Covenants and Regulations (CC&Rs) (or by-laws in Australasia). These are standardised documents that address such issues as members' rights and obligations, fees, insurances, resale process, pets and parking – protective regulations adopted by multiple housing projects of all kinds.

In addition to CC&Rs or by-laws, cohousing groups usually have a set of 'house rules' – regulations that are not legally binding, but better represent the unique 'social contract' that the members have struck. These agreements are mutable, sometimes evolving over years of discussion and fine-tuning. They explicitly address participation in cooking for common meals, attendance at meetings, contributions on committees and at workdays, and policies pertaining to guests and the use of common facilities. These kinds of exerted expectations can be problematic as one member laments, "I am very concerned about the ongoing disaffection over the policy that requires each community member to cook every cooking rotation. The conflict over this agreement is beginning to cause serious rifts in our community".[2]

In addition to both these agreement types, some groups have a 'mission statement' or declaration of community values that better represents their philosophical or ethical commonality. These are often written when a project is being developed, as a means of reaching agreement on deeply felt issues and subsequently to attract like-minded members. It is in this statement that environmental values are usually articulated, although 'house rules' can certainly be applied to such matters as waste reduction and the use of toxins. One group has a 'Community Values Statement' in five sections: 'Community Participation', 'Children', 'Safety', 'Environment' and 'Design and Build'. The final two sections are included here in full.

Environment

Where we walk we leave a footprint. May we walk lightly in the world. The global ecosystem is undergoing rapid and dramatic change as a result of human behavior and pollution. The choices we make affect the air we breathe, the water we drink, the food we eat and also that of others. Our community intent is to strive toward choices that benefit us directly as individuals and minimize our impact on the Earth and others. This statement represents our group stance to the world community (eg. visitors, newspapers, publications) of which we are a part. We shall endeavor to act through policy and design to promote health, safety, and harmony within the community and with the Earth. This is a statement of community values.

Design and Build

As persons in community we wish the physical environment to reflect and sustain the quality of our community. Where possible and feasible we shall strive to design and build with an eye towards long-term cost effectiveness, design integrity, and durability in harmony with community aesthetics. We shall strive to place the quality of materials and systems ahead of expensive design and short-term cost savings. We understand that to do so the community may increase its initial costs in order to achieve enhanced liveability and long-term savings in the labor and expense of community operation and maintenance. We acknowledge that as a community we support each other through our combined resources and seek creative ways for all member households to afford decisions that benefit us all over the life of the community.[3]

This statement is included at the very beginning of a document titled *Participation Manual: Version Seven*. It acts to remind long-term members of their commitment to the environment, and to new members it delivers a very clear message apropos the community's expectations of individuals. The statement is clearly intended as a means of *influence* to ensure that pro-environmental behaviours become normative.

The role of 'experts'

During the development phase and for the life of the community there is opportunity for members with established environmental practices to influence others who are less committed. This can happen informally through discussion, or more formally through education and leadership. The influence of one or a few 'greens' in a group may or may not be significant, depending on the social dynamics of the group and the personalities of those involved. Yet the potential for raised consciousness and behavioural change as a result of learning from others is always present.

Tom Lent, a member of Berkeley Cohousing during their development phase, provides a good example of a committed individual being an agent for change (see Chapter 8). This group has developed one of the most environmentally benign projects so far built in the United States. During construction Lent spent considerable time and effort researching strategies, locating sources of alternative building materials and monitoring the construction process. His leadership was critical to ensuring that the group's pro-environmental aspirations for the project were realised. Brian, of Quayside Village, is another good example of the kind of 'expert' who can inform and inspire a whole community – in this case with his knowledge of, and enthusiasm for, recycling.

Expertise of a more general kind is also highly valued in cohousing and often volunteered or pressed into service of the whole community. Through informal discussion, education programs and consensus decision-making, 'functional knowledge' is diffused – albeit unevenly – throughout the group. The greater the extent of knowledge and skill available to a group, the greater can be the benefit. The cohousing population is extremely well educated. In North American cohousing, for example, approximately 10% of adults have a doctorate, 40% more have graduate degrees and a further 30% have undergraduate degrees. In all, a remarkable 80% of American cohousing residents are tertiary educated compared with 30% of the national population (Table 15.1).[4]

Demographic characteristic	Cohousing population (N = 1090)	Overall population (1990 US census)
Education		
Percentage with a college degree	80%	30%
Employment		
Those without full-time renumerate occupations	50%	45%
Percentage of full-time employed with professional occupations	75%	18%
Percentage with casual service or blue collar work	9%	50%

Table 15.1: Demographic characteristics of the American cohousing population.

Amongst those with full-time employment, the proportion of professionals is far higher and low-paid employment is far less common in cohousing than in general. Although a similar proportion is without full-time employment, for many in cohousing this is a lifestyle choice. Indeed, there is considerable diversity of employment type in American cohousing, with 22% working part-time, and 16% working from home. The range of vocations is also significant (Table 15.2).

Field	Percentage	Field	Percentage
Education (School and Home)	12.2%	Architecture and Engineering	4.4%
Management and Commerce	8.8%	Environmental Science	4.0%
Medicine, Nursing and Health	7.2%	Counselling and Social Services	4.0%
Higher Education and Research	7.0%	Economics and Finance	3.6%
Publishing and Librarianship	7.0%	Physical Sciences	3.4%
Computer Science and Support	6.8%	Visual and Performing Arts	2.4%
Building and other Trades	6.6%	Planning and Development	2.0%
Therapy & Alternative Healing	6.4%	Casual Employment	2.0%
Government and Public Admin	5.4%		
Law and Mediation	4.8%	Others	2.0%

Table 15.2: Distribution of vocations in American cohousing (N=504).

Through their appreciation of, and access to, the knowledge and experience of other members of the group and the high level of expertise available to them, cohousing members find themselves in a somewhat privileged place of learning and personal development.

Exchange: reciprocal learning and socialisation

> "In cohousing, new information and practices are frequently discussed at all age levels".
>
> "We have spent more time sharing ecological ideas and tips because we all know each other and spend time together".
>
> "The easy communication with friends and neighbours encourages car-pooling, shopping for others, as well as satisfying social needs".
>
> "By communicating more about it and sharing ideas, so I am encouraged to live more ecologically".
>
> "Children grow up with more ecologically sound models as the norm".
>
> "I see the difference when 32 units are doing it. I would feel I was letting the community down if I took the easy way out".

The process of *exchange* is somewhat different from that of *influence*. Influence is either exerted or imparted. Exchange occurs in a more diffuse manner and involves two-way interaction or *mutuality*. Commonly in cohousing it occurs in the informal discussion of ideas and sharing of experiences. Levels of exchange depend upon the quality of the relationships within the group, being more likely to occur in an atmosphere of mutual respect and receptivity. Through daily contact with neighbours, learning is continually reinforced; a condition that residents suggest is conducive to lasting change in their environmental attitudes and practices.

In the previous section, it was noted that the extent of influence is to some degree dependent on the diversity of educational background and expertise prevalent in each community. Similarly, the potential for exchange will be greater if there is diversity of age, background and life experience. In North American cohousing the average age amongst adults is considerably higher than the national average – 42 years compared with 35.[5] This occurs because groups have so far failed to attract many adults below the age of thirty.[6] Home ownership (a privilege in the US though more widespread in Australasia) is seldom available to people in their twenties who have not yet had time to establish a career or a credit rating.

Apart from this shortfall, the age distribution in cohousing is evenly spread, with roughly equal numbers of members in their 30s, 40s, 50s and 60s. There is also a smattering of 70+ 'elders'. Whilst there is a reasonable age spread, there is limited diversity of background in most cohousing communities. In the Unites States, for example, Afro-Americans are significantly under-represented, comprising just 1% of the cohousing population compared with 11% nationally. Indeed, the American cohousing population is 95% Caucasian. There are also relatively low proportions of other minorities such as gays and lesbians (2.5%) and the disabled (1.6%). This data, in combination with moderate to high personal income levels (Table 15.3) place cohousing residents squarely within the American white middle class.

	Less than US$10,000	US$10,000-US$19,999	US$20,000-US$29,999	US$30,000-US$39,999	US$40,000-US$49,999	US$50,000-US$59,999	More than US$60,000
Number	5	22	61	77	56	41	59
Percentage	1.5%	6.8%	19%	24%	17.5%	12.8%	18.4%

Table 15.3: Gross annual income of residents with full-time employment (N=321).

Australasian and Japanese cohousing is likely to be even less diverse since that is the nature of the general population. At Cascade Cohousing (located in the remote island state of Tasmania) residents are entirely of white Anglo-Saxon heritage – many with quaint English names like Higginbottom and Jenkins. If real diversity has been achieved anywhere, it is in Canada at both Quayside Village and WindSong Cohousing (see Chapters 2 and 3).

Yet residents in almost every community talk openly of the considerable group effort invested in seeking diversity and lament their lack of success.[7] Ironically, the same people often suggest that enough variation *has* been achieved (in members' attitudes, priorities, preferences, and aspirations) to already challenge group cohesion. One resident writes,

> Our community faces a special challenge when it comes to decisions about money, due to our success in achieving considerable diversity of income level among members. The more well-off among us need to temper some desires while learning to contribute, at times, more than their proportional amount to meet a community need.[8]

Perhaps there is a lesson here for cohousing groups that aspire to the greatest possible diversity as a matter of principle. While it is usually true that traditional villages and urban communities are socially (though not ethnically) diverse, many thrive on commonality as much as diversity. In part, rural communities and close-knit urban neighbourhoods work because people enjoy rubbing shoulders with others like themselves, who confirm their values. Perhaps cohousing communities should be seeking a balance of diversity and commonality rather than attempting to maximise diversity for the sake of it.

Socialisation

Socialisation is a subtle, almost inadvertent process of learned behavioural change; but it is effective nonetheless. It is a process by which people acquire values and behaviours that ensure the stability of the group or society. In long-established urban neighbourhoods, for example, public life, social institutions and local traditions constitute the fabric of society, which perpetuates normative values, attitudes and behaviours. Normally socialisation begins within the nuclear family as children are introduced to the values and behaviours of their parents. In many traditional societies child socialisation also involves an extended family or community of unrelated others. Child socialisation is expected to produce competent 'social actors' who fit into society as it is construed by relevant adults.

In contemporary intentional communities, child socialisation is not so straightforward. Parents concerned about the suppression of their children's natural development are often ambivalent, not only about how to socialise their children, but whether or to what extent they *should be* socialised. Differences of approach to child rearing have proved particularly problematic for cohousing groups. "There are few issues that spark as much passion, conflict and controversy," suggests one parent. In one community where residents were agonising over their children's antisocial behaviour, a parent posted the following plea on the community notice board:

> Is anyone else frustrated by how our children are interacting? On any given day, a group of kids will fight amongst themselves for an hour, trying to play a game, but unable to consense on the rules. Or everyone picks on the scapegoat. Is this something they just have to work out themselves? Or could we be doing more to help them learn to enjoy each others' company? Are we limiting their growth by not intervening or meddling when we do intervene? I would like to hear the sound of laughter, not tears. If I hear back from enough parents and others who agree, and want to change things, I will set up a meeting to discuss what we might do.

The notice elicited the following responses amongst others:
- We teach more by modelling cooperative behaviour than by talking about it;
- I feel strongly that having community standards for public behaviour would be really beneficial;
- I think we need to let them work it out – this is how they learn to solve their own problems;

and in response to the previous comment,
- Read Lord of the Flies!

As difficult as these negotiable matters might be, cohousing parents overwhelmingly value the contact that their children have with an 'extended family' of diverse unrelated adults and, of course, so do the children. A teenager offers his perspective on the experience of growing up in cohousing:

> I learned about many things I had never given any thought to. Things such as homosexuality, environmental consciousness, the undisputedly best way to watch Star Trek, rock climbing, vegetarianism, and above all how to truly love thy neighbor.[9]

Another teenager, a seventeen-year-old girl from N Street concurs:

> Growing up in such a unique community, has taught me to appreciate the simpler things in life. With no television or video games to occupy my time, I have turned to friendships with the adults and children around me. I am grateful to have such an extended family that cares for me and is willing to help me. I feel that my ability to bond easily with others has helped me become the multi-faceted person that I am today.[10]

Many residents expressed the belief that substantial progress toward a sustainable society will only come about with generational change and that children growing up in cohousing are more likely than those in the mainstream to inculcate environmental awareness and social sensitivity. Evidence for this was offered by one resident who noted that children there seemed not to be possessive about their bikes, leaving them permanently 'parked' outside the common house and available for general use.

Changes in television viewing habits provide a further example of the realignment in children's values that can occur in cohousing. Many parents have noted the greater pleasure their children were taking from interaction with other kids, and the resultant reduction in the hours spent in front of TV. "The television watching regime in our household collapsed when we moved into cohousing", says one particularly thankful parent. Because children play outdoors for hours each day, it can be expected that childhood obesity (of increasing public concern in both Australia and America) will be less prevalent in cohousing than among the general population.

It is important to distinguish between child and adult socialisation within a community context. Children are enculturated, whereas adults are already acculturated and their socialisation in a new group or society will be more complex and potentially more problematic. "While an individual presumably sees advantages in joining the group, that person may have deeply held convictions, and certainly will have behaviour patterns, somewhat at odds with the group's".[11] For adults, the process of socialisation is interactive and reflexive. Even though they might join voluntarily, their socialisation will involve a complex process of implicit negotiation as the differences between the individual's normative values and behaviours and those of the group are resolved. There is likely to be considerable extra resistance where the expectation to change is perceived as peer pressure. One thing that can keep people from community meals, for example, is the associated peer pressure to be involved in the cooking. "If you have a set-up where you have to cook in order to participate in common meals, those who can't or don't want to cook will drop out," argues a long-term cohousing resident.

Behavioural change

In contemporary mainstream suburban life, the habits and practices of neighbours, friends and relatives have been shown to be an important influence on recycling behaviour. Cohousing residents similarly report that fellow members inform and influence their own pro-environmental practices. Such 'social learning' is a vital precursor to pro-environmental behavioural change.

The kinds of environmental practices most likely to be positively affected by interaction with others include recycling, composting and energy and water conservation. The former two are also influenced by the provision of systems, as discussed in Chapter 14. The latter two, however, are less public behaviours. Energy and water conservation practices happen mostly in the home, out of view of the community. Improvements in such practices are therefore likely to give a more accurate picture of any profound change in fundamental attitudes and values.

To quantify changes in energy conservation practice, residents were asked two sets of questions, one of their behaviour before moving into cohousing and the other of their behaviour since.
- To what extent did/do you turn off lights when they are not in use?
- Was/is the heating or the thermostat turned down on winter nights?
- When replacing light bulbs, to what extent did/do you install energy saving units?

Changed water conservation behaviour was estimated on the basis of responses to the questions:
- To what extent did/do you turn off the tap whilst brushing your teeth?
- To what extent did/do you shower quickly or take shallow baths in order to save water?
- To what extent did/do you install low-flow faucets (i.e. taps) and showerheads?

Once again, the differences between prior and current tendencies were calculated and then averaged to produce an indication of changed energy and water conservation behaviour in each community. Results showed a consistent 5-6% improvement in energy conservation practices across all of the communities surveyed and a 9% average improvement in water conservation behaviour, although this figure was much more variable from one cohousing project to the next. While these may not seem like huge improvements, it must be remembered that many cohousing residents have high environmental awareness before moving in to cohousing.

While cohousing projects are generally initiated by a core group of committed visionaries with common environmental concerns, the majority of residents join for quite pragmatic or even self-serving reasons. It is these members whose attitudes and behaviours are most transformed. The underlying effect of community life on their environmental awareness and pro-environmental practices is likely to be significant, if not profound. What quantitative evidence can be found for this?

Figure 14.7 gives an indication of the change in four areas of pro-environmental behaviour with respect to increasing cohousing experience. The X-axis represents the length of time members had lived in cohousing, irrespective of the age of the particular community in which they reside. The graph suggests that the longer residents live in cohousing, the greater the likelihood of improvement in their pro-environmental practice. The flattening of the graph suggests, albeit crudely, that the rate of improvement is likely to slow after a few years and, one would assume, eventually stabilise as long as community life remains viable.

The trend revealed here may indicate that it takes time for communities to hone their systems to everyone's satisfaction. Perhaps it's an indication of the time it takes for new members to acquire knowledge and skills. One would not expect newcomers to cohousing to suddenly have their environmental praxis[12] transformed. Rather, their environmental awareness would be raised progressively over months or years, and in the process, their pro-environmental practices could be expected to improve. They might gradually modify their behaviour to accord with their deepening environmentalism.

Perhaps the graph reveals that it takes time for trust to develop amongst community members...that others are 'pulling their weight'. Or perhaps, more generally, it indicates that members' pro-environmental behavioural change and their commitment correlates with a community's strength of social cohesion, which itself takes time to develop. This theme will be explored in the next chapter.

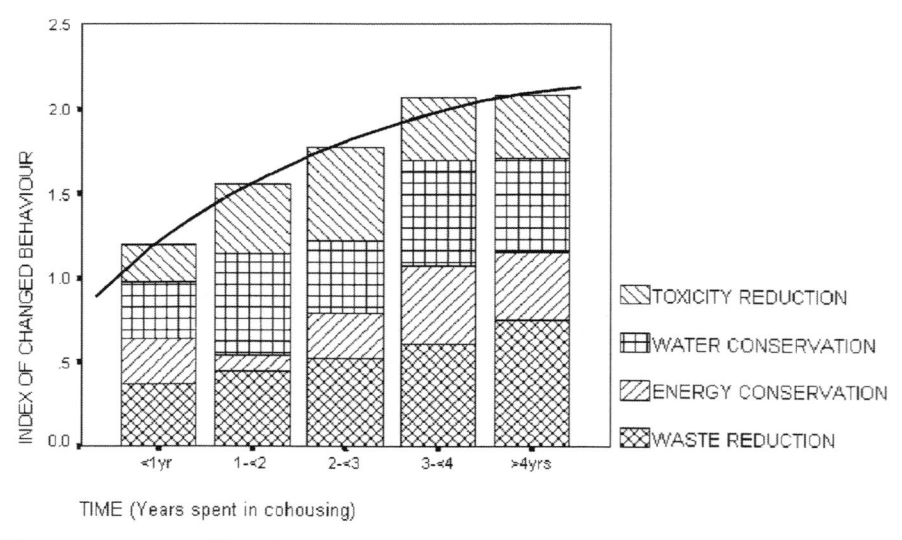

Figure 14.7: Progressive modification of pro-environmental behaviour over time.

Notes:

[1] The New Shorter Oxford English Dictionary, 1993.

[2] Ellen, R. (1996). "Reconsidering our Cooking Policy". Nyland News: The Call for Whatever(September): 7,8.: 7.

[3] Winslow Cohousing Group (1993). Process and Communication Cluster Document: Participation Manual, Version 7. Winslow.

[4] Using data from the author's 1996 survey and the 1990 US census.

[5] The former figure is taken from the author's 1996 survey and the latter, from the 1990 US census.

[6] The stand-out exception here is N-Street, where the high renter population is comprised mostly of young students.

[7] Paiss, W. (1995). "The Challenge of Creating Multicultural Communities". CoHousing: The Journal of the CoHousing Network 8(1): 6-8.

[8] Mandel, D. L. (1996). Southside Park Cohousing: Program Narrative. Sacramento:3

[9] Schneider, B. (1996). "Growing up in Nyland". Nyland News: The Call for Whatever (October 1996): 12.

[10] Personal communication.

[11] Metcalf, W. J. and F. Vanclay (1987). Social Characteristics of Alternative Lifestyle Participants in Australia. Brisbane, IAER.: 249.

[12] Praxis means practice that is informed by knowledge or understanding. It's a neat way to describe the 'package' or totality of an individual's environmental awareness, understanding and practices.

16 Relationship: close sharing and social support

Being in relationship implies both *association* and *connection* between two or more entities.[1] In a cohousing context, association assumes an intentional or purposive guise, most overtly expressed through *sharing*. Given the potential in cohousing for the expression of caring, the connection between members and the bonding of the membership as a whole is most clearly expressed through *support*. *Sharing* and *support* are dimensions of their social *relationships* that cohousing members said had significantly enhanced their pro-environmental practices.

Sharing: defusing the consumerist imperative

> "Having common laundry facilities makes me aware of doing frivolous loads of laundry as I have to share the space, time, work etc with others".
>
> "Sharing things reduces the need for so much. Sharing can reduce consumption of resources and the time we spend on material things – freeing up time to do the things we would really like to do!"
>
> "There's less consumerism in cohousing; it's easy to borrow things we don't have and to lend to neighbours things we have which they don't".
>
> "We use community tools and appliances instead of having our own".
>
> "We car-share instead of buying a new car. We rent half of a neighbour's".
>
> "With like minded people around a lot of resource sharing happens naturally".

To *share*, means to possess, use or occupy jointly with others, whereby some manner of give-and-take or reciprocity is implied.[2] Sharing is a defining feature of cohousing. It involves explicit or implicit agreements made by the group (or a subgroup of households) which enable efficiencies to be developed and mutual benefits to be derived. Sharing builds social relationships but is also dependent upon them, in that the degree to which residents are willing to share depends upon the trust and goodwill they have established.

Sharing in cohousing occurs in at least two ways:
- informal sharing between residents of their private possessions; and,
- formalised sharing of community-owned indoor and outdoor facilities and amenities.

Informal sharing

Discussion of sharing in the cohousing literature is often limited to use of the common house, the most visible expression of community-wide cooperation. Yet willingness to share and cooperate is pervasive in a viable community, as one cohousing resident explains:

> A one-car family can always borrow another in a pinch instead of owning two. We often join forces and carpool on outings. We have three lawnmowers instead of 25. Quite a few of us don't have TVs, but when the TV-less want to watch something special, there's always a willing neighbor who'd like the company. Very few of us have guest rooms, but one family's guests will often stay in the home of a neighbor who's away for the weekend.[3]

Cohousing lore holds that sharing reduces household consumption. It is supposed to enable each household to live in a smaller dwelling with fewer goods and with less need to buy items that they can share. One member notes, "we're always lending each other our camping equipment, tools, books, videos, missing ingredients for a dish in progress, thus diminishing our consumer addictions and saving trips to the store".[4] Items anecdotally said to be communally owned or readily shared include lawn mowers, garden equipment, carpentry tools, washers, dryers, freezers, televisions and video recorders.

Indeed the data supports this view, revealing a reduction in the quantities of some of these items per household. Residents were asked to report the numbers of certain items they owned before moving into cohousing and the change, if any, in that number since (see Table 16.1, particularly the final column). Responses revealed negligible change in the numbers of household refrigerators, televisions and dishwashers; a moderate (one quarter) reduction in the number of freezers, washing machines and dryers; and a significant (three quarters) reduction in the number of lawn mowers owned privately.

Item	2 fewer	1 fewer	nil	1 more	2 more	3 more	Net change	Total # owned	% change
Refrigerators	-	22	230	28	-		+6	281	+2 %
Televisions	2	35	204	37	1	1	+3	360	+1 %
Dishwashers	-	40	195	45	-		+5	184	+3 %
Freezers	-	31	238	11	-		-20	70	-22 %
Dryers	-	82	176	21	1		-61	153	-29 %
Washers	-	79	183	18	-		-61	171	-26 %
Mowers	7	122	148	3	-		-133	45	-75 %

Table 16.1: Changes in household ownership of goods.

An even greater benefit may well be derived from the ready sharing of smaller items. "Before buying a consumer item we check first to see if someone here already has one we can use," comments one member. At least one community has operationalised this process by circulating a list of building, gardening, camping, cooking and other equipment that each household owns and is willing to share (Table 16.2). Members refer to the list should they want to borrow an item and approach one of the relevant households.

Category	Item	Lender Unit #	Category	Item	Lender Unit #
Gardening	Hand trowel	A5,A6,B1,B4	Outings	Backpack	A6,A7,B1,C7,D3
	Lawn mower	A6		Bicycle tools	A7,B1,C7,D3
	Leaf rake	A2,A5,A6,B1,B3		Car bike rack	A5,A6,B1,C5,C7
	Weed scythe	C4		Maps	A6,B1,B4,C7,D4
	Wheelbarrow	A2,A4,A6,B1,C4		Snowshoes	D3
Building &	Back belt	A6,B1,B3		Tents	A7,B1,B4,D2,D3
maintenance	Bucket	CH,B1,B3	Cooking	Coffee pot	A6,D5
	Jigsaw	A6		Oversize mixer	CH,D4
	Sewing mach.	A6,B3,B4,C7,D3		Wok	A6,B1,B4,D4
	Staple gun	A6,B1,C7	Other	Blow up bed	C4,D5
	Toilet plunger	A5,B1		Single futon	D5
	Toilet snake	B1		Folding tables	B1,D3,C6,C7
Cleaning	Mini vacuum	A7,C4			
	Rug cleaner	B1	To add your valuables to the list, call Ken.		

Table 16.2: Part (about a third) of a lending list of household items available to others.[5]

There is enough evidence to suggest that the consumerist imperative that seems endemic in the West is significantly diffused in cohousing. Cohousing residents are generally much less concerned with material acquisition – the size of their dwelling, the model of their car, the most fashionable clothing or the latest home entertainment system. They value consumer goods simply for their functionality, not their monetary worth or perceived fashionability. Especially during the first one or two years, cohousing communities commonly shed excessive quantities of duplicated consumer items that members no longer want or need (Photo 16.1).

Photo 16.1: Items left in the Swan's Market common house about to be redistributed or donated to a worthy cause.

The notice on the wall reads:

Stuff Disposal Week –

Sun–Tues: Take it if it's yours.

Wed–Sat: Take it whether or not it's yours.

Sunday: It goes to MOCHA's white elephant sale!

(Note: MOCHA is the nearby Museum of Children's Art)

Shared facilities

Shared facilities, such as those found in a typical common house, take considerable coordinated effort to operate and maintain. They represent the commitment of cohousing groups to the ideal of cooperation and are critical to social development and group cohesion. The extent and make-up of shared facilities varies widely in cohousing. Some communities have built multi-purpose, full-featured common houses and others more modest ones. Sometimes the indoor facilities are located in one building, the common house, though usually they are spread between two or more buildings. Table 16.3 is an inventory of existing and proposed shared (indoor) facilities in each of the communities (at the end of 2003).

The list is ordered according to the 'count' of built facilities (2 points) and proposed but not yet built facilities (1 point) in each community. However, cross-community comparison on the basis of this data should be undertaken with great caution. There is complex reasoning behind a group's choice of common facilities. The size of the community, its demographic mix and financial capacity are obvious factors. In Tokyo, for example, economic and cultural factors have severely limited opportunities for dedicated shared space. Interpretation is further hampered by the incompleteness of some common facilities at the time of the evaluation. Earthsong Eco-Neighbourhood, for example, has been making do with a pre-existing farmhouse until its common house is built.

The columns of Table 16.3 are ordered according to the total 'count' of built and proposed facilities in all of the groups evaluated. The ordering and banding suggest a prioritisation of common facilities, from those deemed essential (laundry, social space, kitchen and dining room) to those considered highly desirable (guest room, kids' room and workshop) and so on. Apart from the laundry, the most highly valued amenities are those associated with the development of social relationships. Groups appear to recognise the link between available amenity, the social interaction it engenders and the building of group cohesion. A most poignant outcome of the analysis, however, is the low importance attached to teenage facilities. This can no doubt be rationalised in communities with low numbers of teens but this finding supports anecdotal evidence for the needs of teenagers being poorly met in cohousing.

	Kitchen	Dining Area	Laundry	Social Space	Guest Room	Kid's Room	Workshop	Office	TV / VCR	Library	Games Room	Craft Room	Hot tub / Pool	Exercise Room	Teens Room	
WindSong Cohousing	**	**	**	**	**	**	**	**	**	**	**	**	*	**	**	29
Marsh Commons Cohousing	**	**	**	**	**	**	**	**	**	*	**	**	*			24
Puget Ridge Cohousing	**	**	**	**	**	**	**		**	*	**	*				20
Berkeley Cohousing	**	**	**	**	**	**	*	**	**	**						19
Songaia Cohousing	**	**	**	**	**	**	**	**					*		*	18
N Street Cohousing	**	**	**	**			**		**	**	**		**			18
Cascade Cohousing	**	**	**	**	**	**	**		**	**						18
Swan's Market Cohousing	**	**	**	**	**	**	**						*	**		17
Quayside Village Cohousing	**	**	**	**	**	**		**					**			16
Earthsong Eco-Neighbourhood	**	*	**	**	*	**	**	**		*					*	16
Cohousing Cooperative	**	**	**	**	**	*	*	**								14
Kyōdō no mori Cohousing	**	**														4
Total count	24	23	22	22	19	19	18	14	12	11	8	7	6	4	4	

Table 16.3: Schedule of existing and proposed common facilities.

(** = built facilities, * = intended facilities)

The area analysis offered in Table 16.4 is also revealing and to some extent addresses anomalies in the previous table such as the incomplete state of some common houses and the critical mass (related to community size) necessary for the viability of particular facilities. The measure, *area of common space* includes all built facilities, not just those in the common house. Observation and anecdotal evidence suggests that communities with a high common to private space ratio enjoy and make good use of their common house but struggle to optimise its use. Those groups with low ratios of common to private space tend not to 'hang out' in the common house and are constrained by space limitations when the whole community comes together. The data suggests that a ratio of common to private space somewhere between 0.13 and 0.17 is optimal. Whilst not wanting to take the numerical analysis too far, it seems reasonable to suggest that a hypothetical 'average' cohousing community of 18 households should seek to build a common house of around 280 m².

The sharing of resources requires a considerable commitment of time and energy in cleaning, maintenance, improvement and management. All groups start with the premise that everyone who is able should contribute a certain amount of time in their 'civic duty' to make the community successful. However, the means by which groups get the work done varies widely, with each group evolving a different arrangement over many years. Some groups maintain a loose, informal understanding, while others strictly regulate and monitor the relative contribution of their members. In some communities, individual members sign-up for particular tasks, but in most, groups or teams take responsibly for a building, an area of the property or a package of tasks (see Chapter 17).

	Number of households	Area of common space (m^2)	Common space per household (m^2)	Average dwelling size (m^2)	Ratio of common to private space
Marsh Commons Cohousing	17	418	25	105	0.24
Swan's Market Cohousing	20	465	23	95	0.24
Songaia Cohousing	13	325	25	127	0.20
Cascade Cohousing	15	280	19	101	0.19
Puget Ridge Cohousing	23	372	16	95	0.17
Quayside Village Cohousing	19	240	13	80	0.16
WindSong Cohousing	34	557	16	115	0.14
Berkeley Cohousing	14	169	12	87	0.14
Earthsong Eco-neighbourhood	17	200	12	92	0.13
Cooperative Cohousing	11	130	12	108	0.11
N Street Cohousing	17	170	10	110	0.09
Kyōdō no mori Cohousing	12	25	2	90	0.02
Mean	18	280	15	100	0.15

Table 16.4: Area analysis of common versus private space.

Support: restoring 'traditional' personal relationships

> "There's plenty of support – emotional and practical – for environmental views".
>
> "Simple things happen, like a neighbour's trip to the grocery store turns into picking up milk for me (that's one less trip)".
>
> "The community supports ecological practices naturally and encourages the children to do so".
>
> "Cohousing offers significant support to a simpler more sustainable lifestyle".
>
> "Cohousing supports my efforts to live closer to what I believe is right".

In their influential book, *Habits of the Heart*, the authors (Robert Bellah *et al*) characterise 'classic' or 'traditional' personal relationships as those with three principal dimensions: *social*, *practical*, and *moral*. Good friends, they argue, must:
- value one another's company (i.e. enjoy social support);
- be useful to one another (i.e. provide practical support); and
- share a commitment to the common good (i.e. effect moral support).

They suggest that all three aspects have been suppressed in contemporary Western society. Such "habits of the heart", they argue, "made sense more readily in the small face-to-face communities that characterised early American society".[6]

Yet, it is *exactly* this tripartite social relationship that is the norm in cohousing.
1) Social support – diminished in contemporary society through reduced propinquity – is restored in cohousing through ready-found 'caring and sharing'.
2) Practical support is ubiquitous in cohousing through close-knit neighbouring.
3) Moral support is the collective consciousness in cohousing that maintains support for, and validation of, individual members by the group.

Many cohousing residents report that the support of friends, neighbours and the community at large is the single greatest influence upon their environmental practices.

Social support

While most cohousing residents have intimate relationships with one or a few unrelated others with whom they can share personal problems, communities recognise that not all members are so connected. Hence, men's, women's and parent's support groups are common. Some cohousing communities have a committee for the purpose of addressing the personal needs of their members. Radically changed circumstance and emergency situations are often the catalyst for such support. Loss of employment may trigger a loan from an emergency support fund. Accommodation within the community will be found for one of a couple undergoing separation. A cooking roster may be developed to provide meals for a family in need. A single mother, for example, reported not having to cook for two months after the birth of her child.

Social support can be critically important in times of tragedy, trauma or dire need (see Chapter 8). In one community, the 'Caring and Sharing Committee' wrote a page-long article in their newsletter describing the plight of a member suffering Alzheimer's Disease and his carer-partner. They recommended a long list of ways in which members could assist the couple: keeping in touch, calling by, running errands, offering to give the carer a break, taking them out, offering companionship, getting involved etc. The potential for this kind of deep, therapeutic caring and support is inherent within small-scale communal societies, as Rosbeth Kanter has famously documented.

> In many ways the intense love and care, the close coordination of production and consumption, the participation in and sharing of power, the integration of home and work, and the elimination of private property often characteristic of fully developed utopian communities makes them well suited to attacking problems of therapy.[7]

Practical support

Practical support in cohousing can occur in countless ways. There is willingness to care for their garden or feed their cat when neighbours take a vacation. Ready advice is given and time spent helping neighbours to install new software, fix a leaky faucet or move heavy furniture. Such mutual aid can save money, alleviate stress and imbue relationships with substance. It is an essential ingredient of the 'social glue' of most cohousing communities.

Practical support is probably best illustrated by informal childcare. In cohousing, the amenity and safety of common open space and the close proximity of children of similar ages elevates outdoor play beyond watching television as most kids' preferred past-time. Parental willingness to let children play freely outdoors is only possible, however, with the tacit support of a significant proportion of the rest of the community. Knowing that adults are somewhere around, that an informal neighbourhood watch is being kept on the commons and that other houses are open to their kids offers parents a peace of mind that is rare in contemporary society.

Having relationships of trust with a number of close neighbours enables parents to spontaneously, or by regular arrangement, trade baby-sitting and childcare duties. This can be particularly invaluable for single parents. At one community, for instance, a midwife called to duty at 2am knows she can call a neighbour who will immediately come and sleep over with her children. Retired members of many communities and those working at home become surrogate parents, feeding neighbours' kids after school and supervising their play until parents return from work. The elderly become surrogate grandparents. The community becomes a surrogate family.

To a large extent, the availability of such support depends on the diversity of work circumstances and lifestyles. It requires that not all adults commute to 9-to-5 jobs. As previously noted, cohousing has considerable diversity of this kind. Only 50% of adults work full-time. Those employed part-time comprise 22%, full-time students, 11 % and homemakers, 5% of the adult population. Another 5% are retired, 4% are unemployed and 4% have independent means of support. A considerable proportion of residents spend significant amounts of time at home. Sixteen percent make their living from home on either a full-time or part-time basis and about 20% more are based at home as students, homemakers, unemployed or retired.

Moral support

Whether it features in a mission statement or not, all cohousing groups agonise over matters of *equity*, with some members suggesting that it is one of "the *three 'e's* of sustainability" along with environment, and economics. Equity is taken here to mean "the common good" or the even-handed treatment of all, and in particular, community support for the needs of minorities. Gays and lesbians, for example, have found cohousing to be a haven from homophobia and discrimination. Two lesbian mothers once wrote in their community newsletter, "cohousing...offered a safe, nurturing environment for our 'alternative' – we like to think normal – family. We are free to be ourselves here and feel accepted as a family".[8]

In practice, however, real equity proves as difficult to achieve in cohousing as it does elsewhere. Wheelchair access to at least some units is possible in most projects but only a few (eg. Quayside Village and WindSong) have purpose-built ground floor units with full and easy accessibility. Almost all common houses are on two levels, making disabled access to some facilities impossible or difficult. Notably, where disabled members have joined the group during a project's development phase, greater effort has been made to meet their needs. At one community, for instance, the involvement of a disabled child during development of the project resulted in all units being made wheelchair accessible so that he could freely visit his friends.

Such consideration is very rare however as only about 2% of the cohousing population have a serious physical or intellectual disability. This is undoubtedly an issue which could be better addressed in future cohousing projects – as a means of 'future-proofing' dwellings against aging if not as a show of moral support for disabled visitors. Even more difficult to accommodate are the needs of members with ailments such as hypersensitivity to chemicals and synthetics. Whilst they and other residents concerned with indoor air quality can specify benign materials and finishes within their own dwellings, such consideration is not often extended to the common house.

Affordability

Housing affordability is also considered as a matter of equity. Cohousing groups equate entry-level access to cohousing with moral support for less wealthy members. Against a background (during the 1980s and '90s) of unparalleled decline in housing affordability, founding members of *every* group said they had aspired to relative affordability and strove to keep base-level housing costs as low as possible. Groups minimised dwelling size and standardised or replicated house design. Some groups limited customisation on the assumption that varying the design for individual households would increase costs for the whole community. Other strategies included infrastructure rationalisation, design for adaptive reuse and the use of recycled materials.

Yet it seems that cohousing is still not particularly affordable. Table 16.5 offers a basic analysis of the cost of entering cohousing. Total project cost has been divided by the number of dwellings in each community to produce an average dwelling cost. This is then divided by the average dwelling size to produce an average dwelling cost per m^2. Once again, this kind of analysis must be treated with caution. Fine-grained analysis by location and household income would be necessary before firm conclusions could be drawn about housing affordability. However, the raw data is still revealing.

	Project cost (all in US$)	Number of dwellings	Average dwelling Cost (US$)	Average dwelling size (m²)	Average dwelling cost per m² (US$)
Cohousing Cooperative	$720,000	11	$65,455	108	$606
Cascade Cohousing	$1,360,000	15	$90,667	101	$898
WindSong Cohousing	$3,800,000	34	$111,765	115	$972
N Street Cohousing	$1,960,000	17	$115,294	110	$1,048
Marsh Commons Cohousing	$2,540,000	17	$149,412	105	$1,423
Puget Ridge Cohousing	$3,350,000	23	$145,652	95	$1,533
Earthsong Eco-Neighbourhood	$2,400,000	17	$141,176	92	$1,535
Quayside Village Cohousing	$2,400,000	19	$126,315	79	$1,599
Songaia Cohousing	$2,700,000	13	$207,692	127	$1,635
Berkeley Cohousing	$2,580,000	14	$184,286	87	$2,118
Swan's Market Cohousing	$5,260,000	20	$263,000	95	$2,768
Kyōdō no mori Cohousing	$5,500,000	12	$458,333	90	$5,093
Mean	$2,880,833	18	$171,587	100	$1,769

Table 16.5: Cohousing affordability analysis.

The first four projects could be said to be genuinely 'affordable'. Australian cohousing, in particular, has achieved a remarkable level of affordability. Cohousing Cooperative would be the most affordable project of all, but is almost fully government funded anyway (see Chapter 11). Their successful cost minimisation can be attributed to a strictly limited budget, efficient replicated architectural design and very tight construction management – all of which is more likely with a publicly funded project. Cascade Cohousing utilised sweat equity to good affect (see Chapter 12). To some extent both projects reaped cost benefits due to location. Real estate values and the cost of construction are lower in Hobart than elsewhere in Australia.

The Windsong Cohousing project enjoyed excellent economies of scale and the cost advantages of close clustering and innovative project management (see Chapter 3).[9] N Street Cohousing demonstrates the cost advantages of retrofit cohousing, although this project also benefited from its location in a low-cost neighbourhood (see Chapter 7). At the other end of the scale, the Tokyo project starkly reflects the distorted real estate values in that city. Similarly, Berkeley Cohousing and Swan's Market illustrate the extent of real estate inflation in the Bay area.

The remaining projects can be said to be more typical of cohousing generally. Homeowners in these communities paid, on average, US$154,000 to join the project. The prices include a share of the commons, of course, which delivers enormous lifestyle advantages. Therefore, comparison with regular housing costs should be highly qualified. The projects were all constructed in the mid 1990s when the national median house price in the US and Canada was around US$150,000.[10] Based on these figures, it seems that cohousing is no more affordable than regular housing, possibly less so. This is a salutary finding given that cohousing is commonly misconceived or misrepresented as a means to affordable housing. The data suggests that it most definitely is not.

One reason for cohousing sometimes being even less affordable than typical family housing is the complexity of the development process and the number of consultants involved. This is well illustrated in the project development cost analysis produced for Earthsong Eco-Neighbourhood (Figure 16.1). Note that the cost of construction of the dwellings alone amounts to just 45% of the total whilst the so-called 'soft costs' (i.e. consultants fees, taxes, administrative costs etc.) comprise more than a quarter of the total budget.

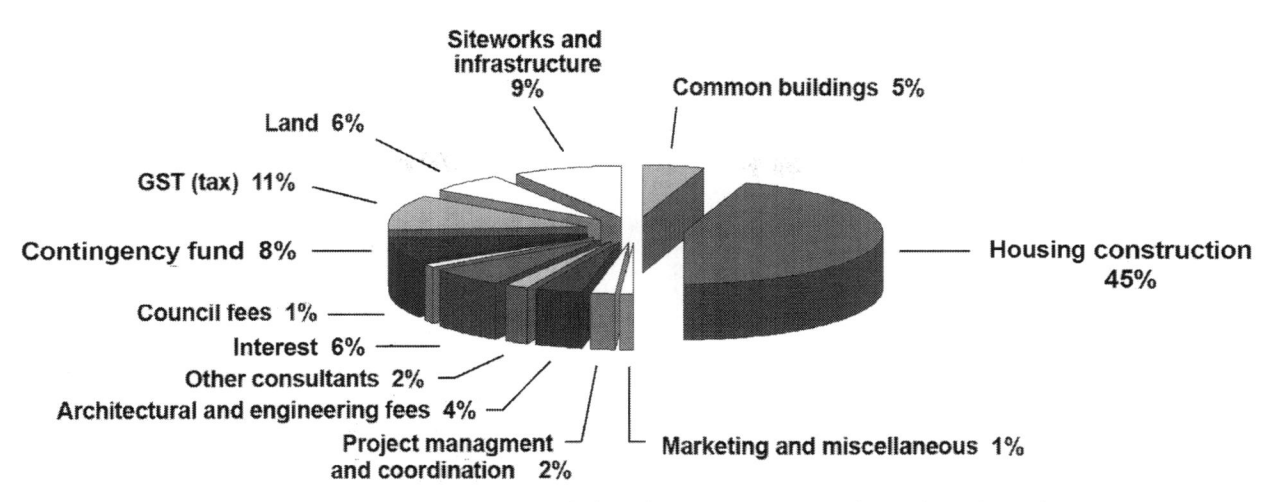

figure 16.1: Earthsong Eco-Neighbourhood development cost analysis (Analysis by Peter Scott).

In recognition of the challenge of affordability, support for low-income members is provided in a number of cohousing communities. A few, including Quayside, WindSong and Berkeley, have successfully raised government subsidies for some units. Others have arranged extra financial assistance from investment companies. Some groups have assisted lower income members with internal loans, subsidies and sliding-scale contribution schemes (for condominium and body corporate fees). Most simply seek to provide rental accommodation for those who can't afford to buy into the community. N Street, for example, with 20 renters in a total adult population of 35, has a high proportion of low-income residents – mostly students. In 1996, 48% had an income below US$20,000 pa.[11] In almost all other cohousing communities, attics or basements are rented out. Although renters usually have reduced voting rights, in every other respect they report feeling fully integrated into community life, and feel no less a sense of belonging to the group.

Notes:

[1] The New Shorter Oxford English Dictionary (1993).

[2] The New Shorter Oxford English Dictionary (1993).

[3] Mandel, D. L. (1996). Southside Park Cohousing: Program Narrative. Sacramento: 2.

[4] Mandel, D. L. (1996: 2).

[5] From the community's guide for new residents and visitors, Life at the Commons, It's Uncommonly Good: A Guide to Living at the Commons on the Alameda.

[6] Bellah, R. N., R. Madsen, et al. (1996: 116).

[7] Kanter, R. (1972). Commitment and Community: Communes and Utopias in Social Perspective. Cambridge, Harvard University Press: 225.

[8] Marian and Joanne (1996). "We're Different, We're the Same". Nyland News: The Call for Whatever(October 1996): 13.

[9] For a fuller analysis, see Hanson, C. (1996). The Cohousing Handbook. Vancouver, Hartley & Marks.

[10] Reuer, J.-P. (1995). Strategies for Reducing Costs in the Development of Cohousing in the United States and Canada, McGill University.

[11] Meltzer, G. (2000). Cohousing: Toward Social and Environmental Sustainability. Department of Architecture. Brisbane, The University of Queensland.

Photo 17.1: Residents engaged in landscaping Kyōdō no mori (Image courtesy of Tetsuro Kai).

17 Engagement: from belonging to efficacy

Engagement can mean "commitment to, or involvement with, people, place or activity".[1] In cohousing, 'commitment to people' and 'involvement with place' together instil a *sense of belonging* to a location-based community. Further, 'commitment to place' and 'involvement with activity' induce participation in community life and a sense of personal *efficacy*. *Belonging* and *efficacy* are components of *engagement,* both with one's circumstance and in society.

Belonging: from association to community

> "We feel and act with responsibility to the community and its primary values".
>
> "The culture created in the community influences my behaviour".
>
> "A community mindset is developing which expresses ecological values".
>
> "We have a group commitment to modelling ecological practices both for our children and the broader community".
>
> "The norms of the community emphasise ecological practice which contributes to our awareness and practice".
>
> "It [environmentalism] is a stated community value".

In socially cohesive communities, the confluence of associations and relationships that members develop with other individuals becomes identified at some point with the group as a whole and transmutes into a sense of *belonging* to that group. A sense of belonging is acquired over time by dint of the *quality* of those associations and relationships.

> As we move [from acquaintance] to association, and from association to community, mutuality reaches beyond exchange to create more enduring bonds of interdependence, caring and commitment. There is a transition, we may say, from reciprocity to solidarity and from there to fellowship.[2]

Belonging to a group, or "an individual's membership of, and acceptance by, a group"[3] associates members with the values of that group in two distinct and reciprocal ways. Firstly, members operate within a framework of the group's explicit and implicit values. In turn, individuals test and evaluate their own values against the expectations of a membership that they know take them seriously as a person and a member.

About one half of cohousing communities have a written mission or value statement (see page 129). In every case these make explicit reference to living in a caring, pro-active relationship with the environment. Such a codification of values effectively guarantees continuity of, and adherence to, the matters of principle and practice that they address. This provides members with assurance that, provided actions fall within certain guidelines, they may freely pursue individual goals as they see fit. Deference to such 'rules' (as opposed to subordination to them) can in fact free people to "do what they do best and to pursue concerns that are for them, truly relevant and problematic".[4]

In all but a few of those communities without a mission statement, a strong unwritten ethos supporting the environmental beliefs and practices of members still pervades. It is the condoning of, and support for, green principles that enables cohousing residents to adopt pro-environmental practices they would not contemplate in more conventional circumstances. An example already mentioned is the 'free box' where garments, kitchen utensils, books and toys can be deposited and/or acquired. This matter-of-fact attitude to material needs enables a reduction in non-essential purchases and encourages living more simply and with less. It directly addresses what many in cohousing believe to be the fetishism of consumerist acquisitiveness that is endemic in wider society.

A mission statement or implicit set of values is important to group identity but it works at a quite esoteric level. Most cohousing communities work hard to also develop and reinforce their identity through shared experience. Due to a realisation that "the bonds of community are strongest when they are fashioned from strands of shared history and culture",[5] groups deliberately build their identity through festive celebration and cultural expression. Traditions and a common history are established, which further build identity and encourage increasing member participation. The same process had been identified in a study of Australian intentional communities:

> Most...groups have a host of traditions which are ritualistically re-enacted at appropriate times. Such behaviour is clearly important to the group, and serves as a symbol of 'groupness'. This behaviour becomes part of the symbolism and traditions of the group.[6]

Cohousing communities often adapt established traditions – creating something new and distinctly their own. At Songaia, for example, May Day is celebrated as Earth Day; an occasion for expressing members' deeply felt ecological values through tree planting, dedication, singing, dancing and feasting (see Chapter 4). The celebratory centrepiece is a neo-traditional May Pole dance. At N Street, Halloween is marked with a procession to the local cemetery – an adaptation of the Mexican 'Day of the Dead' tradition (see Chapter 7). Afterwards over dinner, residents share stories about their lost parents, friends and pets, which at some level are a metaphorical expression of their deepest held values of family life and friendship. In the process, their understanding of each other is deepened and their sense of community reinforced.

Cohousing residents commonly acknowledge and celebrate each other's religious traditions, which previously may have been observed privately. Jews frequently light Sabbath candles at a Friday night common meal and, in turn, will participate in a gift giving ceremony at Christmas. At Quayside Village Cohousing, Abi involves the whole community in his celebration of the annual Nepalese festival of *Tihar* (see Chapter 2). However, religious diversity can occasionally be problematic. Indeed one of the enduring contentions in cohousing involves the scheduling of meetings and other events on days that might coincide with the religious observances of some members. Diversity is, by definition, always going to present such conflicts of interest. However, if they are met with lenience and open communication, such 'conflicts' present further opportunity for members to deepen their understanding of each other's cultural values.

In a socially cohesive community, where relationships are generally supportive and non-judgemental, there is great potential for artistic and creative expression by individuals and groups. The cohousing groups that have most successfully established a program of cultural and creative activities are also those with the most cohesive social relationships. Inevitably, social cohesion takes time to develop, so longer-lived communities such as WindSong, Songaia and Puget Ridge benefit from the richest cultural expression. WindSong and Puget Ridge residents regularly enjoy concerts, plays and talent nights. The Songaia community sing together at formal and informal gatherings.

A normative mainstream focus on individual and familial well-being, when combined with a material conception of the world, has produced the 'great' Australian or American 'dream'. In cohousing, through deepening one's connection with others, such aspirations are dismantled and reassembled into a more altruistic, outwardly focused caring for the well-being of others. The focus of caring shifts from self (and family) toward unrelated others…and from material to social need. In the words of one WindSong resident, "We're learning to trust that less equals more…diminishing the importance of stuff…emphasising connection, not consumption!"

Efficacy: achievement through participation

> "Being here in cohousing allows me to participate fully in the group effort".
>
> "I enjoy working with others to enhance our surroundings".
>
> "We have to make decisions about how to solve problems and move forward".
>
> "Daily we feel encouraged that we are making a difference because all of us care and take action. This is exponentially inspiring!"
>
> "It is empowering to do composting and water conservation as a group because it is easier to see that we make a difference".
>
> "It is much easier in cohousing to live closer to our values and beliefs".

Efficacy is defined as "the ability to bring about an intended result".[7] This final theme is perhaps the most intangible and difficult to assess. Yet it is the most important, given the tenuous link between environmental consciousness and behavioural change (outlined at the beginning of Chapter 1). In this section, the means of bringing about an intended result is investigated in terms of personal participation in community affairs.

Cohousing, by definition, involves members in a process of designing and developing a housing project themselves – albeit with the help of professionals and consultants. When cohousing groups first form, it is with this intention. Yet most have little idea of the difficulty of such a venture. The experience of the Songaia and Marsh Commons groups illustrate just how challenging and traumatic the process can be. Of course, the opposite can also occur. The development of Puget Ridge, for example, proceeded smoothly, if not joyously. Table 17.1, shows the development time line for each of the projects. It highlights the similarities and differences between them in terms of the total time taken and the different kinds of challenges faced by each.

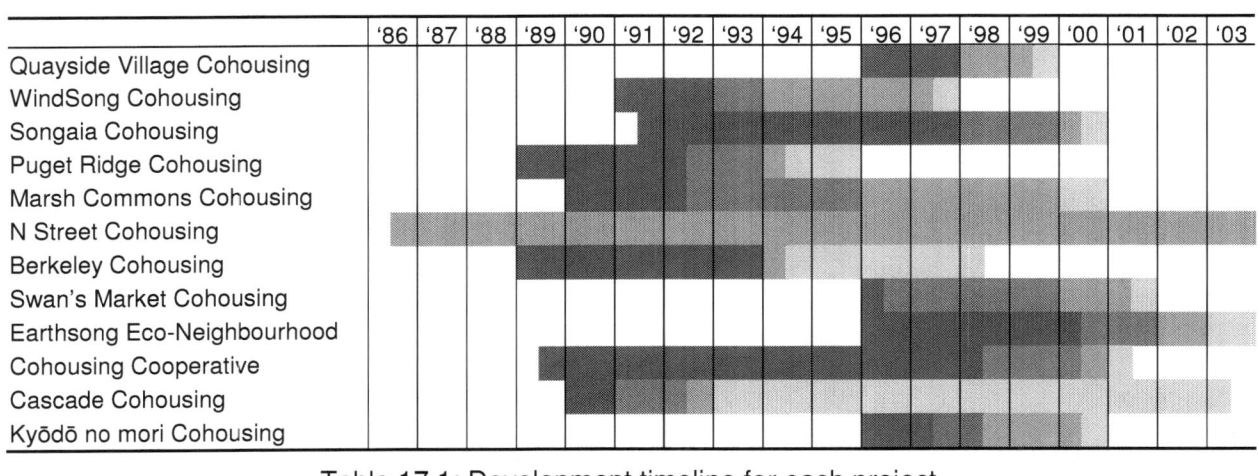

Table 17.1: Development timeline for each project.

Project inception – land acquisition
Land acquisition – start of construction
Start of construction – initial occupation
Initial occupation – project completion

Chapter 17: Engagement

Songaia and Cohousing Cooperative spent the greatest proportion of their development timeline in early machinations over project feasibility and fund-raising respectively. Marsh Commons and Swan's Market each had a drawn-out construction phase – the former due to toxic contamination of the site and the latter due to the unique complexities of the project (being a small part of a much larger mixed-use development of a heritage building). Cascade Cohousing had by far the longest period between initial move-in and project completion because members built their own houses and the common house over a ten year period. These examples indicate just how unpredictable and potentially thorny the development process can be and so highlight the critical importance of group process – communication, decision-making and dispute resolution methods in particular.

Most founding members enter cohousing development with a poor understanding of group process. Some may have gained prior experience in collective decision-making and conflict resolution. However most will not have and their assumptions will be naive. "Decision-making and responsibilities are shared by all members" suggested the marketing literature of one community, arguing that this "puts all members on an equal footing, avoids power struggles [and] encourages everyone to participate by communicating openly".[8] In fact, genuinely open communication (let alone transparency), which is critical to such processes, requires a separate and resolute agreement of its own. Groups like Puget Ridge and WindSong that make such a commitment at the outset enjoy a smoother ride through the project development phase. Their success builds mutual trust and confidence in their agreements and processes which, following move-in, launches a more vigorous participatory management of the project.

> Trust, or the capacity to make credible commitments, is a very effective arrangement for enabling participants to cooperate. Many problems in common-pool resource situations (the so-called 'tragedy of the commons') have been solved thanks to self-monitoring and self-enforcing patterns of human interaction.[9]

Does the political and social microcosm that is cohousing exhibit these characteristics? Participation in common meals, social events, general meetings and voluntary workdays was reported as follows.

Event	Never	Seldom	As often as not	Usually	Always
Common meals	1.7 %	11.8 %	28.6 %	41.6 %	16.2 %
Social events	-	4.6 %	22.5 %	58.1 %	14.7 %
General meetings	1.4 %	5.5 %	13.9 %	50.3 %	28.9 %
Voluntary workdays	0.9 %	7.8 %	26.0 %	50.6 %	14.7 %
Mean	1.0 %	7.4 %	22.8 %	50.2 %	18.6 %

Table 17.2: Reported participation in community activities (N=346).

This data indicates high levels of participation in community events. Of all the activities, general meetings held fortnightly or monthly have the highest reported levels of participation. Attendance at community meetings holds particular significance for the application of environmental values. The translation of environmental concern into practice is made more complex for individuals and households in cohousing because they cannot act independently. The group as a whole determines many of the lifestyle choices with environmental implications. Notwithstanding the role of the mission statement in guiding these and other choices, prolonged and often intense discussion of group goals and priorities precedes most decisions.

Consensus decision-making, if properly functioning, allows an individual's aspirations to at least be heard, if not met. At best, each member of the group will identify with choices made and feel that they represent their personal aspirations. At worst, some will feel that although particular decisions are less than ideal, they can at least live with and abide by them. This may be limiting or frustrating for some, but for the less assertive majority the process can be empowering, leading to increased self-efficacy and greater opportunity to manifest environmental concern than would be possible in more conventional circumstances.

In addition to their 'civic' role in the life of the whole community, cohousing residents are inevitably involved in administrative tasks at the committee level. The number of committees and their titles, sizes and responsibilities vary widely amongst cohousing groups but there are commonalities worth noting. Almost all groups have an administrative core of the following four committees:
- A Board (though it may not be called that) responsible for legal and management matters;
- Process Committee to facilitate collective decision-making and monitor community cohesion;
- Landscape Committee to coordinate and implement decisions about gardens and landscaping;
- Common House Committee to coordinate and administer shared facilities and resources.

A second tier of committees is found in about two-thirds of communities:
- Social Well-being Committee to facilitate the improvement of social relations;
- Maintenance Committee to monitor and maintain buildings and site infrastructure;
- Finance Committee, responsible for the commercial and economic concerns of the community;
- Common Meals Committee to oversee food procurement and cooking procedures.

A third tier of committees is found in about half of the communities:
- Children's Committee, which looks after the needs of the children; and
- Design Review Committee to preside over architectural and building proposals.

Cohousing groups allocate management responsibility in many different ways. Some do not have a Finance Committee, for example, because they entrust the Board to deal with financial (as well as legal) matters. A few groups have the Common House or Social Committee administer common meals instead of a committee constituted solely for the purpose. Some groups spread responsibility widely. One cohousing community, for example, has sixteen committees. Others amalgamate their committees into fewer and larger groups with multiple responsibilities.

The total number of committee positions varies with community size, though the average number of positions per adult member varies between one half (i.e. half of the members sit on committees) and two (i.e. members sit on an average of two committees) with the mean being exactly one. This fits with the loose expectation found in most cohousing communities that adult members serve on at least one committee.

Cohousing communities continually adjust and refine their administrative structure, which may change with shifting need and sometimes undergo radical overhaul. The devolution of decision-making invariably changes over time. Typically, during the early years, committees defer most decisions to a meeting of the group as a whole. Later on, as the administrative load is rationalised and trust within the group is developed, the committees take greater responsibility for decision-making on behalf of the community.

For many residents, involvement in committees can mean that a whole new range of skills (managerial, organisational, communication and presentation) is developed. Members grow to appreciate the potential of collaborative effort and their personal efficacy within a mini-democracy. Facilitation, consensual decision-making and conflict resolution processes become normative. Members learn to deal with professionals, local government and bureaucracy at all levels.

Groups develop political leverage in the process of lobbying a particular cause and in some cases, not only politicise their own members but the surrounding neighbourhood as well. Individual and collective engagement with their circumstance is a palpable outcome for participants in cohousing development and management. Members gain a profound appreciation of their power to bring about change and to align their lives with their values – they become *empowered*. This acquired capacity to align lifestyle and values particularly applies to environmentalism, as one cohousing resident suggests:

> Cohousing is a fit for my values and lifestyle. Never have I felt my visions and ideals so in line with my everyday life. Many problems in the world are related to over-consumption by Americans. Cohousing provides an opportunity to use fewer of the world's limited resources while living in a community of kindred spirits.

Empowerment, or the progressive gaining of control over their circumstance by individuals and households, is the crux of the matter. Apropos environmental concerns, it is the link between awareness, attitude and behaviour. Empowerment dissolves ambivalence and enables the application of environmental values in practical ways.

As a 'case study' vehicle, cohousing has demonstrated a physical, instrumental and social context within which pro-environmental attitudes and behaviour are nurtured and sustained. Residents are able to fashion their physical surroundings to accord with their aspirations in ways not available – or even conceivable – within mainstream society. The architecture and site planning facilitate interaction, which builds familiarity. Social intercourse is encouraged and further supported by intent. Familiarity facilitates 'consciousness raising' and the spreading of 'functional knowledge'. Relationships of substance evolve, leading to increased sharing, support and trust.

In a trusting society – one in which members are prepared to "surrender their instinctive habits of distrust, where they are prepared to have faith in their neighbours words" – there is a lot of enthusiasm and motivation for improvement and change.[10] Through collective action bonding occurs, which cements attachment to people and place and grows a 'sense of community'. Feelings of belonging feed a sense of self and further encourage participation in 'civic' life, which in turn builds skills, confidence and a sense of self-efficacy. Empowerment provides impetus for the application of awareness and attitudes in practical ways. In the next chapter empowerment will be considered in detail using a conceptual model that relates aspects of cohousing life which, to this point have been considered separately.

Notes:

[1] The New Shorter Oxford English Dictionary (1993).

[2] Selznick, P. (1992). The Moral Commonwealth. Berkeley, UC Press: 362.

[3] The New Shorter Oxford English Dictionary (1993).

[4] Selznick, P. (1992:265).

[5] Selznick, P. (1992:361).

[6] Metcalf, W. J. (1987). Dropping Out and Staying In, Griffith University, Brisbane: 355.

[7] The New Shorter Oxford English Dictionary (1993).

[8] Mathew, R. (1997). "Quayside Village Cohousing: Construction set to begin in mid July". CoHousing: The Newsletter for Cohousing in Western Canada 5(3): 2,3: 2.

[9] Misztal, B. A. (1996). Trust in Modern Societies. Cambridge (UK), Polity Press: 214.

[10] Pagden, A. (1988). The Destruction of Trust and its Economic Consequences in the Case of 18th Century Naples. Trust; Making and Breaking Cooperative Relationships. D. Gambetta. Oxford, Basil Blackwell:130

18 Empowerment: lessons from the cohousing model

> [Empowerment is] an intentional ongoing process centred in the local community, involving mutual respect, critical reflection, caring, and group participation, through which people lacking an equal share of valued resources gain greater access to and control over those resources.[1]

Empowerment

Empowerment (as the above quote makes clear) is the process whereby otherwise disadvantaged individuals and groups progressively take control of their circumstance and gain increased access to resources. It usually involves a challenge to established or dominant relationships of power and is mostly associated with 'grass-roots' or 'bottom up' participation in community action. At a personal level, empowerment can result in the attainment of skills, knowledge and competence and lead to an increased sense of self-efficacy. It is said to be an "antidote to the alienating and disempowering growth of our mass society and its institutions".[2]

Empowerment theory is particularly popular in the disciplines of political and social science, psychology, management, education and health. Discussion here will focus on *community* empowerment, a concept most thoroughly canvassed in the emerging community psychology literature. This construct neatly brings together many of the threads developed in previous chapters and introduces some broader concepts. It is a notion that links personal participation, supporting systems and proactive behaviours to matters of social change. It is, therefore, likely to shed light on pro-environmental behavioural change occurring in cohousing communities. The breadth of empowerment theory – its "heuristic value…across many settings and levels of analysis" – renders it most appropriate to the task.[3] It establishes a theoretical framework within which matters of environmental and social sustainability can be holistically integrated.

Unfortunately, the development of empowerment theory has been uneven. There is a plethora of definitions of empowerment causing it to be confused with other psychological constructs such as self-esteem, self-efficacy, competency and locus of control. Much of the literature fails to connect theory and practice, leaving empowerment-based activists without a solid conceptual framework on which to base strategies and actions. Even though empowerment is widely written about, a lack of empirical testing has limited development of the construct. Such a task is rendered more difficult by the contextual specificity of empowerment. A person, for example, may feel empowered in one setting (eg. at home) and disempowered in another (i.e. at work). Workplace empowerment has, in fact, been thoroughly investigated – albeit from a management perspective. However, the domestic or community variant generally has not. It is hoped that this book will contribute to the furthering of empowerment theory by offering contextual, empirical research of the phenomenon within a residential and community setting.

Most commonly, empowerment is seen to occur within a bounded *social* environment, typically an organisation. An empowering organisation is one that fosters personal development, the process whereby individuals learn and develop competence through practice. Democratic decision-making and clear communication are both critical to the process. Participation in collective action can only set the stage for personal empowerment provided there are "regular and adequate communications of policies and frequent opportunities for discussion of them by all concerned".[4] Involvement in collective decision-making has been shown to have positive attitudinal and behavioural outcomes at a political level. Indeed, the personal and the political are deemed inseparable within an empowerment perspective, and "participation with others to achieve …some critical understanding of the socio-political environment" is a basic component of the construct.[5] Only through individuals being able to relate the personal and the political are the possibilities for action leading to genuine empowerment revealed.

Empowerment is *fundamentally* about medium and long-term adaptation or improvement of one's circumstance; a process by which "individuals gain mastery and control over their lives, and a critical understanding of their environment".[6] It is, therefore, context dependent; a construct that "embraces the notion of person-environment fit".[7] The English community architecture movement of the 1970s, for example, can be viewed as an empowerment process that grew out of the physical conditions of the built environment. Empowerment is encapsulated in the title of an insightful book on the topic, "Community Architecture: How People are Creating their own Environment" by Wates and Knevitt.[8]

Within the Architecture and Planning professions, the relationship between housing and residents' participation in community life has long been investigated. The literature shows that residential architectural design can facilitate greater social contact and a proprietary interest in the immediate built environment, leading to higher levels of participation in community life.

> The built environment consists of architectural and urban planning features such as building size, street width, real and symbolic barriers, and outdoor seating. These may be…related to participation through their impact on resident interaction.[9]

Social contact in public areas enables residents to discuss shared problems, which provides "an impetus toward collective action".[10] The quality or depth of their relationships is critical in enabling individuals "to count on each other… [and] pursue a common goal or purpose".[11] A sense of community that delivers social interaction, information sharing and feelings of solidarity makes it more likely that residents will solve their problems collectively.[12]

> A sense of community…contributes a sense of individual and group empowerment that helps neighbours to collectively act to meet their shared needs. When people share a strong sense of community they are motivated and empowered to change problems they face.[13]

The process is cyclical, as collective participation in turn reinforces a sense of community. Inherently, empowerment has a collectivist dimension and it is this aspect that distinguishes it from similar constructs such as self-efficacy and personal 'locus of control'. Its collectivism is crucial to social change processes. However, social change within communities is a hugely complex matter that can only really be understood holistically or 'ecologically'. 'Ecological' in this sense requires that multifaceted (physical, social and political) aspects of community life be interrelated.

The Community Empowerment Model (CEM)

In the preceding four chapters, the environmental praxis of cohousing residents was analysed within four different domains: *circumstance, interaction, relationship* and *engagement*. These are words with common and variable meaning. In this book their usage is derived from the dictionary definitions outlined previously and repeated here for convenience. As inclusive domains or categories, their meaning should carry all of the richness and nuance of their dictionary definitions.

Circumstance is defined as the "external conditions affecting or that might affect action". Chapter 14 shows that 'circumstance' can set obstacles and offer conveniences that strongly influence pro-environmental behaviour. Empowerment theory further reveals how a group's circumstance can contribute to social *interaction* within it.

Interaction is described as both "the action or influence of persons...on each other" and "reciprocal action". Chapter 15 reveals how interaction is important in raising environmental consciousness and spreading awareness about how to apply one's environmental values in practice. Empowerment theory shows how interaction that advances personal growth builds appreciation of, and deepens social *relationships*.

Being in *relationship* implies both "association" and "connection" between two or more entities. Chapter 16 shows how the sharing and support available in high quality social relationships enhance the environmental praxis of cohousing residents. Empowerment theory further shows that relationships build understanding and trust, leading to a deeper *engagement* with others.

Engagement means "commitment to, or involvement with, people, place or activity". In cohousing, social commitment and involvement with place instil a sense of *belonging* to a community. Commitment to place and involvement in activity induce personal and collective *efficacy*. There is a nexus revealed here between the personal and the 'political'. Chapter 17 describes how a sense of belonging and high levels of real and perceived efficacy enable cohousing residents to successfully manage their own affairs. They are in control. They feel *empowered* to make changes and improvements to their *circumstance*.

The sum of all these connections and relationships can now be represented as a model – the Community Empowerment Model (CEM).

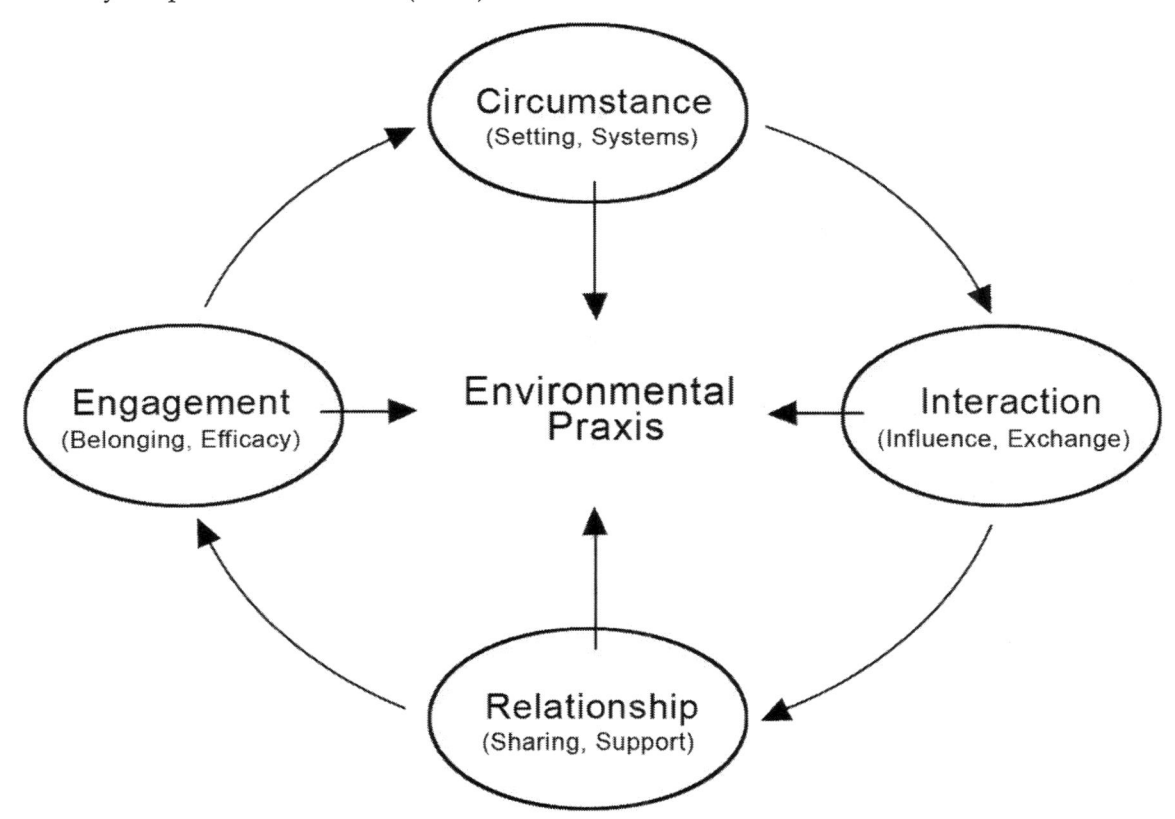

Figure 18.1: The Community Empowerment Model (CEM).

In the model, linking arrows represent the functions 'facilitate' or 'contribute to'. *Circumstance* facilitates *interaction*, which contributes to *relationship* building, leading to *engagement* with *circumstance* – which is the empowerment process. It is iterative and cyclical – becoming more effective and comprehensive over time. Each domain is a separate influence upon environmental

Chapter 18: Empowerment

praxis but it is the iterative and cyclical empowerment process that underpins its effectiveness. In this way, the link between community-based social relationships and effective environmental praxis is revealed.

To put it more explicitly, in a socially cohesive community:
- *circumstance* facilitates human *interaction* which builds meaningful social *relationships*;
- supportive *relationships* in a community context imbue a sense of *belonging* to that community;
- *belonging* (to geographical community and therefore, 'place') induces confident *engagement*;
- and, *engagement* with *circumstance* is the very basis of effective *environmental praxis*.

It is in the nature of such a conceptual model that these connections are represented simplistically. There are numerous subtle relationships between many more dimensions of community life – more than could possibly be modelled in such a manner. The model is heuristic, intended as a means of exploring ideas and further developing aspects of theory. It invites further speculation.

Cohousing and empowerment

Empowerment, the CEM suggests, is the means by which residents take control of their circumstances rather than be indifferent to, ambivalent about, or a victim of them. It brings an awareness of the quality of the surrounding environment coupled with the motivation, efficacy and control of resources to improve it. The motivation to improve environmental quality is the basis of 'environmentalism' in a general sense. In cohousing, an environmentalist feels little of the helplessness, ambivalence or frustration typically felt by well meaning 'greens' living within a rapaciously consumerist society. The community appears as a microcosm within which environmental concern is regularly verified and readily applied. It reinforces green values and practices rather than negates them as normative values and behaviours in Western society are likely to do. "It's easy to be an environmentalist when all around you are also. It's a natural with community living" suggests one cohousing resident.[14]

'Moments' in the empowerment process, as cohousing members progress toward a more effective environmentalism, may include:
- taking a smaller dwelling because workshop, guest room and library are shared;
- learning to compost and recycle because convenient managed systems are provided;
- taking the lead from others more practiced and learning the basis for such practices;
- forging trusting relationships with neighbours which enable the sharing of resources;
- and in the process, becoming less attached to personal possessions and the status of wealth;
- growing instead to appreciate social support and the benefits of collaboration;
- feeling bonded to, safe within and developing a sense of belonging to the group;
- encouraging free expression of personal values sympathetically reflected by the group;
- increasingly participating in the ongoing management of the community and its systems;
- being motivated to contribute to the improvement and maintenance of the surroundings; and
- feeling valued for that contribution and a strengthened sense of personal efficacy.

Empowerment within the context of community induces a realignment of personal priorities. Material consumption diminishes in importance as social relations and environmental quality become more highly valued. Empowerment dissolves ambivalence and overcomes indifference toward the needs of others, leading to the application of concern and caring in practical ways. Personal change is not just behavioural or attitudinal but occurs at the level of deepest held beliefs and values.

The CEM illuminates the underlying psycho-social processes that enable cohousing residents to overcome contradictions inherent in Western capitalist society. It is suggested in Chapter 1, for example, that living with less, in a simpler way, is *so* contrary to deeply held aspirations for material comfort and personal status as to be difficult for most Westerners to comprehend, let alone enact. Anti-consumerist values are, in fact, common amongst members of intentional communities and axiomatic for many communes and alternative lifestyle groups. But in cohousing these values are not so prevalent. Members generally have middle-class aspirations of home ownership and a comfortable lifestyle. Most are encumbered with mortgages and, hence, locked into commuting to conventional jobs. For most cohousing residents, living with less in a simpler way is learned or adopted through community-based structures and social relations. Priorities change as individuals and households are continually prompted to reassess their essential needs. They will be *forced* to ask themselves,

> Do we really want a large house with guest rooms, games rooms, play rooms, exercise rooms, and party-sized living rooms to clean? Or do we want to be able to accommodate guests, play games or exercise when we wish, have somewhere for the children to make a noise and a mess, and a convenient place to throw a party? Do we really want a kitchen full of gadgets, or have delicious meals as easily as possible? Do we really want an electronic security system and dead latches on every aperture, or do we want a safe environment in which to live? Do we really want our homes to be our castles, or do we want loving human relationships? Do we really want an automobile, or do we want easy and convenient access to jobs, shops, leisure and cultural activities and friends? Do we really want exotic vacations in distant lands, or a satisfying, stress-free life in beautiful surroundings?[15]

Whilst some of the data presented in preceding chapters might suggest only a moderate improvement in pro-environmental practices, it must be borne in mind that (a) cohousing folk are often fully practicing 'greens' prior to moving into cohousing and (b) all the cohousing communities featured here are in their infancy. Relationships of trust, which underpin many collective practices, are still being established. Our conditioning makes close living and sharing with others difficult. Sharing requires trust, but trust is built on sharing.

Unfortunately, trust in conventional social and political institutions is almost completely eroded away. In the late 1950s, trust was said to be 'sky-high'. Seventy-three percent of Americans said they trusted the government to do the right thing "most of the time".[16] By 1997, the proportion was just 30%. Now it's likely to be even lower. The same erosion of trust applies at a personal level with 60% of people now saying "you can't be too careful in dealing with people".[17] Rebuilding trust at the level of community is, necessarily, a slow and painstaking process.

Yet, whether or not it forms part of their mission statement, this is implicitly what cohousing groups seek to do. Members seek to develop trust in each other and the group's institutions, which encourages sharing and cooperation, practical and emotional support – and generosity of spirit. Over time, this can lead to more caring and intimate social relations, which can diffuse preoccupations with individual well-being and turn one's focus outward toward the welfare of significant others. This 'brings home' the need to maintain and improve the quality of the surrounding physical environment for the benefit of those significant others…which is a form of environmentalism. Concern may broaden into an altruistic focus on the well-being of people and their circumstance generally. Thus, the seeds of a more comprehensive or global environmentalism may be sown. In this way a sense of community, empowerment and environmentalism are linked.

> Whether we live in the centre of a large city or the edge of a forest, the physical environment starts at our front doors, making environmental issues those which are concerned with our surroundings – both physical and social – rather than those which are in some way related to 'nature'.[18]

Cohousing and social change

To what extent might cohousing-based empowerment contribute to any transformation toward a more sustainable society or, indeed, to social change generally? That cohousing facilitates personal growth in its members does not necessarily mean that it can or will contribute to social change within broader society. It is entirely possible that a community-based social awareness could be as inwardly focussed as a conventional preoccupation with well-being of self and family. Western liberalism's exaggerated individualism combined with a materialist worldview has bred the 'great American, Australian and Western European dream' focussed on ever-increasing private wealth. Might not cohousing communities develop a similar preoccupation with their own welfare whilst remaining unconcerned about broader social and environmental issues?

In Chapter 1, it is suggested that cohousing groups differ from 1960s and '70s communes and the majority of contemporary alternative lifestyle communities in one critical respect; they *elect* to remain fully embedded within mainstream society. Whereas utopian communities of the past generally imagined leading or influencing society by *remote* example, cohousing groups seek to *connect* with society in multiple ways and 'influence (if that is their ambition) from within'. Cohousing projects are generally built in urban or suburban areas. Some contribute to, if not lead, urban renewal and transformation. Their physical boundaries are permeable so that (in the case of Cohousing Cooperative for example) members of the public are encouraged to pass through the site on their way to school or the shops. Cohousing residents make full use of schools, shops and services in the locality. They contribute to their local economy and are often involved in municipal politics. Upon moving into cohousing, members keep their jobs and maintain their pre-existing social ties and recreational pursuits.

This is perhaps cohousing's most significant deviation from communalist traditions and its basis is, at least in part, a matter of principle derived from a different reading of the process of social change. Cohousing can, perhaps, be seen to exemplify the "New Communities" that will "engage with society and make a conscious effort to pull the 'reality' of the world towards a new 'vision'".[19] Cohousing is acceptable to mainstream society and seen not to threaten traditional family or liberal values. For this reason the influence of cohousing will ultimately not be limited to that of the communities that get built. It has the potential to inform future human settlement way beyond the fuzzy edges of the cohousing movement itself.

This is already evident in Denmark. A recent housing project, *Munksøgaard* (completed in 2001) heralds "the advent of the mainstream ecovillage," according to Hildur Jackson, founder of the ecovillage movement.[20] It's located within a bike ride of *Roskilde*, a city of 45,000 and connected by train to Copenhagen, 35 km away. *Munksøgaard* has the scale of organisation (100 households) and ecological aspirations of an ecovillage, yet its site planning, architecture and social agenda are pure cohousing. The housing is divided into five courtyard-like clusters of twenty dwellings, each with its own common house (Figure 18.2). Each cluster is purpose designed for a select resident demographic. One is for youth and another for elderly folk – this housing being rented from a non-profit housing association. The remaining family housing is in three clusters, one privately owned, one a private co-op, and the other rented. The settlement has all the practical, technological and economic advantages of a large, diverse and socially cohesive 'village' but within each cluster residents enjoy closer sharing and more intimate interaction with like-minded people.

A mainstream developer and contractor oversaw construction of the project, yet ecological building strategies were implemented extensively. It has its own grey water and sewerage treatment plants, district wood heating and solar water heating. Permaculture principles underpin a comprehensive landscaping plan. Residents co-own three vehicles. The project has succeeded for developers, residents and authorities alike, and been promoted in Denmark as a new prototype. "We have recently been awarded a grant," says a founding resident, "to report on the existing difficulties in establishing sustainable settlements, and to identify the laws which need changing…to allow for a more sustainable form of development".[21] It seems that the progressive Danish culture that once spawned both cohousing and ecovillages is now pioneering new models of sustainable human settlement and adapting its laws to facilitate widespread ecologically sustainable development.

The popular success of cohousing in Denmark has resulted in many of its features being incorporated into mainstream social housing as well as new neighbourhoods of private sector housing. These include the provision of shared social spaces and facilities enabling smaller private dwellings, cooperative formal and informal childcare arrangements, an increased range of housing options for non-nuclear households, integration of workplace, residential and recreational functions and increased social opportunities for marginalised groups such as the elderly, the disabled, low-income and single people.

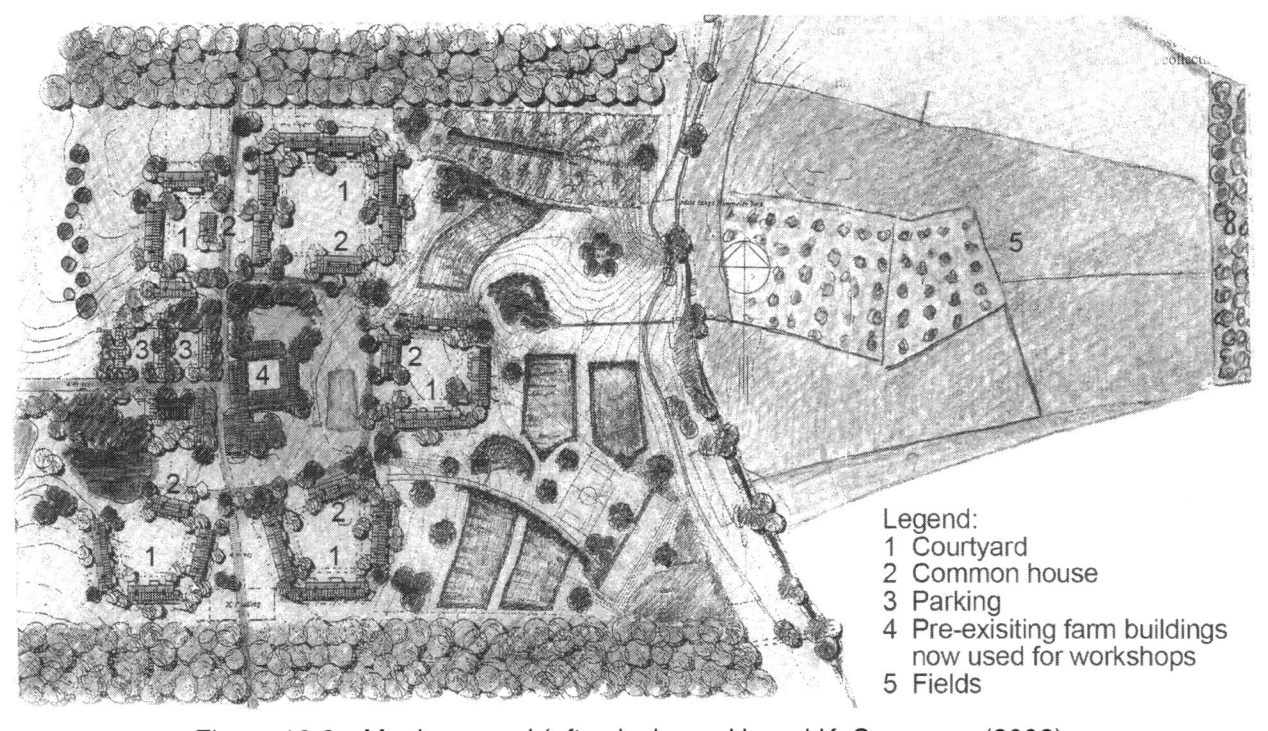

Legend:
1 Courtyard
2 Common house
3 Parking
4 Pre-exisiting farm buildings now used for workshops
5 Fields

Figure 18.2: *Munksøgaard (after* Jackson, H. and K. Svensson (2002).

All of these strategies have been applied in *Egebjerggard*, a fully planned 'new town' near Copenhagen that incorporates a strong social and environmental agenda informed by the success of cohousing. *Egebjerggard* has a distinctly urban character and a legible hierarchy of squares, streets, neighbourhoods and gathering nodes. With 600–700 dwellings on 27.5 hectares, it is twice the density of traditional Danish townships yet it incorporates 8.1 hectares of forest, open space, water bodies and agricultural land, all within a stroll or bike ride of the dwellings. Housing, schools, shops, offices, studios, industries and services are fully integrated. Neighbourhoods of distinctly different architectural character improve legibility, establish solidarity amongst neighbours and strengthen their sense of belonging. Participatory design, sweat equity, and urban artwork are implemented to the same end.

The housing provision strategy emphasises choice. Housing for the elderly is situated within an easy walk of parks, services and buses. Townhouses with private yards are provided for families and apartments or affordable housing for singles, couples, single parents and communal groups. People could choose to live in separate households, in groupings of 5 -10 units, or cohousing-like configurations of 25 – 50 units with a common house, designed to encourage a "mixed residential composition and a variety of mutual learning".[22] *Egebjerggard* exemplifies the humanistic traditions of Danish urban design. Its human scale and social underpinning render it another important model of sustainable human settlement.

The importance of successful examples of ecologically sustainable development cannot be overstated.

> An important aspect of effective social change campaigns may be to inform the audience of "success stories" where change is occurring and yielding benefits. There are many public and private initiatives at the local, national and international levels representing progress toward sustainability that could be publicised in a social change campaign.[23]

Photos 18.1 and 18.2: *Egebjerggard* - images showing integrated town square, shops and offices (left) and a common house overlooking a rainwater detention pond (right).

Fritjof Capra warns of impending ecological disaster for the "polluted, nuclearized, economically imperilled societies" of the West.[24] He argues that the literature on the subject – the "outpouring of books and articles that, taken together, are unique in the world for the breadth and depth of the new-paradigm solutions they propose" – is being ineffective for the want of more concrete examples of sustainability theory being applied in practice.

As a working example of sustainable human settlement, cohousing demonstrates, above all else, a civilised way to live in dense, urban situations where the pressures of propinquitous living with increasingly stressed human beings might otherwise lead to increasing anxiety and social dysfunction.

It remains to be seen just how popular cohousing will become. The recent involvement of housing developers in the creation of cohousing shows that 'community' can have currency in a capitalist marketplace. Popular American futurist, Faith Popcorn, has little doubt that cohousing will become widespread:

> [C]o-housing (sic) will Click in the decade and century ahead. In place of real estate agents, we'll have Co-housing Counsellors, akin to certified social workers, who will match up would-be neighbors or housemates. We'll have Co-housing Clearinghouses on the Internet or 900- number phone lines, where people can post openings in co-housing communities and screen applicants. And maybe someday we'll be watching the evening news on Election Night and hear reports on how the "co-housing vote" is swinging. Because co-housing – and the tightly knit new Clans that it creates – promises to be that big a phenomenon. [25]

However, even if cohousing does not become as widespread as Popcorn envisages, it still has the potential to contribute significantly to the future development of ecologically and socially sustainable human settlement. This theme will be further explored in the next and final chapter.

Notes:

[1] Perkins, D. D. and M. A. Zimmerman (1995). "Empowerment Theory, Research, and Application". American Journal of Community Psychology **23**(5): 569-579: 570.

[2] Perkins, D. D., B. B. Brown, et al. (1996). "The Ecology of Empowerment: Predicting Participation in Community Organisations". Journal of Social Issues **52**(1): 85-110: 86.

[3] Perkins, D. D., B. B. Brown, et al. (1996: 86).

[4] Saegert, S. and G. Winkel (1996). "Paths to Community Empowerment: Organising at Home". American Journal of Community Psychology **24**(4): 517-550: 546.

[5] Perkins, D. D. and M. A. Zimmerman (1995: 571).

[6] Zimmerman, M. A., B. A. Israel, et al. (1992). "Further Exploration in Empowerment Theory: An Empirical Analysis of Psychological Empowerment". American Journal of Community Psychology **20**(6): 707-727.

[7] Zimmerman, M. A. (1990). "Taking Aim on Empowerment Research: On the Distinction Between Individual and Psychological Concepts". American Journal of Community Psychology **18**(1): 169-177: 173.

[8] Wates, N. and C. Knevitt (1987). Community Architecture: How People are Creating their own Environment. London, Penguin Books. See also Towers, G. (1995). Building Democracy: Community architecture in the inner cities. London, UCL Press.

[9] Perkins, D. D., P. Florin, et al. (1990). "Participation and the Social and Physical Environment of Residential Blocks: Crime and Community Context". American Journal of Community Psychology **18**(1): 83 – 115: 85.

[10] Perkins, D. D., P. Florin, et al. (1990: 88).

[11] Speer, P. W. and J. Hughey (1995). "Community Organising: An Ecological Route to Empowerment and Power". Ibid. **25**(5): 729-748: 737.

[12] Perkins, D. D., B. B. Brown, et al. (1996:90).

[13] Chavis, D. M. and A. Wandersman (1990). "Sense of Community in the Urban Environment: A Catalyst for Participation and Community Development". American Journal of Community Psychology **18**(1): 55-81: 73.

[14] Personal communication with a Nyland Cohousing member, 1996.

[15] Hollick, M. (1997). Achieving Sustainable Development: The Eco-Village Contribution. Perth, University of Western Australia: 105.

[16] de Graaf, J., D. Wann, et al. (2001). Affluenza: The All-Consuming Epidemic. San Francisco, Berrett-Koehler: 64.

[17] de Graaf, J., D. Wann, et al. (2001: 64).

[18] Weston, J. (1986). The Greens, 'Nature' and the Social Environment. Red and Green, the New Politics of the Environment. J. Weston. London, Pluto Press: 14.

[19] Poulter, S. and J. How (1991). New Communities. Diggers and Dreamers. Sheffield, Communal Network: pp. 23-32.

[20] Jackson, H. and K. Svensson (2002). Ecovillage Living: Restoring the Earth and Her People. Devon, Green Books: 162.

[21] Jackson, H. and K. Svensson (2002: 164).

[22] Perks, W. T. and D. R. Van Vliet (1993). Assessment of Built Projects for Sustainable Communities, Canada Mortgage and Housing Corporation: 110. Note that the size of these clusters was deemed the minimum necessary to support a common house without requiring the participation of all residents

[23] Corson, W. H. (1995). "Priorities for a Sustainable Future: The Role of Education, the Media and Tax Reform". Journal of Social Issues **51**(4): 37-61: 56.

[24] Capra, F. (1984). Green Politics. NY, Dutton: 194.

[25] Popcorn, F. and L. Marigold (1996). Clicking: 16 Trends to Future Fit Your Life, Your Work and Your Business. New York, Harper Collins: 2.

19 Sustainable Community: applying the lessons

> It is "up to us" to show that there are other, better, viable alternatives. Rather than destroy, reform or convert the forces which maintain violence and injustice in society, the aim is to make them so redundant and so irrelevant to human purposes that they will whither and die.[1]

This book offers findings and speculation resulting from an investigation of cohousing, a new form of collective housing that directly addresses matters of social and environmental sustainability. Analysis of multiple data sets has generated a conceptual model that reveals the nexus between the social dynamics of communal group and the environmental praxis of its members. The process of empowerment has been invoked as the means by which residents take control of their circumstance and are able and motivated to improve their environment – which is the essence of effective environmentalism and a means by which excessive consumerism can be recognised and diffused.

The book argues that empowerment and grass roots community development are critical to the process of social change toward a future sustainable society. Key to these processes is their collectivist or communalist dimension. David Ronfeldt believes that 'collaborative networks' will become the principle organisational instrument underlying post-industrial society. He argues that civil society will be the realm most strengthened by the implementation of such networks, "auguring a vast rebalancing of relations among state, market, and civil-society actors around the world".[2] Happily, there is evidence that such a sea change is already well underway, at different levels and in different contexts.

Collaborative networking has certainly characterised the rise of a particular phenomenon central to this book, 'voluntary simplicity' or its variant, 'downshifting', i.e. people choosing to live more simply and with less – usually with a commensurate reduction in income. The voluntary simplicity (VS) movement (or perhaps more correctly, trend) is commonly anchored within small, localised, discussion groups or 'study circles' with no greater agenda than the social and practical support of participants. Groups meet regularly in the homes of members to share experiences and develop strategies for living less material and more meaningful lifestyles. In the process they feel empowered and build a sense of community. Gerald Celente of the US Trends Research Institute said of VS in 1996, "in our seventeen years of tracking trends, never have we seen an issue gaining such [widespread] acceptance".[3] In Australia, a 2002 survey found that 23% of adults aged between 30 and 50 had downshifted during the preceding decade. Clive Hamilton, Executive Director of the Australia Institute ("Australia's foremost public interest think tank"),[4] makes the following observation.

> Given the pressure to define success in terms of increasing income and displays of consumer goods, it is astonishing to find that such a large proportion of the population has rejected the materialist preoccupation of Australian society and chosen to emphasise other, non-material aspects of life.[5]

Although, the term VS was coined by Duane Elgin in his book of that name, the instigator of the first study circles and catalyst for the 'movement' was Cecile Andrews, a Seattle community college teacher. "The thing about voluntary simplicity," says Andrews, "is that it looks so benign. People don't understand how radical it is. It's the Trojan Horse of social change. It's really getting people to live in a totally different way".[6]

Takis Fotopoulos has vehemently argued that such 'lifestyle' modalities can never contribute to, let alone constitute, a coherent social movement due to their lack of a political agenda and a clear set of goals, strategies and ideals.[7] Yet, whilst indiscriminate use of the word 'movement' is clearly problematic, it seems equally problematic in 2004 to deny the existence of a voluntary simplicity or downshifting 'movement'.

A future sustainable society?

The remainder of this final chapter is unapologetically speculative. It offers a utopian vision of a future sustainable society predicated on the findings of this book and the expectation that, ultimately, the vast majority of human beings will either choose, learn, or *be forced* to live radically differently in order to survive with others in a civilised manner.

A 'limits to growth' scenario demands increased self-sufficiency at the local level. The first, essential step toward self-sufficiency is to reduce material need. This is more viable and more satisfying if implemented collaboratively. Cohousing demonstrates how collaboration in socially cohesive groups provides the requisite knowledge, skills and motivation to live with less and, in a psychological sense, to live as comfortably. Cohousing life offers social substitutes for the satisfactions currently derived from consumerism. But given that an insignificant proportion of the population is likely to live in cohousing as such, how might a future sustainable society otherwise manifest?

Visions of a future sustainable society are often invoked by radical Greens and futurists (such as Shumacher, Bookchin and Sale) and variously referred to as post-industrial, post-scarcity or post-materialist society.[8] Some of the features commonly thought likely of such a society include:

- *Decentralisation* toward a Schumacherian "small is beautiful" scenario whereby people collaborating in small groups take control of their resources and responsibility for their locale.
- Growing numbers of non-traditional households and social sub-groups, with an increased emphasis on *extended family* and *community*.
- The growth of *networking*, 'grass-roots' media and the Internet – all of which promote alternatives to the status quo (previously radical ideas which, with greater exposure, become accepted).

The seminal *Blueprint for Survival* anticipated, in the early 1970s, the growth of just such a future sustainable society. Community-based relationships, its authors claimed, in combination with a renewed sense of citizenship, would supplant consumerist desires and attachment to material goods. Living in small-scale communities would enable individuals to overcome atomisation and anonymity. Members would be less impelled to assert themselves in competition with others because human relationships would be deeper and more empathetic.

That this could happen in conservative, urbanised Australia certainly challenges the imagination, though not that of Barry Jones, a leading Australian intellectual, who envisages a "post-service society, which could be a golden age of leisure and personal development based on the cooperative use of resources".[9] Some such trends are already occurring in Australia. The rise of social activism since the 1970s and the popularity of 'alternative lifestyles' signifies the emergence of a grass-roots 'alternative' culture – one that prefigures "a new sort of society".[10] The increasing rate of ecological and social degradation is itself acting as a catalyst for change even amongst traditionally conservative forces.

Whilst grass-roots strategies generally contest the status quo, they are not, in the twenty-first century, revolutionary. The "new social movements"[11] are not the source of social breakdown and chaos that some of their opponents claim. They value democracy and plurality, and prefer to raise fundamental 'moral' concerns: peaceful non-exploitative relations, the integrity of the environment and rights of equity, accessibility and participation etc. Social activists nowadays continue to address relations of power between society and the state, but are not interested in a politically conceived, frontal assault on the state. Rather, they seek to expand *civil* society. This is just as well, because in conservative Australia, with its political system that offers little real choice, attempts to liberalise government policy generally fail or meet with only moderate success. It is perhaps more effective to have such 'moral' values subversively "seep into institutional structures, transforming their practices and mentalities".[12]

Respected Australian philosopher, Robyn Eckersley, argues that visionary values and aspirations can only spread if they "connect with people's experience", as opposed to being "mere mental compensation for, or a means of escape from, the shortcomings of the status quo".[13] Cultural and artistic expression is an important means of promoting visionary possibilities through 'connecting with people's experience'. There is a long tradition amongst radicals and visionaries of advancing their rhetoric in literature, art, music and film. Contemporary enviro-communalist visionaries need to similarly represent their vision(s) in a variety of cultural forms.

An illustration of the power of cultural expression to raise mass consciousness is played out annually at the Woodford Folk Festival, near Brisbane, Australia. The wonder of Woodford is that for six days in the heat of summer, 100,000 citizens come together in complete social harmony. Despite the challenging conditions (eg. mid-summer camping in the tropics) there is no apparent crime, hardly an angry word spoken and little disrespect of the environment. Those attending are of every background, colour and political persuasion. Woodford provides a window into a world where ethnic traditions are treasured, racial diversity is celebrated, political difference is respected and people of every kind enjoy each other's company. The human spectra represented include: black-white, young-elderly, straight-gay, radical-conservative, alternative-mainstream etc. However, the blurring of traditional polarities is such that they almost entirely lose their meaning.

The musical and artistic expression is important, of course. However, its value lies not just in the entertainment provided by a few 'star' performers. Woodford provides an opportunity for a rich sharing of cultural expression of all kinds. Musicians, poets, storytellers, artists, craftspeople, academics, indigenous elders, religious leaders and the 'great unrecognised', all openly share their skills, knowledge and wisdom in workshops, forums and participatory performance. The Woodford ambience encourages widespread cross-pollination of artistic expression such that, even for the professionals, the greatest reward is likely to come from spontaneous performance in ad hoc combinations of artists where ideas are developed, boundaries extended, and fresh enthusiasm gained. It is at events such as Woodford that cultural and artistic expression profoundly moves forward and becomes richer. Established traditions are reinforced and new ones initiated.

Woodford provides a safe environment for the exploration of alternative values, visions and aspirations. Discussion of 'alternatives' is a feature of a comprehensive program of intellectual exchange. Each year, many first time festival-goers experience the social cohesion and generosity of spirit that pervades the festival. Many leave the event having reassessed their own privatised lifestyles in the light of the 'sense of community' that the festival generates. Sadly, most return to their mainstream existence in the socially bleak Australian suburbs.

But need it be that way?

Sustainable community: a grass-roots perspective

> Contemporary Australian society seems overwhelmed by social problems. At a time of apparent economic prosperity, community anxiety about family breakdown, drug abuse, gambling, youth suicide, violence and home invasion continues to mount. …These social problems broadly reflect steadily increasing

> loneliness, alienation and social exclusion. Since the late 1960s our society has seen the collapse or erosion of many of the social structures around which people built relationships, personal worth and belonging.[14]

So wrote Australian parliamentarian, Lindsay Tanner, in a newspaper article entitled *Anti-social disease is spreading: Welcome to Lonely Street, Australia*. Tanner argued that during the 1950s and '60s, material well-being was the "guiding story" of Australian society. During the 1960s, however, personal growth and individual freedom emerged as another 'guiding story'. It has recently become clear, he continues, that "simplistic concepts of liberation no longer provide the answers to our contemporary social problems".[15] A new guiding story is required, Tanner argues…one with social objectives that ensure a 'sense of belonging' through participation in community life and in society.

Tanner advocates "building a new community framework to counter alienation, social exclusion and loneliness". He calls for a halt to the progressive dismantling of community-based structures (sporting clubs, neighbourhood centres, playgroups, residents' associations and community health centres etc.) as a long-term effect of capitalism and in the current climate of economic rationalism. Rather, Tanner demands that strategies be established for *boosting* community development in urban and suburban areas. Social scientist, Jim Ife, concurs:

> The challenge of developing community-based structures in urban and suburban areas is a critical one…Finding adequate strategies for community development in such locations is therefore, a major priority, and unless this can be achieved the potential of a genuine community-based alternative will not be recognised.[16]

A 1970s proposal aimed at achieving such an outcome for the city of Melbourne advocated decentralising the city into a network of foci of graduating scale.[17] A hierarchy of nodes would be established: a central business district (CBD), district or regional centres, local or suburban foci and neighbourhood centres. Such a strategy, it was suggested, would create locally comprehensive clusters of urban facilities providing satisfying social and community contact at the scale of the neighbourhood and suburb. The scheme aimed to rationalise the distribution of work, leisure and cultural opportunities in a way that emphasised qualitative growth and reduced dependence on travel.

> The strong feelings of identity, respect and friendship that can spring from personal involvement with others provide the only creative basis from which people can be weaned from excessive reliance on quantitative growth measured by…the turnover of commodities, or the rate of touring mobility crammed into each day.[18]

The local foci would combine high-density residential accommodation with light industry and a transport interchange. Conveniences such as shopping, welfare, health, educational and other services would be available there, as well as entertainment, cultural and recreational facilities. Local foci would be closely coupled, via an extensive shuttle-bus service, with a network of neighbourhood centres. These would operate at the scale of the suburban block and would coordinate such activities as childcare and shopping. This would facilitate daily contact as a means of alleviating the isolation and boredom of suburban living. The close coordination of the two scales of participation was seen as a means of liberating the captive sector of the community (such as single parents, children, the disabled, the poor and the elderly) by providing, in microcosm, a "magnetic and accessible world of affairs".

While the proposal was fundamentally sound and well-meaning, it was still representative of the deterministic 'top-down' planning paradigm of the 1970s – an exercise in 'community planning' born of the traditional relationship between the professional and society. It failed to elaborate the necessity for *grassroots* community control at the local level over reconfiguration of the urban environment, opting instead for the sort of governmental concern for community welfare that has shown since the '70s to effect little social justice.

Genuine grassroots strategies and outcomes whereby community development springs and grows from *within* the community would be fundamentally more radical. The CEM can be utilised here, to conceptualise such a process. Empowerment occurs slowly and iteratively as people get to know each other and become sufficiently bonded as to be able to mobilise their forces. Therefore, the establishment of caring and supportive interpersonal relations and the consequent building of a sense of community should precede or at least accompany structural measures. Rather than the allocation of services, such a 'social planning' process should begin by encouraging greater interaction between people in everyday life. "Informal discussions can be the beginning of a deeper consciousness raising dialogue, and can be a first step towards effectively empowering a person to become active at community level".[19]

The creation of neighbourhood centres is an obvious first step in the process. "Without such a focal point...it is hard to see how a good deal of other community development could take place".[20] Neighbourhood centres provide a relaxed, informal setting for socialising, childcare, information sharing, group discussions and so on. From there it becomes feasible, even in an otherwise conventional suburban setting, to establish a centrally located 'common house' with workshop, office space, computer room, laundry or vegetable garden that would enable many people's social and vocational aspirations to be met, efficiently and affordably, close to home. Through self-management of such resources, relationships would be built and networks strengthened.

A socially cohesive neighbourhood of participating members might collectively own garden and woodworking tools, washing machines, lawn mowers, books, recreational equipment, games, bicycles, computers and even vehicles. Individuals or households might take responsibility on behalf of the whole community for the storage, care and maintenance of particular items. This not only allocates responsibility, but also creates a role for a person in the community; perhaps someone who might otherwise feel marginalised.

Cohousing has demonstrated how these measures work well at the scale of the neighbourhood. It provides the requisite economy of scale, but is small enough for residents to get to know each other and develop sufficient trust. The long and difficult cohousing development process is not a prerequisite for cohousing-like outcomes, however, as the so-called *retrofit* cohousing model discussed in Chapter 7 demonstrates.

N Street Cohousing has parallels in Australia, one of which involved four families living in Thornbury, Victoria, who decided to demolish their fences and establish a community with the following features: a "luxurious" shared vegetable garden and compost mulcher; a large play space for children; the sharing of a lawnmower, washing machines, sets of tools, a dog, a cat and a rabbit; the conversion of garages into a food store, a tool shed, a workroom and a rumpus room for the kids; and monthly shopping for bulk food items (Figure 19.1).[21] The people involved became close, supportive friends. The operation of their small cooperative helped build a sense of community and provide members with the time and facilities for satisfying, non-domestic pursuits. The community still exists at time of writing and has grown to include six households.

Normative values of private ownership and consumerism are the greatest obstacles to increased collaboration, sharing and trust. Yet collaborative alternatives are essential, claims Jim Ife, "if we are to move towards a society where there is a lower level of material consumption (which from an ecological point of view is inevitable) without a corresponding reduction in the quality of life".[22] Critical to the process of developing the necessary trust, is due and fair process in the management

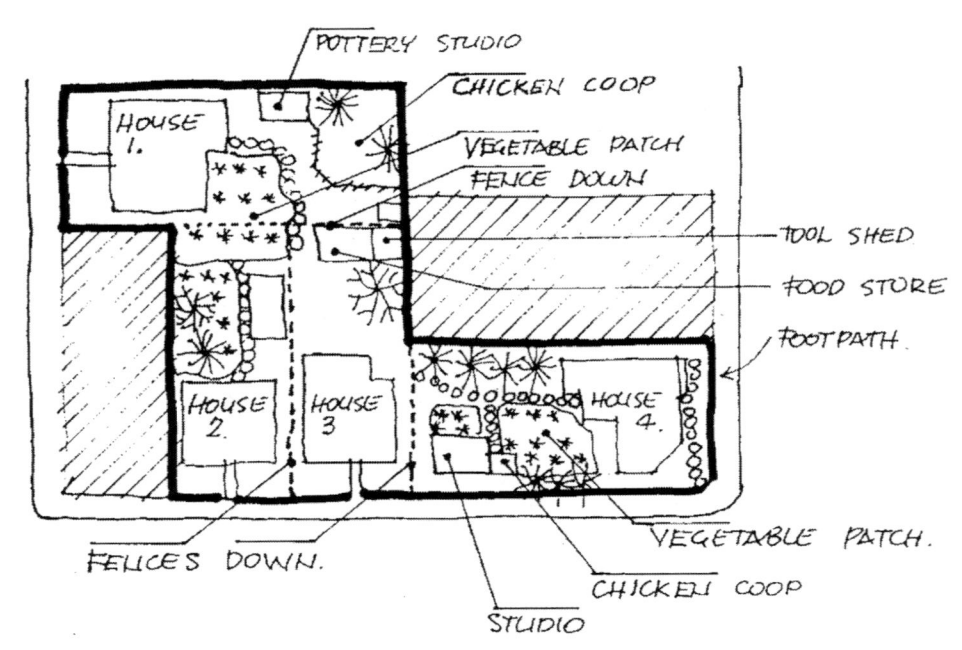

Figure 19.1: An example of retro-fit collaborative housing in Australia (after Baird 1984).

of community resources. Participation will only be encouraged if communities configure decision-making processes and formal meeting procedures to make them accessible and inclusive. Conventional procedures can be very alienating. Consensus-based decision-making processes are more likely to overcome disincentives to participation.

As community development takes effect and relationships of trust are established – along with agreements and instrumentalities that ensure fair and due process – more radical changes could be considered. Communities comprising several neighbourhoods (at the scale of the district, perhaps) might grasp the authority and take the responsibility to initiate and manage resources and services in a way that best suits their purposes. Schools, libraries, halls, shops, parks and recreational facilities could become the responsibility of the community rather than a single bureaucratic or commercial interest. This would serve to better integrate and coordinate community activities and facilitate the acquisition, production and distribution of essential resources.

The latent human resources of the community could be used to provide readily accessible services to help solve individual and collective problems. In the process, professional monopolies would be dismantled and the contribution of all community members would be more valued. Education, for example, could be the responsibility of many people, not just professional educators. People would learn from each other in different contexts and at all stages of their lives, not just when they are young. Health and welfare needs of all kinds could be dealt with at the community level. Dependents might be the community's responsibility, rather than the family's or the State's, and their needs would be met locally. When people needed practical, social or emotional support, they could turn to those with whom they were familiar.

The need for affordable housing is, and will increasingly become, a critical factor in the development of sustainable communities. Yet there are few, if any, areas where the contrast between conventional (consumerist) approaches and sustainable alternatives is so great. The provision of sufficient affordable (let alone socially and environmentally appropriate) housing appears to be beyond the capabilities of conventional instrumentalities and processes. There is a need to reconceptualize the processes involved in housing design, production, use and demolition.

The intervention of middlepersons such as designers, engineers and bureaucrats often constitute a financial and temporal barrier to the procurement of housing. Their attitudes are often embedded within a consumerist ethos that favours brand new buildings, fresh out of their wrapper. A grass-roots perspective, on the other hand, would see building procurement as an evolving, creative and reparative activity. Design might become an ongoing process infused with user input and control. Construction and assembly might integrate with adaptation, extension and upgrading. Housing *facilitation* might be an evolving process that responds to the changing needs and visions of residents.

Wellesly-Miller would make available in vast numbers, a 'start-up' structure based on a common kit of parts. Unique variations would then be instigated by the occupants.

> A 'start-up' structure is built and moved into immediately. Over time the structure is extended and added to, new systems are incorporated, and the older ones integrated or sold. After some time a relatively stable state is reached, and the mature dwelling enters a long cycle of tuning, upgrading and adaptation.[23]

At the level of the district, Wellesly-Miller suggests, a regime of incremental growth according to need could become self-perpetuating as the adaptation of one building stimulated the development of another as parts were upgraded and exchanged. Located within each district might be a facility that is to the house-maker what the library is to the scholar; perhaps an expanded, service oriented timberyard providing not just construction materials, but also planning guidelines, instruction manuals for various building operations and assistance with ordering and estimating.

Clearly, many existing legal and structural mechanisms would have difficulty accommodating these concepts. A radical new approach to building approval would be required, which assesses building *process*, rather than the completed edifice. Similarly, a new regime of building contracts would need to evolve to accommodate varying degrees of user control over the building process. Many would build for themselves; others would contract out the difficult initial stages of set-out, foundations and work up to floor level. Some might wish to work with contractors until the shell is secured and carry out later modifications themselves. Agencies borne of need might be formed to offer advice on matters of design, materials and construction methods in a way that promotes better housing and reinforces self-reliance. A genuine *grass roots* architecture might evolve from within the community itself.

While many of these concepts are 'foreign' in the West, they are not, of course, in the developing world. In developing countries, a half to three quarters of all new housing is built by the residents themselves, who "show resourcefulness and economy rare in the throw-away developed world".[24] Empowerment and collaboration are critical factors in the process. People are aware of their own needs, what they can achieve with available resources and the way in which mutual aid renders seemingly overwhelming tasks possible.

How might utilities (i.e. power, heat and water supply) be accommodated within socially cohesive neighbourhoods, or districts of such neighbourhoods? Electricity can certainly be generated at the local level – and should be from a sustainability perspective, given the inherent inefficiencies of large, remote power stations. At the scale of the single building or housing cluster, solar power generation using photovoltaic power is at last becoming viable. A recently constructed US cohousing project, for example, has installed state-of-the-art photovoltaic roof sheeting. In Australia and elsewhere deregulation of the electricity market has enabled households and small collectives to generate and sell surplus power back to the grid, thus bypassing problematic battery storage and further improving viability. Wind generators are already popular among collectives of farmers and villagers in Denmark. In a future sustainable society of decentralised collaborative communities, they will be another attractive option.

At the scale of single buildings, passive solar design and solar panels are obvious means of heating space and water respectively. District heating *per se* is not new, but has been discredited in the past due to poorly conceived and managed installations in enclaves of social housing. These days, larger cohousing projects and some ecovillages are installing and self-managing their own centralised heating systems. Many are fuelled by wood chips, an otherwise wasted by-product of the timber industry. Others are simply tapping available heat from below grade using subterranean heat wells.

Technology known as Combined Power and Heat (CHP) is also well suited to power generation at the district scale. It already operates successfully in Copenhagen, Stockholm, Stuttgart and Helsinki. Because CHP units operate locally they minimise reticulation losses, are responsive to fluctuations in demand and can distribute 'waste' heat to consumers. Installation in existing urban neighbourhoods is sometimes considered impractical because the distribution of heat necessitates expensive retrofitting. Yet significant savings in piping and metering are available when neighbours collaborate to achieve efficiencies. CHP units are fuelled by gas, which is already available in most Western cities and have minimal harmful emissions. Such systems convert up to 80% of the available energy into useable form compared with about 30% in the case of traditional power stations.

Conventional water supply and sewerage treatment systems are inefficient for the vast distances that water and waste are transported and the enormous amounts of energy consumed in filtration, purification, treatment and disposal. Such systems are linear (i.e. inputs are unrelated to outputs), conveying water from distant catchments to be used just once and then delivered as waste into rivers and oceans. Yet the same chain of supply and disposal can just as easily be a closed loop operating at the neighbourhood level. Earthsong Eco-Neighbourhood, Quayside Village and Kyōdō no mori have piloted urban rainwater management and grey water recycling systems.

These technologies are well suited to building clusters and neighbourhoods. Even sewerage treatment can be safely and efficiently handled by consensual communities. Composting toilets and bio-treatment systems have long been operating successfully in intentional communities and ecovillages in several countries. Similar systems suited to urban situations have been successfully piloted in numerous locations, but seldom applied due to restrictive regulatory control. Some comprise thickly vegetated holding tanks contained within humid, verdant greenhouses. The output water, if not potable, is certainly suitable for grey water usage or horticultural purposes.

All of these technologies become viable when neighbours collaborate and districts of adjoining neighbourhoods coordinate their efforts. It seems unlikely that within any given district there would not be the expertise available to maintain such systems. If not, it would be worthwhile, surely, to train a team of local personnel to do so. They would be employed within their locality and through interaction with friends and neighbours would inform and motivate others to utilise power, heat and water efficiently; catalysing a community of conservers from a populace of consumers.

Concluding thoughts

Debate about the form and fabric of a future sustainable society can only ever be speculative. There can be no best, optimal, preferred or otherwise pre-empted development trajectory, let alone a pre-determined outcome. The desirable characteristics or qualities of a future sustainable society are not *prescribed* in this or any other book. They are not even universally agreed. Nor is a sustainable society going to be a completely static one. Growth and change are inevitable and desirable characteristics of any human endeavour. Yet, a vision of a better world is necessary in order that the first step in the journey be taken with optimism.

At the beginning of the new millennium, there are dramatically increasing numbers of people who are disillusioned and disaffected by mainstream politics, overly bureaucratic institutions and pervasive consumerism. There is massive discontent with warmongering by the US, Britain and Australia, and growing international protest against the ills of globalisation. Many of the most disaffected are working toward an alternative reality – a more sustainable and humane future for themselves, their families, their collaborators and for society. Whether it be in cohousing, ecovillages, neighbourhood centres, or simply in conversation 'over the back fence', people everywhere are collaboratively seeking 'alternative' ways of being in the world.

With the application of modern communications and networking, 'cells' of alternative thinkers and actors naturally coagulate into larger and more viable cells. In 2004, it seems reasonable to suggest that they comprise a genuine social movement. It seems just possible that in time this 'alternative sector' may deliver a paradigm shift and the "forces which maintain violence and injustice in society…will become so redundant and irrelevant…that they will whither and die".[25]

It may be pertinent to conclude with a reminder of the social norms and values of indigenous Australians. Aboriginal peoples might be considered poor from a conventional Western perspective yet they have much to teach us about interpersonal and community relations. "Their material throughput is small, but their security within the group is high. Ideas, information, stories, songs, humour, grief, listening and talking – the human [or *social*] aspects of human existence – are abundant and readily shared".[26] Once we realise that humans might prefer to be pro-social, through sharing, collaboration and participation in the activities of a cohesive human group then there are numerous aspects of society we might choose to redefine. Such changes would be profound. Ultimately, they might deliver a culture far more benign, sustainable and satisfying of basic human needs than any in human history.

The 'good news' is that such changes are already underway, as documented by David Suzuki and Holly Dressel in their book, *Good News for a Change*.

> [N]o matter where people live on the earth, when they focus on this vision of community equality and long term sustainability rather than on wealth or personal financial security, they evolve similar management methods and attitudes that create much healthier and more stable societies. The new precepts for living that they are developing not only are increasing our chances for survival, they have an unexpected dividend; they are helping to discover very deep forms of satisfaction and joy.[27]

Notes:

[1] Kelly, A. and S. Sewell (1988). With Head, Heart and Hand. Brisbane, Boolarong Press: 101.

[2] Ronfeldt, D. F. (1996). Tribes, Institutions, Markets, Networks: A Framework About Societal Evolution. Santa Monica, CA, Rand: 3.

[3] Quoted in de Graaf, J., D. Wann, et al. (2001). Affluenza: The All-Consuming Epidemic. San Francisco, Berrett-Koehler: 178.

[4] Hamilton, C. and R. Denniss (2005) Affluenza: When too much is never enough. Sydney, Allen & Unwin: i.

[5] Hamilton, C. and R. Denniss (2005: 154).

[6] Quoted in de Graaf, J., D. Wann, et al. (2001: 179).

[7] Fotopoulos, T. (2002). "Transitional strategies and the Inclusive Democracy project". Democracy and Nature: The International Journal of Inclusive Democracy 8(1).

[8] See Schumacher, E.F. (1974). Small is Beautiful. London, Sphere Books.
   Bookchin, M. (1990). Remaking Society: Pathways to a Green Future. Boston, South End Press
   Sale, K. (1991). Dwellers in the Land: The Bioregional Vision. Philadelphia, PA: New Society.

[9] Quoted in Baird, J. (1984). By Design: Changing Australian Housing. Melbourne, AE Press: 18.

[10] Altman, D. (1980). Rehearsals for Change: Politics and Culture in Australia. Melbourne, Fontana: 134.

[11] The new social movements anticipate a broad, general social liberation. They carry greater emphasis on collaborative values and lifestyles than traditional ideologies and emerge more from the middle than the working classes. They emphasise environmental and peace issues, feminism, and alternative non-consumerist lifestyles.

[12] Garner, R. (1995). Contemporary Movements and Ideologies. New York, McGraw-Hill: 385.

[13] Eckersley, R. (1992). Environmentalism and Political Theory: Toward an Ecocentric Approach. London, University of Central London Press: 186.

[14] Tanner, L. (1999). Anti-social disease is spreading: Welcome to Lonely Street, Australia. The Australian. Brisbane: 13.

[15] Tanner, L. (1999).

[16] Ife, J. (1997). Community Development: Creating Community Alternatives – Vision, Analysis and Practice. Melbourne, Longman: 119.

[17] White, D., P. Sutton, et al. (1978). Seeds for Change: Creatively Confronting the Energy Crisis. North Melbourne, Vic, Patchwork Press.

[18] White, D., P. Sutton, et al. (1978: 158).

[19] Ife, J. (1997: 149).

[20] Ife, J. (1997: 137).

[21] Baird, J. (1984).

[22] Ife, J. (1997: 185).

[23] Wellesly-Miller, S. (1972). Work Notes on the Need for a New Building Technology. The Responsive House. E. Allen. Cambridge, MIT Press: 19.

[24] Girardet, H. (1992). The GAIA Atlas of Cities: New directions for sustainable urban living. London, Gaia Books Limited: 128.

[25] Kelly, A. and S. Sewell (1988: 101).

[26] Clark, M. E. (1995). "Changes in Euro-American Values Needed for Sustainability". Journal of Social Issues 51(4): 63-82: 80.

[27] Suzuki, D. and H. Dressel (2002) Good News for a Change: Hope for a troubled planet. Sydney, Allen and Unwin: 4.

Bibliography

Alexander C., S. Ishikawa et al. (1977). *A Pattern Language*. NY, Oxford University Press.

Altman D. (1980). *Rehearsals for Change: Politics and Culture in Australia*. Melbourne, Fontana.

Bellah R. N., R. Madsen et al. (1996). *Habits of the Heart: Individualism and Commitment in American Life (Second Edition)*. Berkeley, University of California Press.

Bookchin M. (1990). *Remaking Society: Pathways to a Green Future*. Boston, South End Press.

Brundtland G. H. (1987). *Our Common Future*. Brussels, World Commission on Environment and Development.

Capra F. (1984). *Green Politics*. NY, Dutton.

de Graaf J., D. Wann et al. (2001). *Affluenza: The All-Consuming Epidemic*. San Francisco, Berrett-Koehler.

Dearling A. and G. Meltzer (2003). *Another kind of space: creating ecological dwellings and environments*. Lyme Regis, UK, Enabler Press.

Eckersley R. (1992). *Environmentalism and Political Theory: Toward an Ecocentric Approach*. London, University of Central London Press.

Garner R. (1995). *Contemporary Movements and Ideologies*. New York, McGraw-Hill.

Garreau J. (1991). *Title Edge city: life on the new frontier*. New York, Doubleday.

Girardet H. (1992). *The GAIA Atlas of Cities: New directions for sustainable urban living*. London, Gaia Books Limited.

Goldsmith E. R. Allen et al. (1972). "A Blueprint for Survival". The Ecologist 2(1): 1-43.

Hamilton, C. and R. Denniss (2005). *Affluenza: When Too Much Is Never Enough*. Sydney, Allen & Unwin.

Hanson C. (1996). *The Cohousing Handbook*. Vancouver, Hartley & Marks.

Hollick M. (1997). *Achieving Sustainable Development: The Eco-Village Contribution*. Perth, University of Western Australia.

Ife J. (1997). *Community Development: Creating Community Alternatives – Vision Analysis and Practice*. Melbourne, Longman.

Jackson H. and K. Svensson (2002). *Ecovillage Living: Restoring the Earth and Her People*. Devon, Green Books.

Kanter R. (1972). *Commitment and Community: Communes and Utopias in Social Perspective*. Cambridge, Harvard University Press.

Kelly A. and S. Sewell (1988). *With Head Heart and Hand*. Brisbane, Boolarong Press.

McCamant K. and C. Durrett (1994). *CoHousing: A Contemporary Approach to Housing Ourselves*. Berkeley, Habitat Press.

Meltzer G. (2000). *Cohousing: Toward Social and Environmental Sustainability*. PhD Thesis, Brisbane, The University of Queensland.

Misztal B. A. (1996). *Trust in Modern Societies*. Cambridge (UK), Polity Press.

Perks W. T. and D. R. Van Vliet (1993). *Assessment of Built Projects for Sustainable Communities*. Canada Mortgage and Housing Corporation.

Popcorn F. and L. Marigold (1996). *Clicking: 16 Trends to Future Fit Your Life Your Work and Your Business*. New York, Harper Collins.

Poulter S. and J. How (1991). New Communities. *Diggers and Dreamers*. Sheffield, Communal Network.

Ronfeldt D. F. (1996). *Tribes Institutions Markets Networks: A Framework About Societal Evolution*. Santa Monica CA, Rand.

Rudin D. and N. Falk (1999). *Building the 21st Century Home: The Sustainable Urban Neighbourhood*. Oxford, Architectural Press.

Sale K. (1991). *Dwellers in the Land: The Bioregional Vision*. Philadelphia PA, New Society.

Schumacher E.F. (1974). *Small is Beautiful*. London, Sphere Books.

Selznick P. (1992). *The Moral Commonwealth*. Berkeley, UC Press.

Suzuki, D. and H. Dressel (2002) *Good News for a Change: Hope for a troubled planet*. Sydney, Allen and Unwin.

Towers G. (1995). *Building Democracy: Community architecture in the inner cities*. London, UCL Press.

Wates N. and C. Knevitt (1987). *Community Architecture: How People are Creating their own Environment*. London, Penguin Books.

Wellesly-Miller S. (1972). Work Notes on the Need for a New Building Technology. *The Responsive House*. E. Allen (ed). Cambridge, MIT Press.

Weston J. (1986). The Greens 'Nature' and the Social Environment. *Red and Green the New Politics of the Environment*. J. Weston. London, Pluto Press.

White D. P. Sutton et al. (1978). *Seeds for Change: Creatively Confronting the Energy Crisis*. Melbourne, Patchwork Press.

Index

A
accessibility, 21, 24, 143, 164
acoustics, 25, 49, 126
affordability, vii, 21, 24, 61, 66, 69, 70, 78-81, 93, 97, 101, 143-145, 159, 168
Africa, 13, 14, 112
Agenda 21, 88
agreements, 110, 129, 150, 168
alienation, 3, 15, 165, 166
alternative lifestyles, 3, 4, 6, 158, 164
America, 1, 9, 10, 81, 124, 131, 132, 134, 141, 157
anti-consumerism, 10, 66, 105, 156
apartments, 10, 21, 122, 159
architectural character, 9, 70, 80, 121, 159
architectural form, 4, 6, 9, 99, 100, 119, 121, 123
architectural qualities, 90, 123
architecture, 3, 6-8, 15, 21, 30, 45, 49, 69, 80, 86, 95, 107, 108-111, 115, 119-121, 124, 152, 154, 158, 169
Asia, 13, 14, 77, 112
atrium, 4, 28, 30, 117
Australasia, 3, 125, 129, 132
Australia, 1, 3, 6, 10, 11, 81, 89, 93, 97, 99, 103-105, 110, 118, 119, 123, 134, 144, 148, 164, 165, 167, 169-171
authorities, 7, 12, 158

B
balconies, 22, 112
Barry Jones, 164
behavioural change, 1, 4, 105, 130, 133-136, 149
Berkeley Cohousing, **68-75**, 119, 122, 123, 127, 131, 140, 141, 144, 145, 149
Blueprint for Survival, 1, 164
bofælleskaber, 3, 6, 8, 125
building construction, 11, 25, 29, 30, 38, 46, 47, 54, 57, 69, 70, 87, 94, 99, 101, 110, 111, 115, 124, 131, 144, 169
building types, 10, 122
bulk food, 15, 40, 91, 102, 105, 126, 167
bulletin board, 32, 34

C
Canada, 3, 9, 23, 30, 133, 144
capitalism, 10, 166
car pooling, vii, 15, 42, 91, 96, 116, 132
car sharing, 116
Cascade Cohousing, 10, 93, **98-105**, 117, 119, 122-127, 133, 140, 141, 144, 149

celebration, 41, 42, 66, 148
    birthday, 27, 41, 64, 103, 104
centraal wonen, 6, 8
chickens, 64, 67, 105
childcare, 8, 24, 40, 47, 96, 104, 142, 159, 166, 167
children, 4, 8, 13, 21, 23, 27, 32, 40, 41, 86, 94-96, 103, 104, 117, 126, 132-134, 141, 142, 166, 167
Christopher Alexander, 38, 108
circumstance, 115-128, 151-155
    definition of, 115, 154
clustering, 29, 47, 86, 118, 119, 126, 144, 169, 170
cohousing,
    definition of, 2-5
Cohousing Cooperative, **92-97**, 99, 104, 116, 119, 140, 144, 149, 158
collaboration, 12, 15, 101, 107, 109, 112, 156, 164, 168, 169, 171
Combined Power and Heat, 169
commitment, 2, 6, 15, 27, 43, 62, 70, 83, 97, 102, 110, 111, 124, 136, 140, 147
committees, 25, 42, 49, 50, 124-126, 129, 150, 151
common dining room, 5, 44, 49, 54, 80, 121
common facilities, 2, 3, 5, 7-10, 12, 29, 30, 64, 70, 121, 129, 139, 140
common house, 5, 6, 7, 20, 22, 30, 36, 42-45, 48, 49, 53-58, 62-64, 67, 70, 71, 80, 86, 87, 92, 94, 95, 97-102, 121, 123, 134, 137, 139, 140, 143, 158, 159, 167
    definition of, 5
common interest, 2, 8
common meals, 3, 5, 8, 11, 22, 23, 32, 40, 42, 44, 49, 56, 58, 64, 67, 74, 100-105, 112, 124, 126, 129, 134, 148, 150
    systems, 25, 58, 103, 142
common values, 2, 66, 130, 133
communal living, 3, 4, 6, 7, 9, 10
communalism, 2, 3
commune, 2, 5, 6, 40, 43, 158
communication, 10, 24, 25, 29, 34, 41, 42, 50, 61, 104, 132, 148, 150, 153
community, 1-4, 25, 50, 51, 64, 67, 109, 124, 148, 150, 153, 156, 160, 164, 166
    definition of, 2
community architecture, 154
community design, 4, 9, 11, 12, 15, 38, 79, 86, 109-111, 121, 159
community development, 3, 13, 38, 163-168

Index 175

Community Empowerment Model, 154-156, 166
community life, 3, 5, 6, 24, 38, 49, 58, 126, 135, 154, 165
community psychology, 15, 153
commuting, 99, 157
composting, 86, 105, 115, 124, 125, 129, 135, 156, 167
condominium, 54, 129, 145
conferences, 3, 10
conflict, 25, 34, 104, 130, 133
conflict resolution, 12, 25, 42, 96, 150, 151
consensus, 5, 24, 25, 34, 42, 50, 51, 55, 70, 73, 86, 96, 110, 131, 150, 151, 168
construction materials, 7, 57, 66, 70, 86, 87, 90, 91, 94, 99, 100, 108, 111, 117, 123, 124, 131, 143, 169
consultants, 9, 30, 38, 55, 79, 109, 123, 144, 149
consumerism, 4, 10, 129, 137, 148, 163, 164, 168, 170
consumption, 1, 4, 40, 123, 125, 137, 138, 149, 156, 168
context, 121
contractors, 29, 30, 38, 46, 54, 69, 124, 158, 169
cooperatives, 9, 93
cost saving, 15, 88, 91, 94, 101, 169
Council, 53, 57, 69, 79, 88, 89, 91
courtyard, 4, 20, 22, 25, 45, 47, 95, 96, 112, 117, 158
creativity, 27, 31, 32, 49, 99, 104, 148
cultural expression, 49, 148, 164, 165
customisation, 30, 47, 143
cycling, 66, 104, 116, 117

D
David Ronfeldt, 163
decision-making, 5, 12, 24, 25, 27, 34, 42, 50, 70, 72, 86, 96, 110, 123, 131, 150, 151, 153, 168
demographics, 9, 131
Denis Altman, 10
Denmark, 3, 6-9, 99, 125, 126, 158, 159, 169
density, 7, 10, 21, 81, 107, 109, 116-122, 159, 166
developers, 9, 79, 81, 109, 158, 160
development process, 12, 25, 45, 51, 57, 124, 144, 150, 167
diet, 49, 58, 126
disabled, the, 23, 86, 94, 132, 143, 159, 166
diversity, 38
   demographic, 5, 21, 24, 25, 27, 31, 42, 131-135, 143, 148, 165
   of cohousing, 4, 9, 16, 121
double-glazing, 66, 111
downshifting. *See* voluntary simplicity
Doyle Street Cohousing, 72, 79

Dr Namiko Minai, 12
driving, 1, 115, 116
Duane Elgin, 163
duplex, 21, 37, 38, 64, 65, 73, 122
Duwamish Cohousing, 114
dwelling size, vii, 14, 23, 30, 70, 100, 105, 121, 122, 138, 141, 143, 156, 159

E
Earthsong Eco-Neighbourhood, 11, **84-91**, 119, 122-124, 139, 140, 144, 145, 149, 170
ecologically sustainable development, 1, 158, 160
economy of scale, 23, 94, 124, 126, 144, 167
ecovillage, 11, 85, 158, 169, 170
edge city, 29
education, 11, 13, 46, 89, 130, 131
efficacy, 147, 149, 150-153, 156
   definition of, 149
Egebjerggard, 159, 160
elderly, the, 9, 12, 21, 25, 27, 86, 132, 142, 158, 159, 166
embodied energy, 67, 70, 87, 123
employment, vii, 115, 131, 132
empowerment, 2, 3, 152-157, 163, 166, 169
   definition of, 2, 152, 153
energy, 15, 86, 88, 99, 117, 124, 170
energy conservation, 70, 88, 89, 129, 135
energy efficiency, 23, 83, 86, 99, 105, 115
engagement, 147-151, 155
   definition of, 147, 155
environmental awareness, 1, 4, 11, 129, 132-136, 149, 152, 165
environmental impact, 1, 4, 11, 61, 69, 70, 99, 115, 123, 124, 129
environmental practices, 24, 66, 105, 124, 129, 130, 132, 135-137, 142, 147
environmental praxis, 136, 154, 155, 163
environmental sustainability, 1, 4, 153
environmental values, 1, 3, 66, 129, 130, 147, 148, 150, 152
environmentalism, 1, 105, 136, 151, 156, 157, 163
equity, 143, 164
exchange, 10, 15, 34, 41, 129, 132, 147
expertise, 24, 42, 53, 55, 125, 129, 131, 132, 170
experts, 24, 54, 123, 129-131
extended family, 13, 14, 37, 74, 133, 134, 142, 164

F
facilitation, 25, 51, 55, 96, 168
families, 13, 14, 25, 96, 117, 142, 159
family life, 10, 66, 148
feminism, 8, 97
fences, 10, 61-63, 66, 167, 170

festivals, 40, 41, 165
financing, 5, 7, 9, 25, 30, 38, 40, 46, 54, 69, 93, 94, 96, 110, 112, 124, 143-145, 168
food procurement, 40, 42, 43, 67, 83, 103, 124, 126, 129, 167, 168
free box, 125, 148
Fureai houses, 12

G
gated housing, 15, 97
gemeinschaft, 2
gentrification, 45, 79
Georgie Award, 23, 30
government, 9, 21, 93, 94, 144, 145, 151, 157, 164, 166
grey water, 23, 86, 105, 111, 158, 170

H
Hardiplank, 123
heating, 15, 91, 111, 123, 158, 169
    geothermal, 123, 169
heritage, 79
hierarchy, 5
Highline Crossing Cohousing, 118
Hildur Jackson, 158
HIV/AIDS, 14, 77
home ownership, 10, 157
homosexuality, 132, 134, 143
housing, 1, 7-14, 23, 29, 61, 69, 78-81, 93, 94, 97, 118, 119, 121, 144, 154, 158-160, 168, 169
HUD, 70

I
ideology, 14, 37, 112
income, 5, 21, 58, 93, 94, 132, 133, 143, 145
individuality, 10, 30, 41
indoor air quality, 123, 124, 143
influence, 129-132, 135, 155
infrastructure, 5, 14, 118, 123, 143
    centralisation of, 123
insulation, 57, 66, 70, 100, 111
intentional community, 2-5, 37, 38, 43, 118, 133, 148, 156, 158, 170
    definition of, 2
interaction, 4, 29, 42, 77, 81, 117, 129-135, 150, 152, 154, 155, 158, 166, 170
    definition of, 129, 155
interconnectivity, 4, 15
intimacy, 8, 32, 120, 142, 158
intimacy gradient, 120
intranet, 10, 34, 57, 94

J
Jackson Place Cohousing, 114

Japan, 3, 6, 11, 13, 108, 109, 110
Jim Ife, 166, 168

K
Kenzo Tange, 107
kollektivhuser, 6, 8
Korea, 11, 13
Kyōdō no mori Cohousing, **106-112**, 118, 119, 122, 140, 141, 144, 146, 149

L
land use, 4, 10, 14, 23, 29, 81, 85, 99, 107, 110, 117-119, 126, 159
landscaping, 22, 38, 43, 45, 47, 49, 57, 66, 87, 94, 99-101, 111, 115, 118, 120, 123, 129, 158
leadership, 96, 130, 131
levies, 5, 25
life-cycle analysis, 123
limits to growth, 164
Lindsay Tanner, 165
location, 2, 58, 70, 83, 85, 115, 116, 124, 143, 144
loss of community, 3, 13, 15
lot development, 9, 30
low-income, 7, 9, 12, 21, 77, 80, 93, 145, 159
low-rise, 6-9, 29, 109, 117

M
mainstream society, 3, 4, 6, 10, 83, 134, 152, 158, 159, 165, 170
maintenance, 12, 25, 43, 50, 54, 91, 96, 138, 167
Marsh Commons Cohousing, **53-60**, 117, 119, 122-124, 140, 141, 144, 149
McCamant and Durrett, 4-9, 16, 45, 62, 69, 70, 86, 99, 117, 121
meetings, 4, 22, 27, 32, 34, 38, 45, 50, 51, 55, 57, 58, 96, 97, 104, 109, 129, 133, 148, 150, 151, 168
Metabolism, 107, 110
methodology, 113
micro-climate, 106, 108
mission statement, 21, 23, 29, 99, 124, 129, 130, 143, 147, 148, 150, 157
mixed use, 81

N
Muir Commons, 9
N Street Cohousing, 55, **60-67**, 119, 122, 123, 134, 140, 141, 144, 145, 148, 149, 167
natural light, 57
neighbourhood, 3, 8, 72, 77, 81, 85, 86, 91, 115, 141, 166, 167, 170
neighbourhood centre, 166, 167
neighbourhood design, 4, 9
neighbourhood watch, 142

Index   177

neighbours, 10, 13-15, 104, 110, 120, 142, 152, 154, 156, 159
    outside the community, 7, 9, 10, 25, 38, 42, 81, 97, 111, 151
neo-vernacular, 6, 7, 9, 120
Netherlands, the, 6, 8, 9
networking, 10, 163, 164, 170
New Urbanism, 15
New Zealand, 3, 6, 10, 11, 88, 89
normative values, 1, 156
North America, 3, 6, 9, 10, 125

O

organic food, 15, 23, 34, 40, 57, 67, 83, 85, 105, 109, 124, 126, 129
outreach, 38, 42

P

parenting, 22, 24, 86, 133, 134, 142, 148
parking, 9, 21, 29, 49, 80, 89
participation, 2-5, 94, 103, 115, 129, 148-154, 164, 165, 168
passive solar design, 30, 86-88, 99, 100, 105, 111, 123, 169
paving, 47, 89
pedestrian street, 4, 28, 29, 30, 45, 80, 95, 117, 120
peer pressure, 125, 134
permaculture, 64, 85-87, 158
personal development, 31, 42, 131, 153, 155, 157, 164
photovoltaic power, 57, 111, 169
Pinakarri Cohousing, 93
Pine Street Cohousing, 123
politics, 7, 8, 112, 153, 154, 163-165, 170
post-industrial society, 6, 163, 164
potlucks, 32, 34
privacy, 4, 5, 10, 22, 41, 96, 117, 119, 120, 124
professionals, 9, 29, 131, 149, 151, 165, 168
project management, 9, 46, 79, 144
publicity, 10, 89
Puget Ridge Cohousing, **44-51**, 119-123, 140, 141, 144, 148-150

Q

quality of life, 15, 21, 168
Quayside Village Cohousing, **20-27**, 116-119, 122-124, 126, 131, 133, 140-145, 148, 149, 170

R

rainfall, 89, 100, 121
rainwater, 86, 89, 170
rammed earth, 87
recreation, 32, 41, 57, 96, 103

recycling, 1, 4, 22-24, 54, 57, 70, 86, 89, 105, 111, 115, 123-125, 129, 131, 135, 143, 156
refurbishment, 38, 53, 66, 69, 71, 73, 79, 123
relationships, 1-3, 8, 14, 15, 21, 34, 47, 50, 66, 77, 105, 120, 132, 137-142, 148, 154-156, 163, 167, 168
    definition of, 137, 141, 155
rental units, 21, 24
renters, 62, 64, 66, 145
responsibility, 15, 25, 41, 42, 97, 151, 164, 167, 168
retirees, 25, 49
retrofit cohousing, 10, 61, 64, 66, 67, 144, 167
ritual, 41, 48
Robyn Eckersley, 164
Rosbeth Kanter, 142

S

scale of organisation, 15, 122, 125, 126, 158
Seaside, Florida, 15
self-management, 5, 25, 42, 96, 111, 150, 151, 156, 167
self-sufficiency, 85, 164, 169
sense of belonging, 2, 15, 29, 145, 147, 152, 155, 156, 159, 165
sense of community, 1, 3, 8, 10, 15, 47, 64, 99, 148, 152, 154, 157, 163-167
sewerage treatment, 53, 86, 89, 105, 123, 158, 170
sharing, 2, 4, 6, 8, 10, 12, 15, 32, 40, 42, 61, 81, 95, 104, 105, 112, 123, 137, 138, 140, 152, 156-158, 167, 168, 171
single parents, 7-9, 94, 97, 142, 159, 166
singles, 9, 12, 21, 24, 25, 64, 86, 94, 100, 159
site planning, 3, 4, 30, 46, 85, 86, 95, 115, 117, 120, 124, 152, 158
social change, 2, 10, 14, 66, 97, 153, 154, 157, 158, 160, 163
social cohesion, 6, 15, 24, 42, 43, 49, 64, 123, 126, 136, 148, 165
social events, 126, 150
social interaction, 2-4, 12, 22, 42, 58, 61, 64, 87, 95, 112, 119, 140, 154, *See also* interaction
social movement, 10, 163, 170
social problems, 3, 6, 13-15, 160, 165
social sustainability, 1, 4, 14, 153
socialisation, 25, 132-134
solar hot water, 57, 86, 88, 91, 122, 158
Songaia Cohousing, **36-43**, 118, 119, 121, 122, 126, 127, 140, 141, 144, 148, 149
South Africa, 13
Southside Park Cohousing, 72
spirituality, 38, 40, 66
stewardship, 57, 109, 118

storage, 33, 48, 80, 105, 115, 167
stormwater, 45, 70, 86, 89, 123
Strata Title, 25, 129
suburbia, 10, 119, 135, 165
support, 4, 38, 72, 74, 97, 137, 141, 142, 145, 152
    financial, 72, 142
    moral, 41, 72, 141, 143, *See also* equity
    practical, 10, 15, 24, 31, 72, 141-143, 163
    social, 3, 12-14, 24, 96, 104, 112, 137, 141, 142, 156, 163
sustainability, 1, 2, 40, 86, 91, 143, 160
    definition of, 2
sustainable human settlement, 11, 86, 158, 159, 160, 161
sustainable society, 4, 15, 122, 134, 157-170
sustainable technologies, 15, 23, 53, 85, 86, 91, 122, 123, 170
sustainable timber, 57, 70, 87, 123
Swan's Market Cohousing, **75-80**, 118, 119, 122, 123, 140, 141, 144, 149
sweat equity, 38, 47, 61, 64, 93, 94, 97, 101, 144, 159
Sweden, 6-9

T
Tadao Ando, 108, 111
television, 134, 142
Tetsuro Kai, 106, 107, 109, 146
thermal mass, 87, 100
Tokyo, 107
tolerance, 34, 42
townhouse, 10, 21, 29, 54, 80, 122
toxic waste, 54, 55
toxicity, 70, 87, 124, 143
Toyo Ito, 108
traditions, 14, 27, 41, 64, 66, 96, 103, 148, 165
transparency, 50, 96, 150
transportation, 23, 85, 104, 115, 116, 123, 166
travel, 3, 85, 115, 166
trust, 15, 49, 50, 57, 104, 136, 137, 142, 149-152, 155, 157, 167, 168
Tsukuba method, the, 107, 110

U
United States, the, 3, 9, 10, 11, 89, 118, 119, 121, 123, 131, 132, 144, 163, 169, 170
universal design, 24
urban blight, 77
urban design, 107
urban development, 15, 107
urban form, 1, 8, 159
urban life, 4, 79
urban renewal, 10, 69, 72, 79, 80, 115, 158

utopianism, 10, 163

V
values, 2, 10, 13, 38, 42, 45, 121, 133-135, 147, 148, 151, 156, 164, 168, 171
vegetable gardening, 43, 126, *See also* food procurement
vegetarianism, 23, 67, 103, 126, 129, 134
vehicles, 4, 23, 45, 49, 81, 96, 104, 116-119, 158
vertical landscaping, 22, 108, 111
vision, 4, 10, 30, 38, 40-45, 51, 62, 67, 79, 85, 87, 158, 163, 164, 165, 170
    statement, 11, 24
voluntary simplicity, 3, 40, 129, 148, 163

W
waste, 4, 15, 23, 70, 86, 88, 89, 105, 111, 123-125
waste management, 124
wastewater treatment, 53, 89
water, 89, 111, 170
water conservation, 23, 70, 88-91, 123, 129, 135
WindSong Cohousing, **28-34**, 118, 119, 121, 122, 126, 133, 140, 143, 145, 148-150
Winslow Cohousing, 9
Wonderland Hill Developments, 9
Woodford Folk Festival, 165
workdays, 126, 129, 150
working from home, 57, 115

Y
youth, 21, 41, 158

Dr Graham Meltzer is said to be the world's leading expert on cohousing. He is an architect, academic and commercial photographer who researches and consults in the fields: social and environmental architecture, housing and communalism.

ISBN 1-41204994-6
9 781412 049948

Made in the USA
Lexington, KY
19 October 2010